SINN FÉIN AND THE IRA

SINN FÉIN AND THE IRA

From Revolution to Moderation

Matthew Whiting

EDINBURGH
University Press

Edinburgh University Press is one of the leading university presses in the UK.
We publish academic books and journals in our selected subject areas across the
humanities and social sciences, combining cutting-edge scholarship with high editorial
and production values to produce academic works of lasting importance. For more
information visit our website: edinburghuniversitypress.com

© Matthew Whiting, 2018

Edinburgh University Press Ltd
The Tun – Holyrood Road, 12(2f) Jackson's Entry, Edinburgh EH8 8PJ

Typeset in 10/12.5 pt Sabon by
Servis Filmsetting Ltd, Stockport, Cheshire,
and printed and bound in the United States of America

A CIP record for this book is available from the British Library

ISBN 978 1 4744 2054 9 (hardback)
ISBN 978 1 4744 2055 6 (webready PDF)
ISBN 978 1 4744 2056 3 (epub)

The right of Matthew Whiting to be identified as the author of this work has been
asserted in accordance with the Copyright, Designs and Patents Act 1988, and the
Copyright and Related Rights Regulations 2003 (SI No. 2498).

CONTENTS

FIGURES AND TABLES

ACKNOWLEDGEMENTS

This book originated from my doctoral studies at the London School of Economics and my biggest academic debt there is certainly owed to Bill Kissane, who proved to be an excellent supervisor throughout the whole process. Without his guidance and input this book would certainly be much poorer. I also owe a debt of gratitude to Simon Hix who was hugely supportive and encouraged my interest and understanding of comparative politics, as well as owing thanks to Tony Travers, Denisa Kostovicova and Jonathan Hopkin. Both Michael Kerr and Giovanni Capoccia made invaluable suggestions on publication, which were much appreciated. I would also like to thank the two reviewers who offered excellent and constructive advice on improving the manuscript along the way. Of course, all errors which remain are my own.

In terms of undertaking research for the project, it would simply not have been possible without the many people who agreed to be interviewed by me and freely gave their time and insights. Without exception, all interviewees were very welcoming and open in their assessments and appraisals of the conflict, often going well beyond my expectations to help me understand their perspectives on it. For this I cannot express my gratitude enough. Thanks are also owed to staff at the National Archives in Kew, the National Archives of Ireland in Dublin, the Linen Hall Library and the Public Records Office in Belfast, and the British Library Political Collection at the LSE. I would also like to thank the whole team at Edinburgh University Press who took me through the publication process so expertly, especially Jen Daly.

Finally, I would like to thank all those friends and family members who supported me and listened to me throughout the long period it took to write this book. Johannes Wolff, Stefan Bauchowitz, David Marshall, Mike Seiferling, Jose Olivas Ossuna and Ulrike Theuerkauf have all listened to my ideas at different times and helped me along the way. I would also like to thank Roisin and Sinéad, who have been unfailingly encouraging and supportive, even when I lost motivation myself. Finally, I would like to thank Zeynep and Elif, who have proved the best inspiration in more ways than I could ever hope for.

1. INTRODUCTION

Two contrasting speeches, both by British prime ministers but made twenty-five years apart, highlight the stark nature of the transformation of Irish republicanism from violent revolutionaries to reformist politicians. On 12 October 1984, Margaret Thatcher, surrounded by security officers, declared to the Conservative Party faithful, 'this government will not weaken. This nation will meet that challenge. Democracy will prevail.'[1] The challenge she was referring to was that posed by the IRA's armed campaign and Sinn Féin's anti-system politics. She viewed republicans as posing an unambiguous threat to the legitimate democratic political order. The reason for a particularly visible security presence that day was that she was speaking just hours after the IRA had come close to assassinating her at the Grand Hotel in Brighton during the annual Conservative Party Conference. Some days later Thatcher reiterated this same sentiment even more strongly, declaring that she viewed the bombing as an attempt to 'destroy the fundamental freedom that is the birth right of every British citizen: freedom, justice, democracy'.[2] This was not the only time the IRA came close to assassinating a British prime minister and in 1991, after John Major's close escape from an IRA mortar bomb, he too decried republicanism. He viewed them with 'contempt' and declared that republicans 'have demonstrably failed and every time they even contemplate joining the political process they are rebuffed'.[3]

By 2010, a British prime minister was making a very different speech. Instead of accusing republicans of trying to destroy democracy, Gordon Brown was now praising their co-leadership of Northern Ireland's power-sharing executive and their constructive role in the new Northern Irish democracy. After securing support for the Hillsborough Castle Agreement which enabled the devolution of policing and justice powers, a key milestone in the consolidation of the peace process, Brown stated that 'this is the last chapter of a long and troubled story and the beginning of a new chapter after decades of violence, years of talks, weeks of stalemate'.[4] This speech came sixteen years after the IRA initially declared what was to become a lasting ceasefire and twelve years after Sinn Féin accepted the Belfast Agreement peace treaty. For many, as for Gordon Brown, this represented the completion of the implementation of the peace process, which brought to an end the twenty-five-year conflict in which the IRA killed over 1,700 people.[5] By now, Sinn Féin representatives were part of established politics in both parts of Ireland, they were welcomed in the White House, and were even seen as ready sources of advice about how to broker peace and build democracy in other parts of the world.[6]

When placed in historical context, the transformation of Irish republicanism was highly unlikely. Previous efforts to engage republicans in a peace process had failed or had been rejected out of hand. The Sunningdale Agreement, British Prime Minister Ted Heath's effort to establish an earlier power-sharing settlement in Northern Ireland in 1973, failed to include republicans and republicans dismissed it as a British attempt to maintain illegitimate sovereign power and prevent Irish self-determination. The IRA's official response to the Sunningdale proposal was to claim that it highlighted 'the artificiality of the Northern Irish state' and that 'the mechanism designed to secure what is termed power sharing requires the acceptance of an English politician as virtual dictator of the Six County area'.[7] Sinn Féin's response was even more dismissive, claiming that the proposed power-sharing deal merely 'reinforces injustice and violence, leads to counter violence and postpones the day of true and lasting peace'.[8] Instead republicans maintained that the only way to guarantee peace in Ireland would be for complete British disengagement and Britain setting a clear date for when they would withdraw. Anything short of this was rejected as British subterfuge and perfidy.

Other attempts to broker peace which may have looked initially promising also failed. In 1975, the IRA and the British government negotiated a truce, but one that was to prove temporary and which entered republican folklore as an example of British trickery at its worst. After encountering various problems during the short truce, Britain's motivation came to be seen by republicans as attempting to drag out the ceasefire to run down the capacity of the IRA without ever genuinely engaging in negotiations. This experience rang as a warning bell for republicans for any future internal discussions about talking with the British government or its representatives. From the late 1970s, initially under Prime Minister Jim Callaghan and his Secretary of State for Northern Ireland, Roy Mason, and later under Margaret Thatcher, Britain primarily relied on military responses to combat republican activity, hoping to defeat the IRA and marginalise Sinn Féin. An entrenched belief in military engagement as the sole way to break the deadlock was to become the hallmark of both sides throughout the second half of the 1970s and the 1980s. Even while the British Army was repeatedly warning that an outright defeat of the IRA was unlikely, successive British governments saw republicans as too radical, inflexible and militant to even consider embarking upon any negotiations.[9] The future for Northern Ireland was thoroughly bleak, to say the least.

In spite of such an atmosphere of historical pessimism, by the end of the 1990s republicans turned away from their initial starting point of advocating and using violence, rejecting the existing ruling British institutions as alien and unjust, and making revolutionary claims to an alternative sovereignty. Today they have replaced this with non-violent political participation, acquiescence to be governed by reformed institutions still under British sovereignty, and accommodation with former political rivals. This transformation was personified by Martin McGuinness, a former commander of the IRA in Derry, who served as Sinn Féin's deputy First Minister of Northern Ireland from 2007 to 2017 and who shared power with former bitter rivals like Ian Paisley and Peter Robinson. McGuinness also ran for president of the Republic of Ireland in 2011, coming in third and outpolling many established political figures. This change from radical outsider to mainstream political leader was truly remarkable. McGuinness was not the only notable IRA member to become a politician. Martina Anderson, Martin Ferris, Gerry Kelly, Alex Maskey and Conor Murphy are all notable former members of the IRA who have served in elected office since the Belfast Agreement. It would seem then, on the surface at least, to be all change in republicanism.

But it would be a mistake to see this as some sort of Damascene conversion with republicans decrying their former ways and changing the very fibre of their movement. Indeed several significant continuities remain. Sinn Féin may have agreed to participate in new ruling institutions in Northern Ireland and sit alongside former Unionist enemies in Stormont, but this disguises their singular lack of willingness to tolerate any claims to British sovereignty over Northern Ireland or view anything other than a united Ireland as possessing any legitimacy. An editorial in the official republican newspaper, *An Phoblacht* (The Republic), in 2005 (seven years after agreeing to the Belfast Agreement) stated that while a permanent end to armed struggle represented a change in strategy, republicans must still 'continue to weaken the union with Britain, maximise broad-based national and international support for Irish reunification and implement practical steps towards all-Ireland integration'.[10] One week later, Martin McGuinness offered the traditional republican interpretation of the conflict as emanating solely from British attempts to maintain an illegitimate colonial presence in Northern Ireland.[11] In its official announcement that it had eventually agreed to decommission all its remaining weapons in 2005, the IRA declared 'we reiterate our view that armed struggle was entirely legitimate'.[12] It was later to emerge in 2015 that the IRA remained in existence ten years after decommissioning as a 'social club' rather than an active force – a revelation that led to a temporary crisis in the Stormont Parliament. This is more than mere rhetoric by newly moderate republicans hoping to retain their hardline image, although undoubtedly 'playing to the gallery' was an important way of holding on to core supporters. Traditional republican beliefs remained evident in their new policies and behaviour. It is precisely for this reason that conflicts over symbolic issues have taken on such prominence in Northern Ireland today, where symbols of nationalism and expressions of identity became the primary battleground once violence had ceased.

The ambivalence of extensive strategic change alongside ideological continuity meant that republicanism has been met with scepticism from all sides. Both hardline and moderate Unionists criticised republicans during the peace process for being a wolf in sheep's clothing, donning the garb of moderation while in reality being unreconstructed militarists bent on using the peace process to force a united Ireland upon the people of Northern Ireland. In 1997 when Sinn Féin representatives attended Downing Street to meet with Tony Blair, the Democratic Unionist Party (DUP) leader Ian Paisley denounced this as seeing 'the godfathers of those who planned the bombing of Downing Street, standing outside there and piously pretending they were engaged in a search for peace'.[13] Even as late as 2007, the DUP feared republicans would continue to be involved in dubious events like the Northern Bank robbery or the break-in at the Special Branch headquarters in Castlereagh, with Paisley needing reassurance from the British government before being willing to risk his credibility and embark upon power sharing.[14]

Republicans, meanwhile, were also attacked by disenchanted supporters from within Sinn Féin and the IRA who believed its leaders had gone too far and sold out on core principles and values. High-profile former IRA members like Tommy McKearney, Anthony McIntyre and Brendan McFarlane emerged as leading critics, arguing that republican leaders had in effect accepted partition and given up their republican core by agreeing to abide by the Belfast Agreement.[15] This created a difficult situation for Gerry Adams, McGuinness and other republican elites whereby they were criticised for not going far enough by their adversaries and for going too far by former comrades.

Throughout all this, the leaders of republicanism claimed that the movement had not fundamentally changed but merely entered a 'new phase' of the struggle without losing sight of its original agenda. Gerry Adams reassured supporters that the peace agreement was not the final destination but part of a longer-term strategy to realise a united Ireland.[16] The IRA continued to be thanked and celebrated for their role by Martin McGuinness and others in Sinn Féin. The right to armed struggle to achieve Irish freedom remained, but this right no longer needed to be exercised. Republican leaders instead argued that the Belfast Agreement opened up a new path for fair political contestation by removing elements of systemic discrimination that were inbuilt into Northern Ireland's earlier incarnation. Agreeing to work through new institutional arrangements did not imply accepting the legitimacy of the political unit and, in republican eyes, Northern Ireland remains illegitimate and a reminder of the need for territorial unification in order to realise self-determination and 'true' Irish democracy. Nonetheless, the doctrine is now Irish unity through consent rather than through force. This confusion and sophistry is at the heart of much of republican politics today.

From an empirical (as opposed to a normative) perspective, it is clear that Irish republicanism has indeed become a moderate group. If moderation is understood as abandoning revolution in favour of reform and accepting the principles of democratic politics as the only acceptable rules of the game,[17] then clearly republicanism went through a long process of moderation that subsequently has been consolidated with little or no chance of a return to earlier violent and revolutionary ways. According to the comparative politics literature, the distinction between moderation and radicalism reflects the distinction between those who recognise existing institutions as an appropriate forum for political contestation and those who refuse to do so and instead choose to work outside them, often using political violence. In other words, the radical-moderate distinction is related to whether a group attempts to overthrow the political status quo (revolution) or whether it attempts to work through existing institutions to achieve its goals (reformism). Irish republicanism has abandoned its tactics of building parallel states and refusing to participate in elections and it is difficult to conceive of any way in which it would return to outright violence. Yet how far this transformation entails a change in values and not just behaviour is a core debate that continues to be asked of republicanism today.

The Argument of this Book

All this raises a number of questions about Irish republicanism, which are also of central importance to wider studies of how non-state armed groups transform into peaceful political organisations. Most obviously, the main questions are: What caused the moderation of Irish republicanism and why did it happen when it did? But related and often overlooked questions are: What exactly did this transformation entail, what changed, and what remained the same? The goal of this book is to provide answers to these questions and tease out the lessons of these findings for wider debates.

The 'official' explanation for the change in direction offered by both republicans and the British government is that a mutually hurting stalemate set in between the British Army and the IRA. This led republicans to consider new directions and explore alternative avenues to reach their goals.[18] Republicans could not accept a peace deal any earlier because the ongoing conflict needed to run its course to show that no other outcome was possible.[19] Such approaches usually emphasise the evolution of the IRA's strategy and how it became a more containable threat from the British perspective over time.[20] Variants on this idea are evident in studies which argue that the penetration of republicanism by British intelligence crippled the ability of republicanism to pose a credible military threat or to use this as leverage to achieve their goals. Cases of high-profile informants like Sean O'Callaghan, Dennis Donaldson and Freddie Scappaticci, as well as evidence that emerged in the course of the Smithwick Tribunal, are used to support these claims.[21] There have even been allegations that both Gerry Adams and Martin McGuinness were turned by the British security services as early as the 1970s and that the transformation of republicanism was the product of careful choreography whereby British spooks orchestrated Adams to become the leader of republicanism.[22]

The trouble with such explanations is twofold. Firstly, it is not clear that there was a wide acceptance within republicanism that the IRA had reached a military stalemate with the British Army, especially amongst grass-roots volunteers.[23] Secondly, and more importantly, these approaches fail to take into account the evolving political context in which republicanism was operating. Instead they assume republicanism is primarily reducible to the acts of the IRA and assume that as the IRA was constrained this led to a reappraisal of their political direction. However, as this book argues, this confuses cause and effect, and the changing political context limited the viability of IRA actions rather than the other way round.

Other explanations have focused much more directly on the politics of the transformation of republicanism and these are generally much stronger. The emphasis here tends to be about how the British sought to define the political space in which republicanism competed, gradually co-opting republicans into mainstream politics and shutting down the possibility for the pursuit of radicalism.[24] These studies are similar in focus to comparative studies that look at 'de-radicalisation' and 'de-militarisation' as the product of the shutting down of opportunity structures for violence.[25] The best of these explanations sees republicanism as gradually co-opted through its engagement with civil society, which the British used to tame its potential to engage in violent revolution. While republicans subsequently tried to establish this arena as a confrontational form of politics, their avenues for violent and revolutionary expression were gradually cut off as they became more dependent on local communities for their position of power.[26]

Interplay between the British and republicans is also to the fore in explanations that focus on the dynamics of the peace process as the driver of republican moderation. For Jonathan Powell, who served as Tony Blair's Chief of Staff and a lead negotiator of the Belfast Agreement on the British side, rather unsurprisingly the success of the peace process lay in the ongoing process of negotiations.[27] The argument he offers is that once negotiations have a momentum they will make headway, and therefore the onus was on the British to always keep the process moving otherwise it would fail. Choreography and creating the conditions that allowed key actors to make concessions in a way that was publicly acceptable to all sides was central to delivering republican moderation.[28] For others, the very act of talking to terrorists transformed the conflict.[29] Yet there is more than a hint of the teleological about explanations that see British dialogue and statecraft as the key driver of republican moderation when it is far from clear that there was a coherent plan underpinning British policy (and certainly not before the Major era by which time significant republican moderation had already begun).

Another approach which emphasises interplay, but this time between republicans and the SDLP rather than between republicans and the British, is the powerful and convincing account by Murray and Tonge. This argues that interplay between Irish republicans and their moderate rivals, the SDLP, led to a republican reappraisal of their radical positions and a gradual realisation of the benefits of pursuing a reformist path.[30] The idea that the SDLP 'conditioned' republicans for engaging in a peace process with the British and Irish governments is one readily promoted from within the SDLP itself.[31]

The trouble with existing studies is that they often neglect the wider institutional context in which key individuals made their choices. No one would doubt the importance of individuals and their contributions and, of course, interplay is important to understanding the moderation of Irish republicanism. However, this emphasis neglects how the very act of inclusion within a macro-framework of stable institutions actually elicits moderation. In those studies where institutions are examined, these focus almost exclusively on power-sharing institutional designs that were agreed during the peace process.[32] But institutions are not just the product of interplay between actors over how to be governed – they also regulate and incentivise how actors behave in the first place.[33] In other words, interplay and negotiations take place within an institutional context that incentivises and constrains the decisions and paths chosen by elites.

It is here that the argument of this book differs from existing explanations and offers an alternative understanding of the moderation of Irish republicanism. The argument offered here is that the very act of inclusion within key political institutional processes, namely engaging in party politics and later in democratic bargaining, extracted moderate commitments from republicanism in a gradual and path-dependent process. In other words, simply coming into contact with stable democratic institutions led to moderation. Sustained contact with stable democratic institutions, such as electoral politics and a consolidated framework of democratic institutions, was a vital moderating force. This was path dependent in the sense that once critical decisions to participate were made, it locked republicans into a process of further moderation because they were rewarded for doing so and faced high costs if they changed their path. As a small number of studies have shown, path dependency is a powerful way of explaining British and Irish policy choices and continuities, especially by accounting for long-term outcomes that were sometimes unintended by the actors concerned when they made their original choices.[34] Similarly, a path-dependent understanding of the moderation of republicanism draws our attention to how actors chose to engage in moderation within a generally stable institutional context and the wider British and Irish policy frameworks in which this occurred.

This process began as early as 1981 when republicans first chose to pursue electoral office to build on rising levels of public sympathy following the IRA hunger strikes. Electoral participation, and all that it was associated with, generated increasing returns for republicans and progressively induced them to accept full participation. Once the decision to participate in elections was made, this imposed constraints on republicans by forcing them to: fractionalise their struggle into a series of short-term reformist aims; act as a provider of club goods to their supporters by using the existing system rather than attempting to overthrow it; and court the support of potential allies whose preferences did not support revolutionary action.

Later this moderation went even further when republicans engaged in democratic bargaining to reform the Northern Irish political unit – again a longer-term process than an emphasis solely on the short-term peace process acknowledges. Rebellious masses may strike mutually beneficial bargains with elites that entail abandoning revolution in return for gradual and relatively stable democratic reforms,[35] and this is how republicanism saw its role in Northern Ireland. Throughout the course of the Troubles, republicans' relationships with other actors were changing and this occurred within a wider context of negotiation over the nature of democratic institutions in Northern Ireland. By the late 1980s when a small set of republican leaders explored common ground, initially with the SDLP and later the Irish government and Irish-America, this resulted in a loose pan-nationalist alliance or 'democratic nationalist consensus'. In order to make this possible, republicans needed to make themselves 'coalitionable' – that is they needed to make themselves acceptable partners to these groups in order to realise the benefits of this loose alliance. This entailed revising their use of violence and moving towards accepting reformism. This transformation was then cemented through the formal peace process and the design of power-sharing institutions which reduced the risks for republicans of changing from a violent to an exclusively peaceful political strategy.

In order for political inclusion to be effective in extracting moderate concessions from republicans, it was necessary that a powerful external broker was present to reassure republicans that their interests would be heard against the competing voice of a more powerful British state. In parallel with studies which argue that external brokers make power-sharing agreements more durable,[36] the US played this crucial role for Irish republicans. It did this by reinforcing and affirming republicanism's institutional participation and acting as guarantor at key stages in their moderation. This was difficult for the US given its close relationship with Britain, particularly within the State Department, and given that it also needed to serve as a neutral overseer of the Belfast Agreement during its brokering. Later, US officials also extracted moderation by using their coercive influence to force republicans to moderate at times when they were reticent, most notably over decommissioning.

This book also examines what exactly moderation entailed and what it did not necessarily entail. Moderation meant giving up violence and revolutionary politics and agreeing to work through established political institutions. However, crucially, this did not require that republicanism diluted its ethnic goals or values, which have remained undimmed. Essentially moderation was a strategic adaptation by republicans.[37] Core values such as the valorisation of Irish nationalists' claims to Northern Ireland, a refusal to accept British rule as legitimate and asserting the historical justification of armed struggle, all remained undimmed. This aroused suspicions on the part of their former adversaries about the degree to which republicans were committed to the moderate path. In order to demonstrate their sincerity and commitment to moderation, republicans needed to undertake a series of concrete acts, most obviously decommissioning, accepting policing and responding firmly to dissident republicans. What enabled this form of strategic moderation while still retaining core values and goals was the nature of the British state's response. This was highly tolerant of Irish nationalist goals and accepted the pursuit of Irish unification as a legitimate aspiration, even though it threatened the territorial integrity of the UK state. The state also allowed republicanism to emerge as a political force without looking to suppress the movement. Both of these are highly unusual when viewed from a comparative perspective.

Having undergone a moderate transformation as a result of increased political inclusion, radical Irish republicanism serves as an important case for understanding the precise causal pathways underpinning this process. Other notable cases of rebel-to-party transformations occurred in contexts where democracy was not strongly consolidated. El Salvador (FMLN), Mozambique (RENAMO), Burundi, the Democratic Republic of Congo, and Rwanda (both Hutu and Tutsi groups), and Bangladesh (the People's Solidarity Association in the Chittagong region), are typical examples. In contrast, Irish republicanism's moderation occurred in one of the oldest consolidated democracies in the world with a long history of democratic and pluralist institutions. This completely changed the dynamics of moderation compared to these other cases.

In other cases of separatist conflict, groups have faded due to military defeats or a general depletion of their will over time, rather than as a result of democratic inclusion. ETA in Spain and the National Liberation Front of Corsica stand out as examples here. Other conflicts have remained remarkably resilient and appear to be deeply entrenched, with no sign of inclusion or military defeat on the horizon, such as the PKK in Turkey and Palestinian liberation groups, where they are met with suppression rather than offered inclusion. Against this backdrop of wider reasons for why non-state armed groups moderate, the case of Irish republicanism stands out as being importantly positioned to offer crucial insights into democratic inclusion as a long-term moderating process.

A note on sources is useful here. This book draws on: archival material from the UK, the Republic of Ireland and Northern Ireland; interviews with key players; policy documents; speeches and public proclamations; memoirs; and an extensive newspaper review over the forty years of the focus of this study (especially republicanism's official newspapers *An Phoblacht* and *Republican News*, which was later absorbed into *An Phoblacht*). In terms of interviews, fewer republicans agreed to be interviewed than was ideal despite a large number being contacted. Their assistants explained this as them simply being too busy to take part. To compensate, contemporary original statements by these players are used where possible, often drawing on *An Phoblacht* but also on a range of other documents. The perspective of British and Irish government officials and other key players from Northern Ireland is extensively covered through interviews, and throughout the book a process of triangulation of sources was used wherever possible to construct the analysis and insights offered.

The structure of the book is as follows. Chapter 2 puts the transformation of Sinn Féin and the IRA into a historical context by drawing a comparison with the moderation of the anti-Treaty side of the Irish Civil War and the emergence of Fianna Fáil under Éamon de Valera. The chapter draws out the parallels between these two transformations not only to show the origins of radical Irish republicanism and the political goals it concerns itself with, but also to show what exactly moderation does and does not entail in this context. The decline of the militancy of a sizeable proportion of the anti-Treaty rebels after defeat in the Civil War, and their emergence as the most powerful political force in the Irish Free State who mobilised support around their nationalist programme, is highly instructive for understanding Sinn Féin and the IRA in Northern Ireland seventy years later.

Chapters 3 to 5 focus on the causes of the moderation of Sinn Féin and the IRA today, looking at long-term contact with a set of stable democratic institutions. Chapter 3 looks at the role of elections and demonstrates how republicanism only explored elections after the failure of their alternative revolutionary strategy of parallel state building. However, once the decision to participate was made at the critical juncture of the hunger strikes, republicans were incrementally drawn into more moderate positions through fractionalising their goals into short-term aims and through the need to build electoral alliances. Chapter 4 argues that the transformation of republicanism can be understood as the outcome of bargaining between republicans and other actors within a wider liberal democratic institutional framework. This process was about agreeing to rein in radicalism in return for securing a set of reformed institutions that provided a stable and low-risk basis for political competition in Northern Ireland, while simultaneously rendering the future of Northern Ireland as part of the UK uncertain. This process also entailed republicans changing their relationships with other actors, which had an inhibiting effect upon their radicalism as they reformed in order to make themselves coalitionable. Chapter 5 examines the role of Irish-America and the US government, both in providing incentives for republicans to moderate and in acting as a guarantor of republican interests throughout the peace process. As an external actor they facilitated and solidified the moderation process by guaranteeing republican interests during the uncertain process of moderation and by exerting a coercive influence. A common theme through all these chapters is that moderation was initially strategic, but once this path was chosen it became embedded and linked to increasing returns where the cost of changing path back to radicalism was high. Republican moderation did not entail giving up many of republicanism's long-standing values, yet this was more than just surface moderation and the changes it went through were clearly profound.

Chapter 6 looks at British policy in Northern Ireland throughout the conflict. Rather than seeing republican moderation as the outcome of British co-option, this chapter argues that British policy was often confused and unclear in its goals. However, what was consistent throughout the conflict period was a high degree of tolerance for the politicisation of Sinn Féin (even while simultaneously pursuing repressive measures against the IRA). In addition, by the 1980s successive British governments actively sought to provide a stable set of democratic institutions through which Irish nationalists could legitimately pursue their political goals. These policy directions were not necessarily always pursued with a clear destination in mind. Nonetheless these two factors were the crucial elements of British policy which allowed republican moderation through inclusion to occur without republicanism actually having to change its core values or goals. This is why we see the mixture of change and continuity that is the hallmark of this particular path to moderation. This tells us that moderation can occur when a radical movement is willing to shift tactics while still insisting on retaining its long-term values and, provided this is reciprocated by the state, it allows the movement to pursue separatist goals in return for accommodating to the system.

Chapter 7 concludes by doing three things. Firstly, it summarises the main arguments and pulls everything together. Secondly, it also examines how realistically moderate republicanism has been able to pursue a united Ireland on entry into the Northern Irish Assembly, arguing that this has mainly been at the level of rhetoric with the party more concerned about vote shares. Finally, it looks at the lessons from the case of Irish republicanism for other significant separatist conflicts in the world today, showing the potential applicability and limitations of this framework for elsewhere. It also considers the implications of this case for existing debates around institutional design to regulate conflict and how states should respond to separatist threats.

Notes

1. Thatcher, M. 'Speech to Conservative Party Conference', 12 October 1984.
2. Thatcher, M. 'Speech to Finchley Conservatives. 25 Years as MP', 20 October 1984.
3. Major, J. 'Interview on Sunday 10 February 1991' <http://www.johnmajor.co.uk/page2041.html>.
4. 'Brown hails "new chapter" in Northern Ireland as end to years of violence', *The Guardian*, 5 February 2010.
5. Jonathan Phillips noted that this optimism sat alongside ongoing concern within the Northern Ireland Office (NIO) about the failure to agree over legacy issues and parading.
6. 'Irish republicans to hold peace summit with Kurdish and Basque separatists', *The Guardian*, 10 February 2011.
7. *An Phoblacht*, 30 March 1973, p. 1. *An Phoblacht* (*AP*), translated as The Republic, is the official newspaper of Sinn Féin.

8. Ibid.
9. Interview with Bernard Donoughue; interview with Tom McNally.
10. *AP*, 28 July 2005, p. 3.
11. *AP*, 4 August 2005, p. 7.
12. 'IRA Statement Announcing an End to Armed Struggle', 28 July 2005. Available at: <http://news.bbc.co.uk/1/hi/northern_ireland/4724599.stm>.
13. *The Guardian*, 26 March 2007.
14. Interview with Peter Hain.
15. McKearney, *The Provisional IRA*; McIntyre, 'Modern Irish Republicanism'; Moloney, *Voices from the Grave*.
16. *AP*, 9 April 1998, p. 11.
17. Schwedler, *Faith in Moderation*; Wickham, 'The Path to Moderation'.
18. McGuinness, M. 'The Future of the Union'; Powell, *Great Hatred, Little Room*.
19. This is akin to Waterman's idea that warring parties need to realise no other options are open before settling. Waterman, 'Political Order and the "Settlement" of Civil Wars'.
20. Smith, *Fighting for Ireland?*
21. For example, see Moloney, *A Secret History of the IRA,* or typical headlines like 'Half of all top IRA men "worked for security services"', *Belfast Telegraph*, 21 December 2011. The Smithwick Tribunal investigated Irish Gardaí collusion in the murder of two RUC officers in 1989.
22. 'Spy claims nonsense – McGuinness', *BBC News Online*, 16 December 2005 <http://news.bbc.co.uk/1/hi/northern_ireland/5029768.stm>; 'Wise move by Adams to go public with MI5 agent allegation', *News Letter*, 9 May 2014.
23. Tonge et al., 'So Why Did the Guns Fall Silent?'.
24. McIntyre, 'Modern Irish Republicanism'.
25. Berti, *Armed Political Organizations*; Van Engeland and Rudolph, *From Terrorism to Politics*.
26. Bean, *The New Politics of Sinn Féin*.
27. Powell, *Great Hatred, Little Room*.
28. Spencer, *From Armed Struggle to Political Struggle*; Dixon, *Northern Ireland*; McGrattan, *Northern Ireland*; Gormley-Heenan, *Political Leadership and the Northern Ireland Peace Process*.
29. Bew et al., *Talking to Terrorists*.
30. Murray and Tonge, *Sinn Féin and the SDLP*.
31. Farren, *The SDLP: The Struggle for Agreement in Northern Ireland*; Farren and Haughey, *John Hume: Irish Peace Maker*.
32. McGarry and O'Leary, *Explaining Northern Ireland*; Garry, 'Consociation and its Critics'; O'Leary, 'The Nature of the Agreement'.
33. Alexander, 'Institutions, Path Dependence and Democratic Consolidation'.
34. McGrattan, 'Dublin, the SDLP, and the Sunningdale Agreement'; McGrattan, 'Modern Irish Nationalism; Ruane and Todd, 'Path Dependence in Settlement Processes'.
35. For example, see Huntington, *The Third Wave*; Di Palma, *To Craft Democracies*; Acemoglu and Robinson, *The Economic Origins of Dictatorship and Democracy*.
36. Hoddie and Hartzell, *Strengthening Peace in Post-Civil War States*; Kerr, *Imposing Power-Sharing*; Walter, *Committing to Peace*.
37. Whiting, 'Moderation without Change'.

2. RADICALISM AND MODERATION IN THE HISTORY OF IRISH REPUBLICANISM

Republicanism is not inherently radical. A republican ideology has provided the foundation for the 1937 constitution of modern Ireland, a decidedly stable, highly democratic and largely uncontroversial political system. Yet the 1937 constitution was written by Éamon de Valera who in 1921, in the name of 'pure' republicanism, fought against the decision of his former comrades to accept the Treaty offered by Britain to Ireland to end the War of Independence, which offered a limited Free State status rather than full independence. Even after being on the losing side of the resulting Irish Civil War over the Treaty, and with declining public appetite for ongoing conflict, de Valera continued to reject the legitimacy of the Irish Free State. However, with his decision to form Fianna Fáil in 1926 and to challenge the Treaty system from within, de Valera and his followers went through an important process of moderation. Significantly, this did not entail changing their values towards the legitimacy of the Free State or apologising for their history of violent radicalism.

The parallels with the transformation of Sinn Féin and the IRA in Northern Ireland seventy years later are striking. These two transformations highlight that the boundaries between moderate and radical strands of republicanism are not always clear-cut or self-evident. The transformation of radical republicanism in both instances was concerned with redefining republicans' relationships with institutions and violence, while at the same time remaining committed to their ideological goals.

The Meaning of Moderation

A moderate refers to 'those who don't rock the boat and . . . ultimately they accept limited reforms that protect the power bases of the current elites', while a radical 'is typically used to label those who demand more substantive systematic change and strongly oppose the power configurations of the status quo'.[1] In other words, the distinction is akin to that between revolutionaries and reformers. The process of shifting from revolution to reform is multi-layered and multi-dimensional, with a radical group moderating on some issues at a different pace than on other more resistant issues.[2] While undoubtedly an important part of moderation is giving up revolutionary ways in favour of accommodation to the existing system, this alone is not sufficient to define moderation. In fact, it is possible that a party may only appear to moderate purely in order to win power and it may subsequently try to impose an authoritarian order upon society. The fear here is that some actors behave in a moderate way while actually retaining radical beliefs. Declaring a cease-fire or agreeing to participate in elections is often not proof enough for critics who want formerly radical groups to condemn their past behaviour, espouse a fundamental change in their values, and express a normative commitment to the existing political system before the transformation is accepted as credible.

In order to capture this distinction between sincere and insincere moderation, scholars have distinguished between behavioural and ideological moderation, arguing that both behaviour and values need to change before a group can be considered genuinely moderate. The meaning of behavioural moderation is intuitively grasped, but the meaning of ideological moderation is somewhat trickier. Wickham defines ideological moderation as the 'abandonment, postponement, or revision of radical goals that enables an opposition movement to accommodate itself to the give and take of "normal" competitive politics'.[3] Similarly, Tezcür sees ideological moderation as 'a process through which political actors espouse ideas that do not contradict the principles of popular sovereignty, political pluralism, and limits on arbitrary state authority'.[4]

Yet the moderation of different phases of Irish republicanism shows that a radical separatist group does not necessarily have to undergo any value change or alter its goals in order to become moderate. Rather a strategic change in behaviour away from using violence and from attempting to overthrow existing institutions is sufficient. Nationalist movements are often characterised by core ethnic values which the group and its supporters view as non-negotiable, not least because if these values and goals are diluted or compromised then the group ceases to be a nationalist group. Because of these non-negotiable values, it is analytically limiting to consider a nationalist party as having moderated only after having changed its core values and abandoned claims to territorial sovereignty.

Irish republican moderation is best understood as a process of agreeing to work through existing institutions but without actually forsaking its ethno-national values. This does not prevent republicans from being sincere and committed to their moderate path. Abandoning their ethno-national values and goals was not necessary because there is nothing inherently anti-democratic in making an alternative claim to sovereignty. Even in its radical form, Irish republicanism was not outright anti-democratic and there is nothing which made it incompatible with political pluralism. Whether talking about the defiance of the rebels associated with the 1916 Rising, the anti-Treaty side of the Irish Civil War, or provisional republicanism in Northern Ireland, they were all committed to establishing a democratic political system and expressed a belief in democratic values. Their use of violence, while undoubtedly radical and beyond the acceptable boundaries of any democracy, needs to be contextualised. Radical republicans considered themselves to be radical democrats, fighting to liberate Ireland and realise Irish freedom in a way that the Treaty or the partition of Northern Ireland prevented. This led Hart to describing radical republicanism as 'ademocratic' rather than anti-democratic.[5] This meant that a removal of violence and agreeing to participate was sufficient for moderation, even while retaining a rejection of existing sovereignty and retaining the (no longer exercised) right to armed struggle.

RADICALISM AND THE ANTI-TREATY POSITION

If we are to identify critical junctures that sent Irish nationalism down a radical and confrontational path, then Irish republican leaders and activists trace it to the Easter Rising of 1916. This small, violent and initially marginal insurrection against British rule played out mainly in Dublin, resulting in the deaths of over 160 British soldiers and sixty-four Irish Volunteers. It generated huge public sympathy following Britain's harsh security response and execution of the Rising's leaders. When this was combined with growing anti-British sentiment over the possibility of conscription of Irishmen into the British Army, support for a peaceful struggle for Irish independence by working through the Westminster Parliament was lost. In this way, the revolutionaries of 1916 shifted the dominant tactics used by Irish nationalist politicians to date. They now bypassed the need for British consent and instead emphasised the pre-political right of Ireland to sovereign self-determination, justified with reference to an exclusive Irish national identity and culture.[6] The Rising was the beginning of a new phase of radical republicanism characterised by

> the elevation of physical force violence as practised by a conspiratorial clique; the emphasis upon military gesture performed in the name of the people (but without their mandate) in order that the gesture should convert the peoples and thereby produce subsequent legitimation; [and] the construction of a cult of willing martyrs.[7]

The political party at the forefront of this new radical republicanism was Sinn Féin, formed eleven years earlier in 1905.[8] Retaining a rigid commitment to republicanism and the use of violence was to prove difficult for Sinn Féin following its popular expansion that followed in the wake of the Rising. The banner that held this disparate group together was Irish self-determination free of Britain, but beyond this unity was hard to find. Those groups that gathered under the Sinn Féin label included the military Irish Volunteers and the Irish Republican Brotherhood, agrarian factions and interests, organised labour, feminists, anti-partitionists and the Gaelic League. It embodied both urban and rural interests, landed and landless interests, farmers and workers. As Hart argues,

> this omnibus 'Sinn Féin' flew a republican flag but it could also stand for simple self-government, political and social reform, an end to corruption and profiteering, a voice for youth and women, an alternative to the Irish Parliamentary Party, a hard line against partition, a prophylactic against conscription, land for the landless, or Gaelcization.[9]

There were those within the leadership who wanted to use the party as a vehicle to create a forceful republican movement, but gathering support from a diverse array of groups, each with different preferences beyond their common general commitment to Irish independence, put a limit on how forceful the party could become. This is illustrated by the fact that the party could not unanimously agree its long-term policy for the government of a united Ireland. Therefore, in 1917 the party ended up adopting a compromise formula and declared its aim to be 'the securing of international recognition of Ireland as an independent Irish Republic, but once that status was achieved, the Irish people may by referendum freely choose their own form of government'.[10]

Early radicalism was absolute, by which I mean that it had characteristics that would make this group radical in any party system. But, crucially, it was not anti-democratic. Its radicalism lay in its total rejection of existing institutions as a way to subvert British rule in Ireland and its use of violence. However, it would be a mistake to think of this as a rejection of democratic political institutions as a whole. Hence, in the 1918 general election, Sinn Féin sought an electoral mandate for their plans to withdraw its MPs from the Westminster Parliament and form an alternative parallel assembly in Dublin. The election provided an overwhelming victory for Sinn Féin, gaining seventy-three out of the 105 seats available to Irish MPs, a result that republicans claimed retrospectively endorsed the Rising. Newly emboldened by what de Valera saw as a mandate from the people for his vision of republicanism, Sinn Féin refused to take their seats at Westminster and instead established the First *Dáil Éireann* (Irish Assembly) in 1919.

The establishment of the parallel Dáil was a central tactic to this phase of radical republicanism. Through this entity Sinn Féin representatives sought to undermine the authority of the existing British system of rule and simultaneously replace it with one that would assert the authority and competence of a self-determined system of rule. As such, it both attacked the British state and acted as a way of establishing the infrastructure for future Irish rule.[11] The reality of the Dáil, however, was of a somewhat poorly attended assembly of limited remit. It met for only a total of twenty-four sessions between 1919 and

1921 and even then attendance was limited, with thirty-four of its members in prison, and only two members had ever sat in a parliament before. Its real power lay in its propaganda value and in making a difference in those areas where the British state was limited, especially the courts and local government, which it exploited to great effect.

Emanating from, and contingent upon, an alternative claim to sovereignty and rejection of existing ruling institutions, was the violent dimension of republicanism. Once mobilised this was to prove very difficult to rein in. The Rising embedded the belief within the IRA that initially unsupported acts of violence against the British could serve to shake the populace out of their lethargy and pave the way for politics. With the declaration of the War of Independence (1919–1921), the military dimension began to rise in importance. The new Dáil had an ambivalent relationship with the army Volunteers. The Volunteers were initially reluctant to come under civilian control, doubting the republican commitment of some Sinn Féin members, preferring to act outside of civilian subordination. However, by August of 1919, the Volunteers agreed to swear an oath of loyalty to Dáil Éireann, thereby enhancing the legitimacy and authority of both groups. This led to their transformation from the Irish Volunteers to the Irish Republican Army. There is much doubt as to how much control the assembly actually exerted over the IRA during the War of Independence and the Dáil did not take responsibility for their actions until March 1921. What is more, coming under Dáil command, even only rhetorically, did not imply that the IRA felt the need for an electoral mandate to secure the freedom of their country. But it did show that the IRA was not intent on military rule but saw its role as the equivalent of the official army of a future independent democratic Ireland.

In the 1921 election, Sinn Féin competed as if they were elections to a Second Dáil and won 124 unopposed seats to cement their political hegemony. It was under the auspices of the Second Dáil that Sinn Féin accepted Britain's offer of a truce which came into effect in July 1921 and led to the negotiations that culminated in the Anglo-Irish Treaty and the onset of the Irish Civil War (1922–1923). The Treaty offered a method of ending the War of Independence by granting Ireland its own parliament and dominion status within the British Empire and agreeing to the withdrawal of the majority of British troops from Ireland. But it also had a number of contestable features, including: the need for all Irish deputies to swear an oath of fidelity to the King of England in his capacity as the head of the Commonwealth; the establishment of a Governor General's office; the retention of the right to appeal to the British Privy Council; and Britain's retention of certain key ports in Ireland. Additionally, it allowed Northern Ireland, which had been created by the Government of Ireland Act of 1920, an opportunity to opt out of the Free State, which it duly accepted.

If radicals are those who aim to overthrow a system while moderates agree to work through existing institutions, then the Treaty settlement led to a break in republicanism, splitting them into moderate and radical camps.

Those who accepted the Treaty were broadly willing to settle for less than their ideal republic in the short term while the rejectionists insisted on continuing to agitate for complete Irish self-determination. This is not to say that the anti-Treatyites rejected compromise with Britain entirely, as evidenced by de Valera's alternative proposal *Document No. 2*, which suggested establishing an 'external association' relationship with Britain within a republican constitution with no mention of the British monarch. However, the anti-Treaty camp was rigid in refusing to endorse anything it saw as a compromise on Ireland's ability to exercise self-determination and national sovereignty.

The contrasting thinking behind those who became moderate through participation and those who remained radical by continuing to agitate is highly illuminating. It was not that the pro-Treaty side accepted the legitimacy of the British settlement, but rather they were willing to accommodate themselves to the new political order. The pro-Treatyites, led by Michael Collins, argued that it could act as a stepping stone towards establishing a republic, his perspective being that the Treaty 'gives us freedom, not the ultimate freedom that all nations desire and develop to; but the freedom to achieve it'.[12] In contrast, critics of the Treaty argued that this settlement represented an abandonment of the republican ideal as declared in 1916 and which the First and Second Dáil represented. The oath of fidelity to a British monarch was particularly galling to this viewpoint. According to de Valera, 'The Free State Constitution made them subject to England ... No man who stood for the independence of the country or who had any sense of personal or national self-respect, would take an oath to a foreign king'.[13] So both sides viewed the Free State as a political unit that needed to be more republican – the disagreement was over the method of how to do this.

Debates over whether to accept or reject the Treaty reveal the complexity of the moderate-radical divide. Those who rejected the Treaty and maintained a rejectionist stance did so in the name of protecting Irish democracy, even though they were actually rejecting the majority will of the Irish population. After a period of internal debate within Sinn Féin and a vote in the Second Dáil, which the pro-Treaty side won by sixty-four votes to fifty-seven on 7 January 1922, Collins and his supporters formed the executive of the first government of the Irish Free State. Even after the vote, anti-Treatyites led by de Valera stood by their rejection of the Treaty. De Valera and his followers rejected the Dáil's decision to endorse the Treaty, arguing that it was not in the power of this parliament to dissolve itself in favour of a settlement that failed to deliver a republic. From this perspective the settlement agreed in the Dáil was based in part on Britain's threat of war if the Treaty offer was refused and thus coercion was at the heart of the decision. For de Valera this undermined the idea that the majority decision to support the Treaty was an act of Irish self-determination.[14] What is more, the IRA's decentralised nature enabled the majority of members to reject the Treaty even though Michael Collins endorsed it, with local IRA units asserting that the Minister of State no longer had any control over their direction.

There is evidence that the population at large sought a peaceful resolution to this disagreement within the context of a unified Sinn Féin party, as indicated by the results of the pact general election of 1922 between the two sides of the Treaty division.[15] However, such unity was never achieved at the elite level. Following the formation of a pro-Treaty Free State government, the anti-Treatyites refused to participate, their forces occupied the Four Courts and civil war broke out. The fighting lasted from 28 June 1922 until 30 April 1923 and resulted in a military victory for the pro-Treaty forces following a difficult guerrilla war waged by the anti-Treaty IRA, which included the death of Collins in an ambush. Crucially, although the pro-Treaty side may have secured a military victory, this did not result in the elimination of the political ideas underpinning the anti-Treaty grievances.

The anti-Treatyites were not simply anti-majoritarian or indiscriminately militarist, but rather there was a clear ideological underpinning to their position.[16] De Valera did not see his actions as overriding the popular will but rather he saw Collins's decision to endorse the Treaty as an executive *coup d'état* against the second Dáil where the majority of the people did not necessarily have the right to do wrong when it came to fundamental law like Irish sovereignty.[17] The portrayal of the anti-Treaty IRA as motivated by frustration and criminality was largely propagated by the pro-Treaty government and overlooked the ideological basis to their rejectionist stance.[18] The pro-Treaty leaders had not managed to establish a normal political order that was widely accepted as legitimate and it was this illegitimacy of the Free State from the perspective of some Irish nationalists that gave the anti-Treaty position volition. That the anti-Treatyites were not a marginal political movement is evident from the result of the 1923 election, where even following defeat in the Civil War, de Valera led a reorganised Sinn Féin to 27.4 per cent of the vote. This exceeded their expectations, especially given that many anti-Treaty leaders and candidates were in prison at the time, their political activities were subject to state repression and harassment by the police, and they were short of funding.[19]

The Treaty settlement fundamentally changed the scope for republican radicalism by creating a decidedly different political context to that prior to the War of Independence. Following their Civil War defeat, a reorganised Sinn Féin party tactically attempted to carry on where it had left off previously, but this time it was focused on defying an Irish state rather than the British one. Once again it operated an abstentionist policy, refusing to take seats in the new Free State assembly. Sinn Féin returned to the tactics of building the institutions of a parallel state.[20] Using a strategy of outright resistance, it hoped its parallel institutions would grow in size to swallow the Free State institutions and assume de facto government. The party also continued to swear loyalty to the Second Dáil to which de Valera was elected president. In this way the anti-Treatyites attempted to propagate the myth of a pre-existing republic which was more legitimate than the Free State. The difference between this attempt and the earlier parallel Dáil between 1919 and 1921 was that this one never gained popular acceptance or effectiveness on nearly as wide a scale. As Bob Briscoe, a future parliamentarian under de Valera's leadership, said 'de Valera was still president of the Irish republic, a shadow government which governed nothing. He was president of Sinn Féin, a shadow political party which took no part in politics'.[21] In this changed political context, de Valera and his followers began to reappraise their strategy.

THE EMERGENCE OF FIANNA FÁIL AS MODERATE REPUBLICANS

The process of the moderation of the anti-Treaty position began not because its leaders were permanently defeated by pro-Treaty and British forces, but it stemmed from an internal strategic reassessment by de Valera who thought reformism would be a more likely way of achieving anti-Treatyite goals. Moderation was also about changing strategy without changing values. Declining Sinn Féin and IRA membership, combined with the failure of their parallel state strategy, was rendering the anti-Treaty position marginal to Irish political life while the new Free State was gaining traction and acceptance from the population. What is more, the new Free State was becoming a relatively accommodating political system for a post-Civil War society. Rather than pursuing repression of the anti-Treatyite view in the aftermath of the Civil War, Free State institutions allowed for reintegration of this perspective at a later date.[22] Anti-Treaty radical republicans may have been defeated but they were still respected, both by their former colleagues and within the electorate, and they were seen as having the potential to contribute to the political life of the Free State. Their policies, as long as these were pursued in a reformist manner, were acceptable to the pro-Treaty side who, after all, sought an Irish republic too.

The first step in the moderation of the anti-Treaty position was participation. Within Sinn Féin, de Valera began to argue that abstentionism and pursuing a parallel parliament was holding the movement back. Instead, he asserted that if the oath of allegiance was removed there would be no obstacle to participating in the Free State parliament as long as they retained their long-term goals.[23] De Valera believed that nearly half of the electorate were prevented from expressing their preferences in elections and two-thirds were opposed in spirit to the existing regime. In order to allow the electorate to express their true preferences it was necessary to remove the oath of fidelity and enact a new constitution for Ireland. Following a vote at the 1926 Sinn Féin annual conference, de Valera's motion to abandon abstentionism was defeated and so he and a large cohort of party members left to found a new party, Fianna Fáil (Soldiers of Destiny). From the outset Fianna Fáil's desire for full participation was clear and the use of violence as a tactic was rejected by the new party. Even though the pro-Treaty Cumann na nGaedheal government refused to abolish the oath, de Valera's party eventually took the oath as an 'empty formula' and entered the Free State parliament in 1927. Although the IRA remained in existence after the Civil War, it declined as a threat to the security of the state and members showed reluctance to reintroduce the gun into Irish politics. Nonetheless, militants in the IRA showed no sign of following de Valera and upon hearing of the possibility of participating in the Free State parliament, the IRA withdrew its allegiance from the Second Dáil in 1925, moving outside civilian subordination entirely.

With participation, the absolute radicalism of rejection and violence was replaced by Fianna Fáil's relative radicalism – it now participated but it still remained radical compared to other parties in the system and to the extent to which it tried to undermine the Free State. The party rejected the legitimacy of the Free State settlement and vocally criticised it; it continued to assert the right to have fought on the anti-Treaty side in the Civil War; it had an ambivalent relationship with the Free State army and police; and it developed a populist social and economic programme that was more socially radical than that offered by other large parties in the Free State parliament, except perhaps by Labour.[24] Yet alongside this Fianna Fáil was now willing to accommodate itself to the existing political system and de Valera even warned his future deputies against the deliberate obstruction of Free State parliamentary business.[25] This was what characterised the shift from absolute to relative radicalism.

Once within the system, Fianna Fáil's position of opposing the system from within while retaining an ambivalence towards the Free State institutions was not sustainable, albeit aspects of its ambivalence were slow and gradual to evaporate. In order to secure power the party needed to moderate to make itself 'coalitionable' to potential partners in government. Then once in power the party passed a series of policies eradicating many of their grievances against the state. The June 1927 general election saw Fianna Fáil enter the Free State parliament as the second largest party behind the incumbent Cumann na nGaedheal. No party won an outright majority and Fianna Fáil had the possibility of forming a coalition government with the Labour Party. An agreement was struck that secured Labour support and in return Fianna Fáil agreed not to pursue its constitutional reforms during that term of government apart from abolishing the oath.[26] However, the Cumann na nGaedheal government survived a vote of no confidence by one vote and soon after held snap elections and secured an overall majority.

By the 1932 election, Fianna Fáil formed a minority government with Labour Party support in return for agreeing to pass some of Labour's policies, and de Valera became head of the Free State executive. When Fianna Fáil deputies turned up at the assembly to assume governmental office, some of them were armed in anticipation of any hostilities they might encounter, but Cumann na nGaedheal, the army and police stood aside and allowed a peaceful transition of power.[27] This was the beginning of sixteen years of Fianna

Fáil government that institutionalised de Valera's vision of an Irish state and thus ascribed the state with a legitimacy it had hitherto lacked. Between 1932 and 1938 Fianna Fáil essentially undid all the aspects of the Treaty settlement that it found disturbing, except partition which became more entrenched. In 1932, they withheld land annuity payments to Britain; in 1933 they removed the oath of fidelity; in 1936 they removed all mention of the King and Crown's representatives, including the Governor General, from the constitution; they abolished the Senate which was seen as a protection of British power; in 1937 they introduced an entirely new constitution to replace the 1922 Free State constitution, renaming the country Éire; and in 1938 control of the Treaty ports was handed over to Irish authorities. In many respects, though, these changes were actually symbolic more than substantial, highlighting that their radicalism was directed at subverting British rule in Ireland and any vestiges of this that remained, rather than a wholesale overhaul of every aspect of the Free State system.

Yet it would be a mistake to think of Fianna Fáil as suddenly becoming a 'normal' political party even following its ascent to government. Between 1932 and 1937, Fianna Fáil refused to accept the legitimacy of the Free State and they only declared the Irish state to have gained credibility and true self-determination once a new constitution written by de Valera was introduced in 1937. The Free State was accepted as a system of political order and Fianna Fáil's decision to participate was about acquiescence rather than legitimation. It was only accepted as long as it was transitional and as long as it offered an opportunity to gain power. In order to gain Fianna Fáil's acquiescence to work through the Free State's institutions, the system had to offer the opportunity to dismantle its objectionable features and replace them with something more symbolically legitimate that could be proclaimed to embody Irish self-determination. In other words, Fianna Fáil's relative radicalism only evaporated once they got their way on the Treaty and only then did the party become a consolidated moderate actor.

Although the party failed to change its values towards the Free State, this did not mean that Fianna Fáil did not demonstrate a strong commitment to their moderate path, even to the point of defending the Free State from former comrades-in-arms who still defied participation. Soon after entering government, the IRA offered to form an alliance with Fianna Fáil based on the fact that the two groups both wanted to keep Cumann na nGaedheal from power. In 1933 Joseph McGarrity tried to sell this deal to de Valera by arguing that the IRA 'can do things that you will not care to do or cannot do in the face of public criticism, while the IRA pay no heed to public clamour so long as they feel they are doing a national duty'.[28] De Valera rejected this out of hand and instead reiterated his own earlier offer that the IRA dump-arms and members could be integrated into the Irish army, and he continued to make speeches that put distance between himself and the IRA. De Valera also resisted efforts to remove former enemies from privileged positions within the state administration and replace them with more sympathetic colleagues or former republicans.[29] A further test came in the 1930s from the rise of the semi-fascist Blueshirt movement on the right of the political spectrum and the continuing guerrilla violence of the IRA on the left of the political spectrum. Under this pressure, the Fianna Fáil government made use of existing emergency legislation to clamp down on both groups of extremists, Blueshirts and the IRA, with equal tenacity.[30] By 1937, Fianna Fáil were explicitly declaring that there could be no possible ideological objections to the nature of the Irish state and ongoing radical republicanism was stripped of any remaining vestige of legitimacy.

PROVISIONAL IRISH REPUBLICANISM, 1970–2006

The radicalism of provisional republicanism was based on the same three dimensions as in the earlier phase: an alternative claim to sovereignty and a rejection of British rule; a refusal to work through existing institutions; and a belief in the use of violence to achieve their goals. However, the dynamics of provisional republican radicalism were different from the earlier phase. In Northern Ireland in the 1970s this originated more from a desire to defend Catholic communities against an aggressive Unionist state rather than from demands for self-determination. However, the way the movement evolved soon led to an integration of defenderism with self-determination and this formed the backbone of radical provisional republicanism. In 1968 a series of civil rights marches led by the Northern Irish Civil Rights Association began – an umbrella group that had links with radical republicans as well as with many other less radical nationalist groups.[31] The movement was seeking to end voting discrimination and gerrymandering which favoured the unionist community, as well as tackling discrimination in the fields of public housing and employment. The civil rights movement was met with repression by the Unionist government (albeit some limited socio-economic reforms were introduced by Stormont under pressure from Westminster), leading to increased polarisation between the two communities and localised incidents of violence, particularly in Belfast and Derry. On 14 August 1969, after days of rioting and high tension, loyalists mobs burned the homes of Catholic residents living on Bombay Street in Belfast and over 1,500 Catholics were expelled.

This event entered IRA folklore as an example of how they had failed in their duty to defend nationalist communities, an inability blamed upon the desire of the then IRA leader Cathal Goulding to wind down the IRA, end abstentionism and pursue exclusively peaceful radical-left politics.[32] In light of their perceived failures, the acronym IRA took on the insulting definition of 'I Ran Away' in graffiti around Belfast. Against this backdrop, a group of republicans split from their IRA comrades in protest at the political direction they were taking and formed the Provisional IRA (PIRA) and Provisional Sinn Féin in 1969/1970. This new grouping was primarily focused on resuscitating their military prowess and they were decidedly suspicious of the compromising nature of political pursuits. Initially the IRA was clearly the dominant partner in this relationship, having been formed one month before Provisional Sinn Féin, and Provisional Sinn Féin's early role was more about enabling and supporting the IRA in its military efforts to unite Ireland than offering a comprehensive political programme.

It is tempting but entirely mistaken to think of the re-emergence of republican violence as an atavistic throwback to some inherent predisposition to violence. Instead, once again, a perceived or actual social context of disadvantage and repression was the motivation for PIRA volunteers. This was then harnessed by elites who readily offered the doctrine of Irish self-determination as a solution to their ills. PIRA members were mostly urban, working-class activists who saw themselves as defenders of their communities against loyalists, a partisan police force and partisan British soldiers. Volunteers were not the unemployed, unemployable or criminal elements of Northern Irish Catholic society and 'surges in membership were linked to political events rather than to rent seeking opportunities'.[33] The conditions of radicalisation were the Northern Ireland government's response to the civil rights movements compounded by security policies, which were seen as directed exclusively at the nationalist population, especially key events such as introducing internment and the killing of thirteen unarmed Catholic civilians by the British Army during a civil rights demonstration on Bloody Sunday in January 1972. Republican radicalism was a defenderist mentality against British aggression, reinforced by more emotional motivations, such as a family history of republicanism, self-esteem, and a desire for action.[34] That is not to imply that this was a movement devoid of ideology at all levels. The founding leaders of provisional republicanism harnessed local grievances and framed them within the republican doctrine that the British state's denial of Irish self-determination was the real problem. In other words, their short-term interests and the pre-existing ideology interacted to provide radicalised nationalists with a decontesting framework to explain Northern Ireland.

Many of the same characteristics that were central to radical republicanism in the 1910s and 1920s were also central to provisional republicanism. The Provisionals claimed to derive their legitimacy from the 1916 Proclamation and the Second Dáil of 1919, even seeking and receiving the endorsement of Tom Maguire, the last surviving member of the 1921 Dáil.[35] The Provisionals were rigidly attached to the notion of a united Irish republic, and anything short of this was viewed as a nationalist failure. Under this conception, the Republic of Ireland, which had been officially declared in 1948, was illegitimate and an unfinished nation-building project, disparagingly referred to as the 'Free State' or the 26 counties to draw attention to its partial nature. From this perspective, the extant Republic could not be reformed as the existing institutions derived their authority from the illegitimate Anglo-Irish Treaty of 1921. To work through these institutions or attempt to utilise them was seen as giving recognition to partition and British sovereignty claims. The ruling institutions of Northern Ireland, which derived their authority from the Government of Ireland Act (1920), were also rejected out of hand. In this context, republicans claimed to be left with no other course of action than violent revolution.

Violence was the central tactic and Provisional Sinn Féin was subservient to the PIRA in the early 1970s, but that is not to say the movement was apolitical. In 1971, Sinn Féin produced the policy *Éire Nua* (New Ireland).[36] This presented the Provisional vision of how the state should be run in a united Ireland both socially and politically, but without actually providing any concrete steps on how to achieve this. Instead faith was placed in the IRA to secure a military victory to unite Ireland at which point these policies could be implemented. The other dimension to Provisional politics at this time was the familiar tactic of parallel state building. The main components of the parallel state strategy focused on building educational, judicial and political institutions that would insulate the Catholic community from engaging with the British state. Sinn Féin established a dedicated educational department with the aim of inculcating a 'proper nationalist outlook' within the population by challenging what they saw as the dominant and Anglicised version of Irish history and politics. Provisionals also acted as a police force in nationalist areas in Northern Ireland and they established 'Republican Courts' to investigate crimes such as housebreakings, vandalism and hooliganism, petty crimes, shop-breaking, car theft and drug dealing. The most sophisticated dimension to the parallel state strategy was the attempt to establish four provincial parliaments and one unified coordinating advisory council across the whole island of Ireland in a bid to implement a federal vision of a united Ireland.[37] Finally, and further highlighting their parallel governmental aspirations at this time, when Republicans were accused of forcibly collecting 'financial tributes' from residents and businesses of West Belfast, Ruairí Ó Brádaigh, Sinn Féin's president, defended this by simply replying: 'the Stormont government and the Westminster government collect taxes'.[38] This policy was to be a spectacular failure and gain no traction beyond small republican circles, but what is important is that the core of their radicalism was a position of outright rejection of existing institutions.

Once again moderation started as a process of internal reappraisal focused on exploring alternative ways to implement their policy goals in light of popular marginalisation. Fearful of appearing irrelevant to many aspects of everyday politics, an internal critique arose within the party demanding more comprehensive and less utopian policies. This was led by Gerry Adams, who was to become leader of Provisional Sinn Féin in 1983, and other predominantly Northern Irish members of the Provisionals who launched a critique of the policies of the old guard of predominantly Southern Irish members.[39] As Adams was to retrospectively present it,

> there was a recognition that republicans needed to identify their philosophy as being relevant not to the vision of a future Ireland but to the actual

Ireland of today, and that they needed to enlist mass popular support, or at least the maximum support possible, for the republican cause.[40]

Left-wing policies aimed at improving the immediate social and economic position of nationalists, especially housing and employment policies, began to be offered in a conscious rejection of former strategy. Although this did not initially change republicanism's rejection of existing institutions or their non-participatory stance, it did represent a fractionalisation of the overall struggle for a united Ireland into a series of smaller and more reformist-oriented goals.

A process of moderation is not necessarily a planned strategy and this accounts for its ambivalence, as is evident from the Provisional's decision to pursue a dual political-military strategy in 1981 following the hunger strikes (see Chapter 3). This new direction did not have a premeditated end point of moderation but rather

> the combination of war and politics espoused by senior activists was nothing other than an attempt to raise the overall impact of the movement by combining political ruthlessness with a campaign of terror ... [Provisionals] inadvertently compromised their military capacity as electoral politics made them vulnerable in ways they had not foreseen.[41]

It soon became evident that electoral participation was incompatible with abstentionism and with a dual political-military strategy. Even though they refused to accept the rightfulness of the elected institutions, Sinn Féin still accepted the idea that they needed to win as many votes as possible. What is more, once the emotively charged issue of the hunger strikes was resolved, Sinn Féin's vote share declined to a more modest level of about 10 per cent across Northern Ireland and significantly lower than this in the Republic of Ireland. With Gerry Adams now leader of Sinn Féin, he placed the blame for poor electoral results in the Republic of Ireland upon the abstentionist stance of candidates. Within five years of commencing a dual political-military strategy the IRA and Sinn Féin changed their constitutions to allow candidates to take their seats in the Irish Dáil, albeit while retaining the policy of abstentionism from Westminster and Northern Ireland. This was a contentious process and the policy was initially rejected at the Sinn Féin annual conference in 1985 before ultimately being endorsed the following year, which acted as an important signal for how the leadership could impose moderating choices.[42] This prompted a walk-out from former leaders Ruairí Ó Brádaigh and Dáithí Ó Conaill who split to form 'Republican Sinn Féin' and the 'Continuity IRA', ironically making it easier for future moderation by removing some hardline internal dissent. The main impetus given to justify the shift in policy was the need to accept the reality of the politics of the Republic of Ireland as this was the best way to achieve republican goals. Republican utopias, it was argued, had a marginalising effect on Sinn Féin within an electorate that uncritically accepted the Republic of Ireland's institutions.

Much of this phase was also about rebalancing the relationship between the IRA and Sinn Féin within the provisional movement. Elections and electoral success was a route for allowing Sinn Féin to emerge from the shadow of the IRA and, as Adams had long hoped, make its own political contribution to the quest for a united Ireland. Needless to say, this was met with resistance from those members who were more militarily inclined, and Sinn Féin needed to give several reassurances that electoral participation would not divert resources away from the armed struggle. This was why endorsements of the electoral campaign by senior militarists like Martin McGuinness were so important and even Gerry Adams, the strongest proponent of an expanded political dimension, declared 'If the British government listened to the ballot box, no one would be reaching for an Armalite.'[43] The extraordinary convention of the IRA, which was held to change its constitution to allow members to run for the Dáil, began with a pledge recommitting members to the armed struggle. The official rhetoric that emerged was that Sinn Féin's increased political role could complement that of the IRA without eclipsing it. For example, *An Phoblacht* declared that:

> the relationship between IRA activity and political change is clear. It is armed struggle which by its relentless application, by its bleeding white the British presence, will force a London government, or an opposition party, to the inescapable conclusion that they cannot rule us and will have to go . . . However, the way can undoubtedly be shortened – not ended – by victories on the political front delivered by the republican machine behind Sinn Féin.[44]

But in reality this was momentous within republicanism because of the way it diverted power away from the IRA towards Sinn Féin.

Over the next decade, the worst fear of many republican activists in 1986 was realised and the party gradually came to accept constitutional methods for pursuing their goals and abandoned violence (the reasons behind this will be covered in the next three chapters). Following a series of secret talks with John Hume and with the British government, in 1994 the IRA declared what was to become a permanent ceasefire and Sinn Féin entered a prolonged and tense period of all-party talks that culminated in accepting the Belfast Agreement peace accord in 1998. The ceasefire, when combined with their loosening of outright rejection, represented an end to their absolute radicalism, but they still retained many values that polarised republicans from other political actors in the system. Interestingly, this stance became somewhat of an electoral asset, with republicans making considerable gains by pitching themselves as militant defenders of nationalist interests while simultaneously showing themselves willing to participate fully.[45]

What is important to note here is that commencing moderation did not necessarily imply a change in attitude or values towards Northern Ireland or the legitimacy of British sovereignty over Ireland. The Provisionals anticipated that a purely political direction could allow them to better implement their policy agenda. Accepting power sharing in Northern Ireland, even though it remained under British sovereignty, was only undertaken conditionally. It was done in the belief that the aspects of the Agreement that established cross-border bodies with the Republic of Ireland and that enshrined Irish input into the affairs of Northern Ireland, could ultimately act as a conduit to a united Ireland. It was also argued by Provisionals that the Belfast Agreement democratised Northern Ireland, creating fairer political and economic opportunities for nationalists. But there was also a clear desire to avoid the consolidation of the new Northern Ireland, which was seen as a temporary and transitional arrangement. There can be little doubt that this was a weakening of their hitherto rigid commitment to the immediate demand for the republican ideal, but this ideal still remained as a long-term necessity.[46] The Provisional commitment to constitutional politics was decidedly ambivalent for the first ten years in other ways too. This is evident from a return to IRA violence in 1996 before reinstating a ceasefire in 1997; from the IRA's continuing role as an internal republican police force; from its refusal to engage in any decommissioning until Sinn Féin was actually in elected office and not finally completed until 2005; and, even from allegations of running a 'spy-ring' within the new Northern Irish Assembly.

Consolidating moderation became necessary for republicans so that they realised the full benefits of endorsing the Belfast Agreement. Their low coalition potential in the eyes of their Unionist counterparts was preventing a functioning and stable executive containing Sinn Féin from being established. Therefore, adapting their relatively radical stances to become completely accommodating and demonstrating a clear commitment to moderation became necessary. The party pushed hard to devolve policing and justice powers from Westminster to the Northern Ireland Assembly, which was eventually achieved through the Hillsborough Agreement of 2010, following reluctant decommissioning in 2005. The response to dissident terrorism by republican groups, whose origins stem from either the split over ending abstentionism in 1986 or else who left the movement in protest at the endorsement of the Belfast Agreement in 1998,[47] was also indicative of a commitment to their changed direction. Sinn Féin, in their capacity as co-leaders of the Northern Ireland Executive, responded to the threat of 'dissident' terrorist attacks on the Northern Irish state by utilising the justice and policing powers at their disposal to pursue and capture those responsible, even though in some cases these were former comrades-in-arms of the Provisionals who were now in power. This was a confirmation of their agreement to abide by the outcomes of the democratic process in a reformed Northern Ireland – in other words, a firm acceptance of the Belfast Agreement as providing a system of order and choosing reformism over any remaining remnants of revolutionary tactics.

In this way, the process of moderation for provisional republicans, as for their Fianna Fáil predecessors, was one that required increasing commitments to the moderate path in order to make their newly adopted reformist strategy a potential success. Once the path to moderation was embarked upon, this changed their relationship with the ruling institutions and with other actors within the political system, who demanded greater commitments from republicans in return for greater inclusion. Thus, ambiguities were reconciled and steadily eliminated. But moderation was also limited for provisional republicans who remain a step behind where they would ultimately like to go, unlike Fianna Fáil which largely achieved its constitutional goals. Moderation was limited in that it did not entail accepting the new political system in Northern Ireland as final or legitimate, and republicans only agreed to the peace process from an instrumental perspective of aspiring to use it to take them closer to their aims. Where Fianna Fáil was able to achieve this as the head of a single party government in a majoritarian political system with few checks on its power, Provisional Sinn Féin struggle much more to use the institutions instrumentally given the number and extent of minority vetoes built into the system.

What Constitutes Irish Republican Radicalism and Moderation?

Both phases of the moderation of Irish republicanism demonstrate that moderation was an ambivalent and gradual process, yet throughout it did not entail changing core values or goals – albeit the goal of a united Ireland became a long-term, rather than immediate, aspiration. This can be usefully understood by looking to a parallel within the study of anti-system parties. Capoccia argues that anti-systemness can be understood in either absolute or relative terms, and this is similar for the case of republican radicalism.[48] A group can be understood as absolutely radical if some aspect of it is intrinsically radical without reference to the location of other parties within the party system. Such a party would be considered radical even if it was transferred into a different party system. A relationally radical party, on the other hand, may not hold any beliefs or pursue any tactics that render it intrinsically radical but rather its relationship with other actors within that political system render it radical. A group can be considered relationally radical if its supporters are spatially distant from that of neighbouring groups or political parties, if it has low coalition potential, and if the group engages in outbidding or attempts to delegitimise the system. The transformation of both phases of radical republicanism can be seen as shifting from absolute to relative radicalism before becoming moderate.

Republican radicalism between 1916–1926 and again between 1970–1994 embodied absolute radicalism. The values and practices of the post-Rising republicans, and their anti-Treatyite successors in particular, and the values and practices of the early Provisionals ensured that they would be considered radical in any political system. The radicalism of both phases lay in the same facets – a complete rejection of working through existing political institutions and the use of violence, both of which were justified by an alternative claim to sovereignty and their perception of British sovereignty as denying Ireland democracy. Violence became acceptable once it was framed as a necessary tool of the less powerful colonised people fighting for their right to equality against an alien oppressor. Their radicalism also entailed outright resistance against British institutions in favour of parallel institution building, a denial of the existing ruling elite to have any say in the composition and political direction of a sovereign Ireland, and a great deal of 'boat-rocking', both to loosen Britain's grip and to shake apathetic Irish men and women from their complicit acceptance of the status quo. It was uncompromising in its rigid commitment to the ideal Republic, evident from the anti-Treatyite rejection of the Free State and the Provisional rejection of Cathal Goulding's attempt to pursue exclusively peaceful politics in the late 1960s.

Moderation when it came was initially about shifting from absolute radicalism to relative radicalism. Relative radicalism was characterised by an end to outright resistance and violence. Yet that it not to say that Fianna Fáil and Provisional Sinn Féin became 'normalised' political parties. Rather, initial change was inherently ambivalent. While they now participated within the institutions of the Free State and Northern Ireland respectively, both groups continued to deny the legitimacy of these ruling bodies and only participated on condition that they were viewed as transitional to a more acceptable political unit in the long term. The shift from absolute to relative radicalism was about accommodation to a form of political order and certainly not about accepting the legitimacy of the ruling institutions and the form of sovereignty that they upheld. There was a loosening of the commitment to the rigid ideal of the Irish republic in return for the opportunity to use the existing institutions to dismantle those aspects of the system that they found objectionable. It is also important to acknowledge that adaptation was active and consciously pursued, rather than merely being responsive to Free State or British state strategies. Importantly, their legacies of violence and rejectionism ensured that they were viewed with an air of suspicion and other actors were reluctant to build trusting relationships without a demonstrated commitment to the existing institutions. Both Fianna Fáil and the Provisionals existed in a 'grey area' and this explains why they would be simultaneously accused of being too moderate by internal critics and failing to display any real change by their former enemies.

Capoccia, when discussing relational anti-system parties, notes that they have a low coalition potential and indeed this is also true of relational radical parties. In the first general election of 1927, Fianna Fáil had the potential to form a coalition government with the Labour Party but this could only materialise if Fianna Fáil agreed to postpone most of its constitutional programme. By the time Fianna Fáil acceded to power it was as a minority government with tacit Labour Party support, further dragging them into the give-and-take of electoral politics. Similarly, between 1998 and 2007, the Northern Irish Assembly was suspended on four occasions, including for a five-year period between 2002 and 2007, due to the reluctance of the Ulster Unionist Party (UUP) and, later, the DUP to sit in a power-sharing government with Sinn Féin, mainly due to concerns over decommissioning. It was Fianna Fáil's and Provisional Sinn Féin's need to cement these relationships and secure a stake in power that facilitated the shift to demonstrating an active commitment to moderation and reconciling their relative radicalism.

Once each party assumed executive power, even relational radicalism was difficult (or soon unnecessary) to sustain. In the case of Fianna Fáil, whenever the party assumed governmental office it used that power to undertake a series of important symbolic reforms that removed the vestiges of British sovereignty over Ireland to bestow the state with a degree of legitimacy it had hitherto lacked. This culminated in the 1937 Constitution. In the Provisionals case this came with the completion of decommissioning and the signing of the St Andrews Agreement in 2006 which restored power sharing and later devolved policing and justice powers from Westminster to Northern Ireland. This was about embarking upon further accommodation of their relationally radical aspects, largely necessitated by the need to improve their relations and enhance their 'coalition potential' with other political actors in the system. By being given a stake in the political future of the new system, they agreed to end spoiler tactics. In power, it was necessary for both Fianna Fáil and Sinn Féin to present a strong defence against threats from former comrades-in-arms (and the Blueshirts in Fianna Fáil's case) who refused to accept reformism and posed an ongoing dissident threat. Fianna Fáil used extensive security powers to clamp down on their former comrades and defend the Free State while simultaneously undoing it from within, and Sinn Féin has been vocal and active in defending Northern Ireland from dissident terrorist threats while explicitly retaining the goal of transitioning Northern Ireland towards unification with the Republic of Ireland.

Fianna Fáil participated in order to dismantle those aspects of the Free State that it found objectionable, and essentially used the state's institutions against itself. This was made possible by the fact that it was not looking for a complete overhaul of the existing order, but just the removal of the vestiges and symbols of British sovereignty. Ironically, the fact that the Free State took the form of a Westminster-style majoritarian system that concentrated power in the hands of the executive gave the elected government the power to undertake significant change free of checks and vetoes. Additionally, and more crucially, both the anti-Treaty and pro-Treaty sides of the debate were agreed on the desired end point of an Irish republic. This contrasts greatly with Northern Ireland where there is much less ground for consensus over the future of Northern Ireland as a political unit given that the dominant political cleavage is based on the unionist versus nationalist divide. The consociational institutional arrangements enshrine minority vetoes and prevent the concentration of executive power to limit extraordinary change, rendering it close to impossible for Sinn Féin to embark upon the kind of 'constitutional reform from within' that de Valera pursued in the 1930s. Nonetheless, the Provisionals too only acquiesced to be governed by the rules of the Belfast Agreement and only agreed to remain under British sovereignty in the belief that they could use these institutions to democratise the Northern Irish political unit and ultimately use the institutions to transition to a united Ireland in the long term. Therefore, the whole nature of moderation without changing core goals and values was only made possible by the tolerance of the Free State and pro-Treaty side towards the anti-Treaty side's political goals and the tolerance of the British state towards the Provisional's political agenda of a united Ireland.

As such it is important to acknowledge the continuities that remained throughout the moderation process. Many of the core ethno-national values and beliefs remained undiluted. Moderation was not about accepting British rule as legitimate nor was it about regretting its history of radicalism. Instead it was a strategic readjustment to achieve long-standing goals. Expecting or demanding core value change of ethno-national values as part of the moderation process is unrealistic. As Freeden notes when discussing ideology, there are certain core values in an ideology which are 'ineliminable' and if these are removed then that belief system is no longer part of that ideology.[49] For Irish republicanism one of the core beliefs is a rejection of British sovereignty and a belief in Irish self-determination. More peripheral values can change, such as the tactics used to pursue these core values, but expecting a dilution of the ultimate ethno-national purpose is neither feasible nor necessary given that radical republicanism was compatible with democracy and the give-and-take of liberal party politics once violence was set aside.

The ethno-national context of Irish republicanism challenges definitions of moderation, which elevate value change to the centrality of the process. These approaches are overly exacting to the point of possibly missing actual important transformations away from radicalism. There can be little doubt that both de Valera's anti-Treaty followers and Adams's Provisional republicans went through very real and profound changes. Yet throughout this process participation was about an aspiration to weaken the existing state, not to entrench it. Any steps to consolidate the long-term survival of the Free State or the current Northern Irish political unit would have been a fundamental challenge to the nationalist and republican credentials of Fianna Fáil and Sinn Féin and, although they may have been willing to compromise on these credentials, they could not be eliminated entirely. Also neither party rejected its history of violence or its right to armed struggle, even if this right was no longer exercised. The shift from outright resistance to participation in government never entailed legitimising the existing political order or changing their beliefs towards British sovereignty or incomplete Irish sovereignty. Here Lamounier's distinction between acquiescence and legitimacy is vital, where acquiescence is agreeing to the political system but legitimacy is 'acquiescence motivated by subjective agreement with given norms and values'.[50] We cannot assume that the final destination of a radical to moderate transformation is or should be tolerance or pluralism of competing political claims or indeed any other fulsome idea of liberal democratic consolidation where all dissent is seen as becoming part of a 'normalised' political process. Rather, for Irish republicans moderation was a way of pursuing long-standing goals and implementing long-standing values in a new context.

NOTES

1. Schwedler, 'Can Islamists Become Moderates?', p. 350.
2. Wickham, 'The Path to Moderation', p. 206; Schwedler, *Faith in Moderation*, p. 6.
3. Wickham, 'The Path to Moderation', p. 206.
4. Tezcür, *The Paradox of Moderation*, p. 10.
5. Hart, *The IRA at War*; Augusteijn, 'Motivation: Why did they Fight for Ireland?'; O'Boyle, 'Bombings to Ballots'.
6. McGarry, *The Rising*, p. 15.
7. English, *Radicals and the Republic*, p. 7.
8. Laffan, in *The Resurrection of Ireland*, p. 20–25, notes that after 1917 Sinn Féin was only partially continuous with the party founded in 1905 given the extensive nature of the changes it went through.
9. Hart, *The IRA at War*, p. 17.
10. Kissane, *The Politics of the Irish Civil War*, p. 44.
11. Mair, *The Break-Up of the United Kingdom*.
12. *Dáil Éireann Debates*, vol. 3, 19 December 1921.
13. Quoted in Dunphy, *The Making of Fianna Fáil Power in Ireland*, p. 64.
14. Regan, *The Irish Counter Revolution*, p. 48.
15. Gallagher, 'The Pact General Election of 1922'; Kissane, 'Electing Not to Fight'.
16. Garvin, *1922. The Birth of Irish Democracy*, gives the opposing view that this was simply an anti-majoritarian movement.
17. Kissane, *The Politics of the Irish Civil War*, pp. 177–201. Regan, in *The Irish Counter-Revolution*, pp. 68–69, has argued that the Free State had questionable democratic credentials at this time too and that the majoritarian versus anti-majoritarian divide was too obfuscated to be relevant in Ireland at this time.
18. Kissane, *The Politics of the Irish Civil War*, p. 104.
19. Dunphy, *The Making of Fianna Fáil Power in Ireland*, p. 38.
20. Pyne, 'The Third Sinn Féin Party 1923–1926: I. Narrative Account'.
21. English, *Radicals and the Republic*, p. 94.
22. Bowyer Bell, 'Societal Patterns and Lessons'.
23. Kissane, *Explaining Irish Democracy*, p. 172.
24. It should be noted that Dunphy in *The Making of Fianna Fáil Power in Ireland* argues that there were limits to the social and economic radicalism of Fianna Fáil given that it was a mass party embodying Catholic social teachings that prioritised private property and the small bourgeoisie.
25. Kissane, *Explaining Irish Democracy*, p. 177.
26. Ibid., pp. 175–176.
27. Ibid., p. 176.
28. Quoted in English, *Radicals and the Republic*, p. 173.
29. Kissane, *Explaining Irish Democracy*, p. 182.
30. Kissane, 'Defending Democracy?'.
31. Ó Dochartaigh, *From Civil Rights to Armalites*.
32. The best account of this comes from Sanders, *Inside the IRA*, chapter 2.

33. O'Leary, 'Mission Accomplished? Looking Back at the IRA'. This was also the view of British Army intelligence in their 1978 report 'Northern Ireland: Future Terrorists Trends'.
34. Alonso, *The IRA and Armed Struggle*, pp. 18 and 67–101.
35. English, *Armed Struggle*, p. 113, for how they sought the endorsement of Tom Maguire for their cause.
36. Sinn Féin, *Éire Nua. The Social and Economic Programme of Sinn Féin*.
37. Sinn Féin, *Peace with Justice: Proposals for Peace in a New Federal Ireland*.
38. *AP*, August 1971, p. 8.
39. Many see the signalling of the beginning of this process with the speech by long-standing IRA Volunteer Jimmy Drumm at Bodenstown in 1977.
40. Adams, *The Politics of Irish Freedom*, p. 8.
41. Bourke, 'The Politicization of the IRA'.
42. Spencer, *From Armed Struggle to Political Struggle*.
43. *AP*, 16 June 1983, p. 3.
44. *AP*, 12 May 1982, p. 1.
45. Mitchell et al., 'Extremist Outbidding in Ethnic Party Systems is Not Inevitable'.
46. Ruane and Todd, *After the Good Friday Agreement*.
47. See Frampton, *The Legion of the Rearguard*, for an overview of dissident groups.
48. Capoccia, 'Anti-System Parties'.
49. Freeden, *Ideologies and Political Theory*. Freeden, in 'Is Nationalism a Distinct Ideology?', also argues that nationalism is only a partial ideology that needs to be filled out by other ideological beliefs. In the case of republicanism, this is filled out with liberal democracy.
50. Quoted in Przeworski 'Some Problems in the Study of the Transition to Democracy', p. 51.

3. ELECTORAL PARTICIPATION AND REPUBLICAN MODERATION

Liberal democratic elections simply do not allow for revolution. Electoral participation, especially if a party wishes to gain office, necessitates compromises that render radical policy goals unsustainable. Once the decision to participate in elections has been made, radical parties are faced with a choice of either forsaking their revolutionary policies or facing electoral marginalisation.[1] Elections are a tool which largely preserves the liberal democratic state and protects the status quo, closing down the space for radical change. In order to succeed at elections, parties must fractionalise their long-term goals into short-term aims that appeal to a wide sector of voters and they must use the existing system to deliver benefits to supporters rather than attempting to overthrow the system in its entirety. Small and niche parties may strive to offer distinct alternatives compared to mainstream parties,[2] but they still need to be seen to accept the existing system and try to use it to benefit their supporters if they are to be viable parties in the eyes of voters.

This moderating logic can take hold even in the case of parties that originally participated in elections in a strategic fashion with a view to destabilising the system from within. Once the decision to participate is made, parties can become locked-in to this decision in a path-dependent process of increasing returns, whereby the party becomes heavily incentivised to engage more and more with elections and high costs become associated with leaving this electoral path. This process was the driving force behind the moderation of a range of radical parties in Europe, including the transformation of socialists into social democrats and the compromises that rigid Christian Democracy underwent.[3] In this way, the inclusion of radial parties within a stable set of electoral institutions gradually extracts moderation and restricts the scope for radicalism.

Electoral participation had just such an impact upon the radicalism of Irish republicans. The decision to participate in elections in 1981 represented a critical juncture for republicanism. The path it chose pushed it in an increasingly moderate direction, rejecting parallel states in favour of ambivalent electoral participation and seeking to build a support base within the nationalist bloc of voters in Northern Ireland and the Republic of Ireland. Electoral moderation was about moving from rejection to participation and ultimately accepting elections and their outcomes as providing what de Valera earlier called 'a system of political order'. Once this path was chosen, republicans became locked in, with increasing gains to be made through electoral success and high costs associated with any attempt to leave this path, such as being taunted for having failed to get a mandate for violence or becoming entirely marginalised from decision-making around the future of Northern Ireland. This electoral direction was then later reinforced by the consociational arrangements which brought republicans into government.

Electoral participation was a rational choice by republicans to pursue their goals through a new means in the hope of avoiding marginalisation. Elections were also pursued to allow them to implement their policy vision in a way that violence was hindering them from achieving, embracing reformism and accepting the status quo as a route through which to pursue their goals. This occurred in spite of republicans rejecting the legitimacy of the electoral institutions to govern Northern Ireland. Of course it is important to acknowledge that alongside republicanism's electoralism there were also major peace negotiations that restructured the British state, and elections alone did not lead to complete moderation. As such, elections alone were not the sole cause of republican moderation but it is possible to identify a clear set of causal drivers of moderation that stem from the very act of inclusion within electoral institutions.

FROM OUTRIGHT REJECTION TO STRATEGIC REASSESSMENT, 1970–1980

Although radical parties may try to maintain stances of complete rejection, these are unsustainable if open and relatively fair electoral institutions exist. Where such institutions are present, then radical groups are either pressured or seduced into exploring this route for instrumental gains or to avoid political marginalisation.[4] In retrospect, the early years of republicanism can be seen as Sinn Féin coming to the decision that outright rejection and primarily relying on military means to achieve their goals were limiting their success and thus a reappraisal towards existing electoral opportunities occurred. This occurred even though the sovereign authority of these elections was rejected.

The strategies adopted by republicanism in the early 1970s reflected a rejection of electoral politics in favour of an embrace of outright revolution. To the founders of provisional republicanism, *active* political participation was unthinkable. Ruairí Ó Brádaigh was not opposed to electoral participation, having been elected on an abstentionist campaign to the Irish Dáil in 1957 as well as having attempted to be elected to Westminster in the Fermanagh-South Tyrone constituency in 1966.[5] However, in the minds of the new Provisional leadership there was a significant distinction between abstentionist electoral competition and taking up any seats if elected. The early Provisionals were resounding in their rejection, declaring that:

> Since 1921 Sinn Féin policy has been to abolish the Stormont and Leinster House parliaments and restore the 32 county Dáil Éireann. Sinn Féin has always maintained that this cannot be done by recognising and attending these institutions as minority groups: it can only be done by remaining free of them and convening an All Ireland Assembly.[6]

Throughout the first decade of its existence, republicanism was built around three strategies: building a parallel state, the policy programme of *Éire Nua* (New Ireland), and the use of violence. Republicans attempted to minimise their contact with all organs of the 'illegitimate' state by building parallel educational, judicial and political institutions. The politics of rejection also extended to refusing to recognise the jurisdiction of any British and Irish courts. An editorial in *An Phoblacht* declared that:

> we salute and admire the gallant stand made by men and women North and South in British and Free State courts. First – non recognition – Second – turning of backs, clicking of heels, throwing books of evidence – and Third – the shouts of courage, Up the Provos, God Save Ireland, Traitors All.[7]

Alongside this, republicans attempted to establish four provincial parallel parliaments and one unified coordinating advisory council across the whole island of Ireland in a bid to implement a federal vision of a united Ireland.[8] There was even some discussion within Sinn Féin that it should run candidates in Dáil elections but they should take their seats in this all-Ireland parliament, in a hark back to the First and Second Dáils of 1918 and 1921. The failure of these institutions to gain any foothold is evident from the fact that only 147 people attended the first meeting of Dáil Uladh (Ulster Parliament) and 100 attended the first meeting of Dáil Connachta (Connacht Parliament),[9] resulting in British intelligence dismissing the participants as 'hardly appear[ing] to represent a cross-section of Connaught life'.[10]

The attempt to create a federal vision of Ireland was part of a broader policy programme called *Éire Nua*.[11] Essentially this was the brainchild of Ó Brádaigh and was to become strongly associated with his tenure as president of Sinn Féin. *Éire Nua* outlined policies mainly focused on how a future united Ireland should look, working on the assumption that a united Ireland would be achieved by the IRA. These were not policies to achieve a united Ireland, but they were policies to shape it once this came about. It was also decidedly rural in focus, neglecting many urban issues, including issues of discrimination against Catholics in Northern Ireland.[12] As such, the policy programme was limited in scope, as well as showing the limitations to what Ó Brádaigh and Seán Mac Stíofáin thought politics could achieve.

The 1970s saw the highest levels of IRA activity (see Figure 3.1 on p. 48), and 1,010 of the total 1,712 deaths attributed to the IRA throughout the conflict occurred in this decade. A typical IRA statement of this time was issued in August 1971 and declared that 'physical force is and must be the main means of struggle against the British forces of occupation'. In a book published by the IRA in 1973, the justification for violence was considered self-evident and in fact the use of violence was 'a duty':

> War is one of the harsh realities of life and being the weapon by which Empires are built, logically enough this same instrument brings about the oppressor's fall. The moral right to wage war of liberation has never been questioned: the moral right, in fact duty, of challenging a foreign oppressive army of occupation, in our case that of a one-time colonial power Great Britain, has never been questioned in the long and bitter history of Ireland.[13]

Faith was placed in the military leaders of republicanism who were seen as 'purer' republicans and less likely to be compromised than politicians, who were mistrusted and viewed as liable to pursue self-interest. According to an IRA staff report which was discovered in the possession of Seamus Twomey in 1977, then the IRA Chief of Staff, 'Sinn Féin should come under Army organisers at all levels . . . Sinn Féin should be radicalised (under Army direction) and should agitate about social and economic issues which attack the welfare of the people . . . It gains the respect of the people which in turn leads to increased support for the [IRA]'.[14] Similarly, Joe Cahill, commander of the Belfast Brigade of the IRA and future Chief of Staff, warned of the dangers of 'weak-kneed politicians' and the necessity of keeping decision-making out of their hands and firmly in the grasp of military leaders.[15] The belief was that violence would bring the British to a negotiating table where republicans would only engage in negotiations on their terms. Republicanism's terms required a declaration of intent from Britain to withdraw all military personnel, an acknowledgement by Britain of the right of the whole of the Irish people to decide their own future, and an amnesty for all IRA political prisoners. The rigidity of this position was a source of bemused shock to the British government during secret negotiations in 1972. Republicanism's rigidity convinced the British government that the IRA would accept no incentive short of an all-Ireland republic to stop their violence and therefore there was little point in trying to include them in any proposed solution to the Northern Ireland crisis.[16]

By the end of the decade, and after many false dawns where Ó Brádaigh and Mac Stíofáin claimed that the IRA was on the brink of victory,[17] a strong internal critique emerged within republicanism from those who saw the tactics of this phase as actually inhibiting the achievement of their goals. The critique was spearheaded by Gerry Adams, who was to use it to force a leadership change within Sinn Féin and to depose Ruairí Ó Brádaigh, who Adams was to chain to the failures of *Éire Nua*. This leadership struggle also represented an attempt to wrest control away from a predominantly southern-based and socially conservative leadership into the hands of a younger and more socially-radically northern cohort.[18] Adams derided *Éire Nua* and the tactics of parallel states as a form of 'spectator politics' that marginalised republicans from contributing to the direction and shape of Ireland and instead reduced them to the role of watching other political actors, such as the British and Irish governments and the SDLP, influence Ireland's constitutional future.[19]

The 'spectator politics' critique centred on the idea that republicans should not assume that the IRA would be able to secure a united Ireland through military means alone. Instead, an additional political dimension was required in the struggle for independence. For Adams, the isolationist abstraction of pursuing a parallel state failed to secure any popular backing because it did not resonate with the everyday needs and experiences of Irish nationalists. As he was to argue a number of years later:

> the real requirements of success, an ideology of liberation, must develop from real needs and real interests. Most people will not struggle, never mind vote, for abstract things. They will fight to win material benefits, to improve the quality of their lives, to guarantee the future of their children.[20]

This was also starkly presented by Jimmy Drumm – a veteran IRA member from Belfast who first joined in the 1930s – during his 1977 Bodenstown speech, which many people speculated was actually written by Adams.[21] Drumm declared that:

> a successful war of liberation cannot be fought exclusively on the back of the oppressed in the six counties nor around the physical presence of the British army. Hatred and resentment of this army cannot sustain the war and the isolation of socialist republicans around the armed struggle is dangerous.[22]

The solution lay in what Adams called 'active republicanism'. Adams argued that republicanism's biggest failing was not developing concrete policies to realise a united Irish republic – 'you may be able to bomb a British connection out of existence, given many other necessary political conditions, but you will not bring anything into existence'.[23] Improving the position of northern nationalists now became a separate but related goal to establishing a united Ireland. This was a significant reversal on the previous policy, which declared that the position of Northern nationalists would improve once a united Ireland was established and therefore the details of their present position were of secondary importance. Now when republicans talked about building alternatives to the current state, it was not about building utopian ideals that were ascribed worthiness due to their historical purism. It was about developing a set of policies which would fill a social need and improve the position and rights of nationalists by advancing the causes of republicanism.

'Active republicanism' developed policies, for example to advance the position of the workers of Ireland and to improve housing conditions for lower socio-economic groups, and offered general policies to tackle social and economic injustices. In particular, inequality and discrimination in Northern Ireland were central to this project. Adams's reforms were eventually to win out over Ó Brádaigh's *Éire Nua*, which was voted out as official policy at the 1982 Party Conference, in spite of Ó Brádaigh's pleas for it to be retained. This prompted Ó Brádaigh's resignation, believing that he would undermine the office of President of Sinn Féin if he remained in post when the majority of delegates did not support his policies, and Gerry Adams became the new Sinn Féin president.

Contrary to the teleological claims of the likes of Ed Moloney,[24] at this stage there can be little doubt that republicans, including Adams and his followers, did not have peaceful and full electoral participation in mind when developing their critique of the existing policies.[25] However, contingent circumstances coincided with this internal appraisal in a way that was to encourage Sinn Féin to pursue 'active republicanism' through ambivalent electoral participation. British policy was tolerant of greater politicisation of republicanism rather than pursuing the proscription of Sinn Féin, and republicanism already had a history of pragmatic timely forays into electoral competition to suit their own propaganda value. Into the midst of these developments came a critical juncture in the path of republicanism in the form of the IRA hunger strikes of 1981–1982, which offered an unmissable opportunity in the eyes of republican elites to pursue a popular mandate to forward their struggle.

Ambivalent Electoral Participation, 1981–1994

The IRA prisoner hunger strikes provided Sinn Féin with an opportunity to harness an electoral mandate for purely instrumental ends to achieve the short-term aim of reform of prison conditions. From the leadership's perspective, elections offered the opportunity to pursue republican goals through a new avenue and perhaps allow them to implement their policy programme in a way that violence would not. The elections themselves and the parliaments that they were electing were both still considered by republicans to be completely illegitimate sovereign bodies. What is more, pursuing elections did not imply curtailing the military campaign and a dual electoral and military strategy was pursued from 1981 until 1994. When republicans initially attempted to secure votes from broadly 'moderate' Catholics who would normally support the

SDLP, this was done in the hope of radicalising these voters rather than diluting republican policies to meet their pre-existing preferences. In this regard, republicans pursued a decidedly ambivalent form of electoralism.

Yet there is a fundamental tension inherent in ambivalent electoral participation by revolutionary movements. Once electoral participation is seen as instrumental to achieving short-term aims, then it becomes necessary for a movement to avail itself of this opportunity. Electoral parties then need to respond to voters' preferences and expand their policy programmes to gain support, often necessitating moving beyond singular long-term goals. This immediately raises the contradiction that if short-term reforms can be achieved within the confines of the existing political system this undermines the need for revolution and the overthrow of the existing system.[26] This tension manifested itself in republicanism in spite of their attempts to maintain a sceptical stance towards their electoralism.

In the late 1970s, IRA prisoners in the Maze Prison began to protest against the removal of their 'Special Category Status' by the British authorities, which essentially granted them the status of political rather than criminal prisoners. The protest initially took the form of refusing to wear prison uniforms and wrapping themselves naked in a blanket. Within two years this escalated into a 'dirty protest', with prisoners refusing to slop out or leave their cells to wash, instead smearing excrement on the walls of their cells. By 1981, amidst deteriorating conditions and following an earlier aborted hunger strike, a group of prisoners embarked upon a staggered hunger strike, ultimately resulting in the death of ten prisoners. The prison conditions and the intransigence of the British government generated worldwide sympathy for the prisoners far beyond the traditional circles of republican supporters. When Independent MP Frank Maguire died suddenly of a heart attack, republicans decided to field a hunger-striking prisoner as a candidate in the subsequent by-election in Fermanagh-South Tyrone. Bobby Sands was duly elected to the Westminster Parliament on a wave of public sympathy before dying less than one month later. Similarly, IRA hunger-striking prisoners Kieran Doherty and Paddy Agnew were elected to the parliament of the Republic of Ireland.[27] This success was to encourage republicans to contest all future elections in Ireland and Northern Ireland on an abstentionist basis from 1982 onwards, and it became a watershed moment.

Republicanism's initial electoral participation was both strategic and ambivalent. Ó Brádaigh and Adams could see that a widespread level of endorsement would increase their negotiating leverage with the British government. The decision to put forward Bobby Sands for election was framed as a temporary tactic to achieve a specific end and *An Phoblacht* described republicans as merely 'borrowing' the election to secure better conditions for republican prisoners.[28] Their election 'manifesto' was simply a statement of the five demands made by prisoners for better conditions and nothing else. It was anticipated that an electoral victory would draw international attention to the position of republicans in Northern Ireland, expose the perceived hypocrisy of British democracy when it refused to accede to the demands of a democratically elected MP, and serve as a galvanising force for the nationalist community. The exact same motivations were behind the six prisoner candidates who competed in the Irish Dáil election in 1981. A mandate would also increase their access to decision-making processes over the future of Ireland and policy decisions that would impact upon republicanism. This was most evident in the belief that a mandate would increase the pressure for Thatcher's government to negotiate with the hunger-striking prisoners. For example, Owen Carron, Bobby Sands's electoral agent who subsequently won the by-election following Sands's death, presented the Irish government with quite a headache when he requested a meeting in his capacity as an MP, a request that would have been easily rejected otherwise.[29]

This is not to say that the whole movement was uniformly behind electoral participation. Even after the electoral victories of Bobby Sands and Owen Carron, there were those in the movement who argued that republicans needed to hand the seat back to an independent republican candidate once the hunger strikes were over.[30] Some of the old guard of leaders saw the rising tide of electoralism as a threat that needed to be contained, with Seán Mac Stíofáin demanding that a statement clarifying and asserting the policy of abstentionism was necessary.[31] Suspicion of the electoral dimension was not restricted to the elite level, with a minority of grass-roots members questioning where it was taking the movement. In a rather prophetic statement, one IRA prisoner suggested that:

> If we examine both the history of elections and parliaments, we find that they work against revolutionary change by stifling and deflecting revolutionary fervour and maintaining the status quo . . . The procedures of Leinster House and Westminster ensure that even the most honest of entrants will become ensnared in the trappings of power . . . Remember, if voting could change the system of government, it would be illegal.[32]

To counter this discontent, those supporting elections emphasised that participation would not eclipse or restrict militarism and that elections would deliver gains that the military campaign could not. The instrumental nature of their participation allowed republican leaders to reassure supporters this would not be about seeking an electoral mandate for the IRA, which made it clear that 'the validity of our mandate . . . rests after the election, as before the election, upon the illegitimacy of partition and the British presence'.[33] The IRA also made it clear that the organisation was very different to the Official IRA that had been seduced by elections, whereas the Provisional leadership remained sceptical of the ability to democratise Northern Ireland from within and so knew the limits to elections.[34] This debate was to dominate the Sinn Féin conference in November of 1981 and it was only through an assertion of ongoing militarism that the membership was reassured.

Throughout these forays into electoralism, republicanism maintained its right to an alternative claim to sovereignty and its right to use violence against illegitimate British rule. The IRA reminded its members that 'the Republican attitude towards elections cannot be divorced from our total rejection of the six-county state . . . Our attitude to constitutional politics is quite simple and clear cut. There is no such thing as constitutional politics in this country.' However, it went on to claim that:

> there is room for Republicans to examine if the struggle for independence can be improved by an intervention in the electoral process in order to show clearly that people support radical Republicanism and resistance to the British presence more than they support any other collaborationist tendency.[35]

The strategy pursued was the dual use of instrumental electoral contestation alongside violence, a strategy that came to be known as 'The Armalite and the Ballot Box' after a quip by Danny Morrison – former Belfast IRA member, director of publicity for Sinn Féin and editor of *An Phoblacht* – at the 1981 Party Conference who asked 'who here really believes we can win the war through the ballot box? But will anyone object if, with a ballot paper in one hand and the Armalite in the other, we take power in Ireland?'

Initially electoral victories were seen as an endorsement of the revolutionary republican approach rather than republicans seeing an electoral mandate as necessitating a dilution of their policy programme. Morrison argued that:

> The election of prisoner candidates, whose profile as IRA members their opponents and the media emphasised, and the recent local government elections in the North, show that the mood of the people is changing. They are far from war weary, far from defeat and not so far from victory.[36]

Yet such an understanding was unsustainable in the longer-term.

Competing in elections, even in an ambivalent fashion, brought a new logic to bear upon republicanism. Electoralism necessitated making appeals beyond its core supporters, fractionalising its struggle into a coherent set of short-term aims which would act as stages to achieving its long-term goal of reunification, and ultimately trying to secure a sizeable number of votes to avoid political marginalisation. Harnessing the instrumental power of elections required building alliances within the electorate and adopting a 'broad front' perspective to court the support of individuals who might be sympathetic to the position of the hunger-striking prisoners, even if they would not usually be sympathetic to the radical tactics of republicanism itself. Sworn enemies suddenly became potential allies, including SDLP and Fianna Fáil supporters and Catholic liberal professionals, all of whom had been hitherto dismissed as 'Castle Catholics'.[37]

Adams presented the new tactic to the republican base with the argument that:

> The more people we have with us, the fewer we will have against us . . . We must build a united nationalist front against the British government. Of course, we will have differences and should be jealous of our own political philosophies but the five demands of the prisoners form sufficient basis for unity among the nationalist grass-roots of all the parties in this country.[38]

This is not to say that republicans became overnight reformers nor that their inclusion immediately led to moderate outcomes. Nowhere was this more evident than in Belfast City Council in the late 1980s where the election of Sinn Féin members actually exacerbated already existing tensions on the Council between Unionist and nationalist councillors.[39] Nonetheless, electoral participation did mean that suddenly short-term aims and courting voters now had to be addressed by republicans.

Expanding to secure the support of wider interests also required expanding their policy programme, something Adams and his supporters had been pushing for following the failure of the parallel state strategy. Even though the prisoner candidates ran on the basis of five specific demands, this narrow focus soon broadened. After his election, Kieran Doherty's electoral agent announced that:

> during the election campaign we stated we were only concerned with one issue . . . the hunger strikers' lives. Whilst this is by far our prime aim, people have proved by the large vote that they care. It is therefore our duty on behalf of Kieran Doherty and his comrades to help the ordinary people.[40]

Similarly, during Owen Carron's campaign in the by-election following Sands's death he pledged that he would 'spend all his time in the constituency as a full-time working MP, both for the prisoners and striving to solve the everyday problems of his constituents'.[41]

Soon Sinn Féin began to expand a more developed policy programme tackling reform-based issues, including unemployment, housing, welfare and discrimination. Once the decision to participate in all elections was made, Sinn Féin began to produce broad election manifestos. Their 1989 manifesto for local elections in Northern Ireland contained policies on the environment, health, housing, social welfare, women, prisoners and culture. It was a similar picture in the Republic of Ireland and full manifestos were produced for the 1987 and 1989 general elections, also offering reformist policies on a range of issues, but with less emphasis on the conflict (although this was still present). By the late 1990s, these changes had become strongly embedded and comprehensive manifestos containing a range of reformist policies were the norm, steadily increasing in style and sophistication with each election.

Of course new issues were ultimately framed within the core concerns of republicanism, but clearly the emphasis in policy changed with the need to cater for elections. For example, poor housing for nationalists was blamed upon British neo-colonial interests and discrimination stemming from the inherently sectarian nature of partition, but the very fact that the party was now dealing with reforms to housing policy was in itself significant. Tonge has argued that this period exposed tensions in the dual military and political strategy. He cites the example of the 1983 election where Sinn Féin criticised high levels of youth unemployment within the nationalist community while the IRA simultaneously discouraged inward investment for fear it would stabilise the statelet.[42] Additionally, according to the new electoral Sinn Féin, getting better housing conditions could be seen as a blow to British colonial interests and thus reforms within the existing systems were worthy short-term aims prior to abolishing the systems in their entirety. The trouble was that this implied that the existing systems could be reformed and acknowledged that existing institutions could be used by republicans without losing long-term principles.

Once the idea became embedded that elections could provide another route by which to achieve republican goals, then it became necessary to maintain the early levels of success. While Sinn Féin hoped that they would radicalise the preferences of mainstream nationalists, this was not forthcoming.[43] After the hunger strikes were resolved and the popular emotion of this event was quelled, the republican vote share declined. Essentially, beyond a small core of the electorate, the majority of northern Catholics and almost all of the Irish electorate accepted existing institutions as a valid reformist route and were willing to explore interim stages short of a united Ireland. Rather than Sinn Féin being able to radicalise the preferences of the moderates, Sinn Féin was forced to respond to this preference structure to avoid political marginalisation.

The preferences of nationalist voters were decidedly more moderate, with little appetite for radicalism. The preferences of Catholic nationalist voters were not based around an unswerving and overriding Irish identity that necessitated a territorial expression. In the mid-1980s only 61 per cent of Catholics described themselves as having an Irish political identity, having fallen from a high of 76 per cent twenty years earlier.[44] Half of all Catholics opted for joint British and Irish citizenship while only 20 per cent opted solely for Irish citizenship. Only half of nationalist voters were strongly committed to a united Ireland, with power sharing proving a much more popular option for these voters in the immediate future.[45] Support for the use of violence was also limited, with less than a quarter believing armed struggle to be legitimate.[46] Although admittedly survey data typically underestimate the level of support for political violence,[47] when asked about the level of sympathy for groups who had used violence the overwhelming majority of Catholics had no sympathy.[48] With this preference structure in place, Sinn Féin was never going to be able to win widespread support on the basis of denying the existing institutions of Northern Ireland and the Republic of Ireland.

At the same time important developments were taking place in British and Irish policy with the signing of the Anglo-Irish Agreement (AIA) of 1985. Although the motivations for embarking upon the AIA were multifarious and varied both within and between the British and Irish governments, it significantly changed the political terrain in a way that challenged republicanism. The AIA reaffirmed the status of Northern Ireland as part of the UK, but it explicitly acknowledged that the British government would allow Northern Ireland to join the Republic of Ireland if this was the will of the majority if its inhabitants. Additionally, it established an intergovernmental conference, which gave the Republic of Ireland a consultative role in Northern Irish policy, implicitly acknowledging that British unilaterialism alone was not an adequate way to govern the region. This in turn changed the relationship between Britain and Ireland in a more constructive and cooperative direction.[49] The AIA was imposed over the heads of dissenting Unionist politicians and voters, something that was seen as the product of the way it was negotiated directly between London and Dublin, and largely cut out the local Northern Ireland Office (NIO) officials from the process entirely.[50] Indeed, Douglas Hurd was not even allowed to brief unionist politicians on the negotiations at the insistence of the Irish government, which heightened unionist suspicions of the deal even further.[51]

The AIA is often seen as being primarily driven by leading civil servants on each side, notably Robert Armstrong and Dermot Nally, and then subsequently 'sold' to Margaret Thatcher against her natural unionist instincts by her own team.[52] For Douglas Hurd, the Secretary of State for most of the negotiations – although it was ultimately signed by his successor Tom King – the purpose of the AIA was to attempt a new initiative given that a political stalemate had set in. The goal for the British was to get the Irish government to accept that the consent of the majority of the population in Northern Ireland was needed for any change in its constitutional status and to move the Irish away from what was seen as a belief that Northern Ireland would just gradually and naturally be absorbed by the Republic over time. This was to be done without conceding any sovereignty.[53] For Thatcher it was somewhat different. She hoped to use greater Anglo-Irish cooperation to make security gains against the IRA, and to force the Irish government to take some responsibility for the running of Northern Ireland rather than merely assuming positions that were critical of the British government.[54]

For Garret FitzGerald, the Irish Premier, the goal was to gain some input into the running of Northern Ireland and to use this to bolster the position of the SDLP and marginalise the electoral threat of Sinn Féin.[55] The SDLP completely rejected the idea that it needed an electoral crutch against Sinn Féin, and indeed voting patterns at the time support this, but the party welcomed the way it was imposed by the two governments against unionist discontent and that it generally increased intergovernmental responsibility for the future of Northern Ireland while also bolstering the need for democratic consent.[56] In fact, there was significant overlap and cooperation between the SDLP and back-room Irish officials on the purpose of the agreement. Both viewed the AIA as an attempt to tackle unfinished business between Ireland and Westminster dating back to the 1920s and which Irish nationalists saw as laying the foundation for the violence in Northern Ireland at the time.[57]

In spite of reservations by both Thatcher and Tom King,[58] and although both governments claimed it was not implemented fully by its opposing counterparts, the AIA clearly changed the political terrain. Constitutional nationalists were now able to show that the British government would work over the head of unionists and allow Irish input, weakening traditional republican claims that the Unionists had a veto and that the British had a vested stake in retaining control of Northern Ireland.[59] It was also seen in part as the outcome of pressure from Irish-America and efforts to raise international awareness of the conflict.[60] All of this bolstered the constitutional nationalist approach and challenged the need for revolution.

In terms of Garret FitzGerald's goal of electorally marginalising Sinn Féin, the AIA was more mixed. In fact, with the return of Fianna Fáil to power, the Irish government was to soon drop the policy of marginalisation for inclusion. Elections held in 1982 for a Northern Irish Assembly, which Jim Prior instigated in an attempt to relaunch devolution, led to Sinn Féin gaining 10.1 per cent of the vote share and five seats – a result that was seen as a major triumph for their electoral strategy. After the elections, *An Phoblacht*'s editorial (under its newly appointed editor Mick Timothy) celebrated:

> To those sound republican supporters who were genuinely concerned that the leadership's endorsement of Sinn Féin's electoral intervention might in some way mean a diminishing of the importance of armed struggle, it represents a positive affirmation that these two aspects of republican resistance go together without contradiction. They complement each other ... In what came as a sensational election result, for all but confident republican election workers and candidates, Sinn Féin achieved its promised electoral breakthrough.

But such electoral trends did not look sustainable for republicans if they continued with their mixture of violence and a confusingly incoherent combination of revolutionary and reformist policies. Their vote share fell from 13.4 per cent (where Gerry Adams was elected as their one MP) in the 1983 Westminster general election to 11.4 per cent (although Adams held his seat) in the 1987 general election. Worryingly for republicans, SDLP's vote share rose from approximately 18 per cent to 21.1 per cent. In the 1985 local elections, Sinn Féin polled 11.8 per cent (fifty-nine councillors), which fell to 11.2 per cent (forty-three councillors) by 1989. In fact, their foray into the 1982 Northern

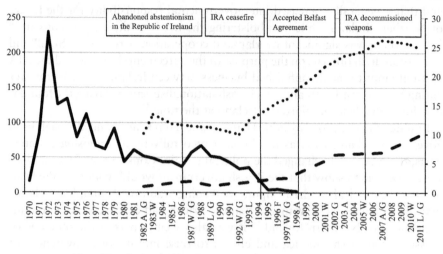

No. of Deaths Caused by the IRA (left hand axis)

····· Sinn Féin Percentage Vote Share in UK (right hand axis)

— — Sinn Féin Percentage Vote Share in Republic of Ireland (right hand axis)

Figure 3.1 The number of deaths caused by the IRA compared against the percentage vote share of Sinn Féin.

Notes: A = Northern Ireland Assembly Election, F = Northern Ireland Forum Election, G = Republic of Ireland General Election, L = Northern Ireland Local Government Election, W = Westminster Election. In proportional elections, the vote share is measured by percentage of first preferences. In addition, Sinn Féin also participated in three other local elections in Northern Ireland not displayed here, but which fit the same trend. The party obtained 16.9 per cent in 1997, 20.7 per cent in 2001 and 23.3 per cent in 2005.

Irish Assembly election was probably their high point during this phase, and their vote share simply stagnated from then on in all UK elections until 1993, when the party began to talk of a ceasefire. Meanwhile in the two general elections in the Republic of Ireland in 1987 and 1989, Sinn Féin polled miserable results of less than 2 per cent of first preference votes (see Figure 3.1).

In light of stagnating electoral performances and a changing political terrain, an unintended consequence of the AIA was that it laid a foundation for republicanism to increase its participation further. Unsurprisingly, republicans decried the AIA, claiming that:

> In one fell swoop this afternoon the Dublin government, led by Garrett FitzGerald, tore up Articles 2 and 3 of its own constitution by agreeing to the loyalist veto over the political future of Ireland and by formally recognising, in an international agreement, the 'Northern Ireland' state. The formal recognition of the partition of Ireland is a disaster for the nationalist cause and far outweighs the powerless consultative role given to Dublin.[61]

But clearly the AIA posed a significant challenge to the traditional republican approach and this coincided with debates within republicanism about its electoral direction. The AIA showed republicans that decisions about the future of Northern Ireland were being taken at an intergovernmental level whether they were part of that dialogue or not, and that the British government was consulting with the acceptable face of Irish nationalism on the future of Northern Ireland. What is more, the Irish government, now led by Charles Haughey, was more inclined towards including Irish republicans in some form of negotiated settlement (even if they were at that time unsure what such a settlement might look like) rather than intent on marginalising them as was the case under FitzGerald.[62] This offered the possibility of some form of inclusion via Dublin, which fed into the other political changes that were putting pressure on republicanism to reappraise the degree of its participation.

Against this backdrop, republicanism began a tense process of reappraising its relationship with state institutions. The first step was to begin recognising the existing institutions in the Republic of Ireland even while continuing to deny their legitimacy. In Ireland in 1979 republicans began to recognise courts in an attempt to get the better of new anti-terrorist legislation. This legislation increased the penalty on conviction of IRA membership from six months' imprisonment to between two and seven years' imprisonment, summarily imposed without needing to produce any witnesses beyond the word of a senior police officer, if the defendant refused to recognise the court. Needless to say, the republican admiration of maintaining a principled denial of the legitimacy of the court was rapidly replaced by strategic recognition. By entering a plea in the courts to deny IRA membership the prosecution was required to present a stronger case with independent witnesses to secure conviction. This led to Jack Lynch, the Taoiseach at the time, apologising to Margaret Thatcher for how the legislation 'backfired by leading the IRA to abandon its policy of not recognising the courts'.[63] Yet, with hindsight, recognition brought republicans into closer contact with the state's moderating institutions. The usefulness of accepting the courts' system soon became evident to republicans who used them to challenge the legality of legislation banning Sinn Féin from the public airwaves in Ireland, albeit unsuccessfully. Recognition of courts in Britain soon followed. When at the 1982 Party Conference a delegate proposed prohibiting Sinn Féin members from recognising the Irish courts, this was soundly defeated by a majority of members.

By 1985, a far more difficult process of recognition was underway – a move to abandon abstentionism in the Republic of Ireland and for any elected Sinn Féin representatives to take their seats in the Dáil. Dogmatists within republicanism, led by Ruairí Ó Brádaigh, argued that abstentionism was an inviolable principle and could not be altered without weakening the ideological foundation of republicanism. According to Ó Brádaigh, 'entry into [the Irish parliament] meant de facto acceptance of the [Irish state's] army, and would enmesh Sinn Féin in constitutionalism. All previous moves by republicans into Leinster House had only strengthened the state and weakened the movement'.[64] There was also the fear that it would damage the IRA by diverting funds, and that it would lead to a need to abandon and pathologise the right to armed struggle.

The counterview was summed up by Tom Hartley, Sinn Féin General Secretary, who argued that 'there is a principle riding above all principles and that is the principle of success'.[65] For Adams, abandoning abstentionism was the next logical step to ending spectator politics. Republicans needed to acknowledge political realities rather than offering vague utopias. That entailed engaging with those political institutions that the people of Ireland accepted as legitimate, even if republicans did not. Adams declared his position as being about recognising the reality of the preferences of potential supporters in Ireland:

> We know that Leinster House ... is a partitionist parliament, but my attitude to it is exactly the same as my attitude to a British court. Fighting a case in the British court does not mean you recognise the legitimacy or sovereignty or validity of that court but that you recognise the reality: you either fight your case or you go to jail. Partition has had an effect in the 26 counties. The state pretends to be a nation and many people believe it is a nation.[66]

Ultimately the reformers won on the back of the argument that Sinn Féin needed to be more competitive electorally and that for republicanism to be successful it needed popular support, which would only come by following the preferences of the nationalist electorate. The IRA lifted their constitutional embargo on members taking seats in parliament and Sinn Féin voted to abandon abstentionism for candidates competing in elections in the Republic of Ireland at its party conference of 1986. Although this decision was made within the context of continually asserting the right to armed struggle, it was not uncontroversial. The sole surviving member of the sacred Second Dáil of 1921, Tom Maguire, withdrew his support and publicly declared that 'I do not recognise the legitimacy of any army council styling itself on the Council of the Irish Republican Army which lends support to any person or organisation styling itself as Sinn Féin and prepared to enter the partition parliament of Leinster House.'[67] Ó Brádaigh and a small group of supporters split from the movement and formed their own rival group 'Republican Sinn Féin', which retained a commitment to abstentionism and returned to the earlier *Éire Nua* federal policy. This split did not really damage provisional republicanism, taking very few of the grass roots with it. If anything, it actually consolidated the power of the Adams-led pragmatists by removing dogmatists who could potentially block any further policy changes.

Explanations which focus primarily on the choreography of this process miss the bigger point, which is that the decision to pursue this policy change in the first place was the product of having to work within certain constraints if elections were to prove useful to republicans.[68] The consequences of increased participation were becoming clear. Anthony McIntrye has argued that a lasting legacy of ending abstentionism was an implicit acknowledgement by republicans that Fianna Fáil's form of Irish nationalism was the appropriate one, that the Republic of Ireland was a complete nation, and that the struggle should be confined to Northern Ireland rather than Ireland as a whole.[69] This greatly undermined their anti-partition ideology. Hitherto, the party had tried to avoid seeing Northern Ireland in an irredentist light for fear of legitimating the existing Republic of Ireland and thus legitimating partition.[70] However, accepting the Republic of Ireland Parliament and now wishing to merge with it suddenly transformed Northern Ireland to an irredentist claim rather than seeing both states as partitioned neo-colonies. Increased participation and all this entailed was undermining the republican stance on partition and the need for revolution in two states.

With hindsight this can be seen as a steady process of increasing engagement once the initial decision to participate was made. This is not to say it was inevitable, but rather once this path of electoral participation was chosen the party was heavily incentivised to remain on it and disincentivised to deviate from it. The major gain of the electoral path was the leverage provided by a popular mandate. By the end of the 1980s, the SDLP was acknowledging that Sinn Féin needed to be included in any solution; the Irish government was aware of the electoral credibility that Sinn Féin possessed and Fianna Fáil was now exploring a more inclusive approach to republicans; and the party itself was attempting to exploit its mandate to further its goals where it could. While some members raised the possibility of moving away from elections and dissented against the increasing recognition of electoral institutions, there were considerable disadvantages to abandoning elections. It was clear that if republicans abandoned electoral competition many in the British and unionist establishment would exploit the failure of republicans to secure a mandate and use this to marginalise republicanism. Additionally, decisions about the future of Northern Ireland were now proceeding between the two governments, and the threat of ongoing British rule with Irish input if no other option could be agreed greatly increased the costs of abandoning politics and returning to a more isolationist policy. Indeed, this was repeatedly raised by Adams and his supporters at the party conferences of 1985 and 1986 in debates over abstentionism. The possibility of increasing marginalisation from the nationalist community and, thus, from the sites of decision-making was raised as a spectre that awaited republicanism if electoralism was rejected.

Consolidating Electoral Moderation through Success, 1995–2010

Accepting elections as providing a form of political order (and therefore violence was not necessary) occurred mainly through the peace process, and there is no reason to think that republicanism's tension between participating in elections while mounting a violent anti-system campaign would have been resolved without the wider peace process negotiations. However, elections were also pertinent in this decision.

In the late 1980s and early 1990s there were some internal critiques of how violence might be hindering vote shares that stubbornly failed to rise even after ending abstentionism. Internal concerns regarding IRA violence first surfaced not by focusing on the right to armed struggle per se, but on the damage caused by IRA operations that resulted in civilian casualties. Danny Morrison has noted the importance on his thinking of meeting a voter in Strabane who expressed support for the policies of republicanism but refused to vote for a party that supported the IRA.[71] Mitchel McLaughlin, former General Secretary of Sinn Féin, when attempting to explain the party's poor performance in local elections in Northern Ireland in 1989, stated that 'IRA operations that went wrong did have an effect because in a sense Sinn Féin is held accountable at the local level for all aspects of the Republican struggle'.[72] The IRA also acknowledged that civilian casualties had a negative impact upon the 'political struggle' and an IRA spokesman stated that:

> There is a greater realisation than ever of the need for the IRA to avoid civilian casualties ... They have given our critics the opportunity to raise once again the proposition that the armed struggle is contradicting and undermining the political struggle. That would never be our intention although, undoubtedly, some operations within the past year have created difficulties for everyone.[73]

When it came to making a choice between these alternatives, there was a greater popular desire for reforms and political advancement than there was for militant action.[74] Essentially, violence was becoming subordinate to electoralism and its efficacy was defined in terms of how it helped or hindered this strategy. Alongside this internal critique of IRA violence, Sinn Féin was engaged in peace talks (to be explored fully in the next chapter) and these two factors influenced the IRA's decision to declare a ceasefire in 1994. This had an immediate and positive impact on Sinn Féin's vote share in elections, which began to rise from 1993 given the widely anticipated nature of the ceasefire.

The peace talks consolidated republicans' attitude to elections as strategic tools to secure their goals. During the course of the peace negotiations republicans repeatedly used their electoral mandate to increase their leverage and criticise the British government and Unionist politicians. The British were accused of stalling the peace process by refusing to negotiate with Sinn Féin without IRA decommissioning, something Sinn Féin claimed violated the electoral democratic rights of their supporters. Much of Sinn Féin's attitude to elections at this time is revealed through the Northern Ireland Forum elections of 1996. The Northern Ireland Forum was an idea that emerged in the peace process and it was an elected body which it was hoped would be used to produce negotiating teams for subsequent all-party peace talks. Indeed it was initially conceived by the British as a way of providing David Trimble with the necessary cover he needed from critics in his own party to negotiate with Sinn Féin by ensuring that all parties to the negotiations had an electoral mandate and therefore a right to be included.[75] Republicans immediately dismissed the idea, labelling it an attempt 'to set in place an assembly with a unionist majority' and a 'delaying tactic' to strengthen the Unionists' position.[76] In fact, so deep were republican reservations about this body that it was one of a series of factors that influenced the IRA to abandon their ceasefire and resume a bombing campaign on the British mainland that was to last between February 1996 and July 1997.

In spite of the depth of these reservations, in April 1996 Adams announced 'we will be taking part in the elections to give leadership at this very crucial time to seek a re-endorsement of our peace strategy and to return a strong republican voice which makes it clear there is no going back to unionist domination'.[77] Following Sinn Féin's highest ever poll of 15.5 per cent the party then gloated 'it was John Major who trumped the elections as a gateway to negotiations and Sinn Féin could not have wished for a more resounding mandate to enter those talks ... Sinn Féin is saying: our voters are not second-class citizens'.[78] Republicans also realised this worked both ways, and that without a mandate they could not secure their goals. When selling the peace process settlement – which fell well short of the traditional goal of Irish reunification – to their own supporters Martin McGuinness stated that:

> A united Ireland was not attainable in this phase not just because of Unionist opposition but because of all the participants only Sinn Féin was advocating and promoting that objective. To the extent that our political strength permitted us to promote all of our positions we did so. A stronger electoral mandate would conceivably have affected the outcome of the talks in any number of ways. We need to learn the lesson of that.[79]

Sinn Féin was also seeing the potential political gains that could be secured through an electoral mandate in the Republic of Ireland. In advance of the Irish general election of 1997, polls were predicting the narrowest of victories for Fianna Fáil, which raised the possibility of Fianna Fáil relying on minor coalition parties to form a government. Prior to the election, Adams declared that:

> in the event of the vote of a Sinn Féin TD being sought to elect a government this party would have a shopping list. This would be based first on the needs of the constituency Sinn Féin will represent, second on the social and economic issues that press down on our communities and overall on the advance of the peace process.[80]

Once again, Sinn Féin was realising that its electoral mandate could give it political leverage to secure policies and, interestingly, the reforms now clearly took preference over the long-term goals. However, political reality soon shook it when it was made very clear by Fianna Fáil that they considered Sinn Féin to be a totally unacceptable coalition partner given its recent radical history.

Following the brokering of the Belfast Agreement, and once the new consociational arrangements were in place in Northern Ireland, Sinn Féin's more moderate electoral positioning was further consolidated. The consociational arrangements encouraged moderation because the size of parties' electoral support was now proportionately linked to executive and legislative power, which acted as a serious incentive for the 'extreme' parties to moderate and increase their vote share.[81] In the first election to the new Assembly, Sinn Féin polled 17.6 per cent of the vote share, securing eighteen seats and two ministries. By the 2003 Assembly election, this had risen to 23.5 per cent, gaining twenty-four seats and four ministries. This trend continued in the 2007 election, with the party securing 26 per cent of the vote share, twenty-eight seats and retaining four ministries. Indeed their vote share rose very slightly in the 2011 Assembly election, gaining twenty-nine seats, before falling for the first time in 2016 and returning to twenty-eight seats, before bouncing back again in 2017 to 28 per cent. Highly significant and momentous in this process was Sinn Féin's eclipse of the SDLP in the 2001 UK general election and confirmed in the 2003 Assembly election. This caused much consternation within the SDLP who viewed this as the product of the British government indulging and propping up Sinn Féin to secure decommissioning and agreement over policing. From this perspective, the SDLP were marginalised from Northern Irish political life by the British because, as Blair said to the SDLP in 2001, 'you guys, your problem is you've no guns'.[82] However, for the British this was more the product of the energy and drive within the republican community compared to the rather more staid image of the SDLP.[83]

Sinn Féin's initial electoral growth was fuelled by harnessing hitherto nonvoters and newly enfranchised young voters.[84] However, later Sinn Féin's growth came from attracting voters who would previously have voted for the SDLP, including expansion into middle-class professionals who traditionally eschewed Sinn Féin.[85] The use of the Single Transferable Vote electoral system also encouraged moderation as the party appealed for lower transfers from other parties within the nationalist bloc. Prior to 1998, SDLP voters were reticent about transferring lower preference votes to Sinn Féin candidates. However, after Sinn Féin endorsed the Belfast Agreement the levels of transfers from the SDLP to Sinn Féin increased markedly. For example, Knox found that in the 1993 local elections in Northern Ireland (the only elections in Northern Ireland using a transferable voting system prior to the restoration of a Northern Ireland Assembly) the SDLP were the only party not to transfer votes as expected, namely to the other nationalist party of Sinn Féin, preferring the Alliance Party.[86] In the first Assembly elections in Northern Ireland in

1998, there was an improving but still generally low level of transfers from the SDLP to Sinn Féin, with 8 per cent of total transfers to Sinn Féin coming from the SDLP.[87] By the 2011 Assembly election this increased to almost 13 per cent of all Sinn Féin transfers, remaining at 13 per cent again in the 2016 Assembly election, and increasing to over 15 per cent in the 2017 Assembly election.[88] There was also a marked increase in the proportion of transfers received from Alliance Party voters during the same time period.[89]

Sinn Féin was also making a judgement to change its strategy on the basis of the ongoing demographic within Northern Ireland. Given that so few Catholics vote for unionist parties and even fewer Protestants vote for nationalist parties, the relative size of religious groups has important political implications. Since the beginning of the conflict in 1969 the number of Protestants has steadily declined in Northern Ireland from a high of almost 60 per cent to just over 40 per cent in 2011. Meanwhile the number of Catholics has increased from 31 per cent to 41 per cent in the same time period (see Figure 3.2). Sinn Féin hoped that a momentum would be built upon a rising tide of nationalist voters and that this would also pressure unionism to reconsider its relationship and position within Northern Ireland.[90] What is more, if the politics of persuading unionism to join a united Ireland failed in a post-Belfast Agreement world, then perhaps demographic change would take care of reunification anyway. This type of calculation may even have seemed to be bearing fruit when the 2017 Assembly election did not return an overall majority for unionist parties.

The trouble with such assumptions was that, as already noted, Catholic voters did not have a strong and uniform commitment to a united Ireland.

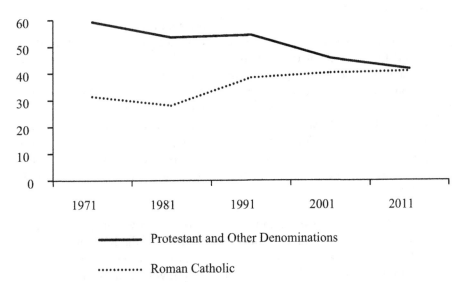

Figure 3.2 Percentage of 'Protestant and Other Denominations' and 'Roman Catholics' in Northern Ireland, 1971–2011.
Source: Northern Ireland Census.

What is more, Protestant voters were more strongly against a united Ireland than Catholic voters were against Northern Ireland remaining under British sovereignty.[91] In other words, the changing demographics did not automatically lead to the gains that Sinn Féin hoped when it made the calculation to participate fully and exclusively in elections. Nonetheless, at the time when the party was making the decision about committing more strongly to electoral competition, this was an important factor in its calculations.

None of this should be taken to imply that increased engagement with electoral institutions was a straightforward process, easily facilitated by increasing vote shares and demographic (mis)calculations. The challenges of accepting the Belfast Agreement are discussed fully in the next chapter, but it is worth pointing out here the internal debates over whether republicans should accept the new Assembly. For many republicans, accepting the Assembly implicitly meant accepting partition and agreeing to work within these confines – even more so than the recognition of Leinster House some twelve years earlier. Indeed, Sinn Féin itself initially opposed the existence of an Assembly during the Belfast Agreement negotiations.[92] The SDLP, however, greatly resisted Sinn Féin's attempt to block an Assembly and soon Sinn Féin stepped aside from engaging in negotiations over institutional designs, leaving this to the Irish government, and focused its energies on issues like prisoner releases and amnesties instead.[93] As such, for some republicans working through the institutions simply would not allow the movement to realise its goals. Instead it was claimed that by entering the new Assembly 'Sinn Féin now risks being co-opted into whatever partitionist arrangements emerge' and that 'Gerry Adams's minimum requirements will not be met' through participation.[94]

In order to generate support for working through the Assembly, the leadership promised to 'test the new structures provided by the Agreement to their very limit' by using them to push for a united Ireland. The leadership also warned that 'without a strong Sinn Féin presence in the Assembly, the North/South bodies and the commitments to equality and rights for nationalists will not be developed'.[95] Key events like the first meeting between Adams and David Trimble were heralded as great republican victories because they represented 'the largest section of unionism finally, belatedly and begrudgingly accepting the rights of non-unionists in the Six Counties to political representation'.[96] The party promised to use the Assembly as a site to further its goals through the

> relentless pursuit of short and medium term objectives such as the establishment of all Ireland structures, the abolition of the RUC and delivery of the equality agenda. The Assembly is a forum where these issues will be thrashed out and through which attention will be drawn to them.[97]

But in reality there were limits to how far Sinn Féin could push the institutions, both due to the checks and balances within the system and due to the incentives for the party to moderate its position. Contrary to pessimistic expectations, the design of the electoral system and awarding executive power in proportion to vote shares did not lead to electoral outbidding. The preferences of northern nationalists were too moderate to sustain this and voters demanded that republicans endorse peace, prosperity and power sharing. Yet at the same time, voters wanted the strongest voice possible to protect their ethno-national interests within the power-sharing institutions.[98] As a result, Sinn Féin needed to moderate in terms of endorsing participation, accepting elections as a form of political order, agreeing to abide by their outcomes, and rejecting violence. However, it never needed to renounce its institutional history of violence or the right to armed struggle and, in fact, its radical tendencies and history became an electoral asset as long as it abided by the principles of the Belfast Agreement. In this way, the elites were able to maintain their long-term goals and merely recalibrate the emphasis that they put upon them, favouring instead the short-term aims of reform and improving the position of the nationalist community within Northern Ireland. This is not to underestimate the very real changes that the party underwent, but it retained its traditional stances on Irish sovereignty and the illegitimacy of British rule and any attempts to stay within the Union. Instead, the means changed in a rational response to a changing environment and in an effort to secure long-standing goals through new departures.

How Change Was Possible

A useful point to consider is how the changes in electoral direction, which were at times incremental and at times dramatic, were possible within republicanism. Party leaders can often find it difficult to get party members to support changes in direction if they are seen to compromise the ideology of the party. When a party's elite wishes to change its policy position in a way that might be seen to be in conflict with previously held ideological principles, the extent to which the leadership is able to impose a new direction depends on institutional constraints such as: leaders' accountability to party activists; the extent to which policy-making is decentralised within the party; whether the party is reliant on activist funding or public funding; the extent to which electoral results depend upon policy positions; and potential coalition outcomes.[99] In the case of the IRA and Sinn Féin, there was a high degree of leadership autonomy from the grass roots and there were high levels of satisfaction and trust in the leadership which allowed it to move in new strategic directions. What is more, the new direction was ultimately electorally successful.

Given that the IRA was a hierarchical military organisation, decisions were made largely autonomously from the input of soldiers who were disciplined and conditioned to follow executive orders. In addition to this, policy decisions by the IRA's Army Council were typically accepted without dispute or questioning because the Army Council, according to republican tradition and lore, was the rightful government of a united Ireland with direct continuity back to the Second Dáil.[100] The Army Council was composed of seven appointed members who determined the policy of the IRA as well as appointing its Chief of Staff, who in turn maintained command over the day-to-day operations of the IRA. In theory the Army Council was subordinate to a General Army Council composed of the rank and file of the entire IRA and which was supposed to meet every two years. However, in reality, all power was really embodied in the Army Council because it was typically too risky to convene a meeting with every member of the IRA for fear of mass arrests and the difficult logistics of such a task for an illegal organisation. Therefore, a small group of leaders at the top of the organisation determined policy and used the authoritarian structure and mythical aura of their position to impose policy upon their followers.

Sinn Féin is a more democratic organisation in terms of its operation, but it too in reality has a highly powerful and autonomous leadership. Sinn Féin's constitution appears to vest power in the membership of the party in many key respects, such as policy-making, choosing the party leader, and selecting candidates to run for election. However, closer examination shows that actual power lies with the leadership of the organisation, namely a powerful twelve-person *Ard Chomhairle* or Party Executive. A case of seeming branch member power actually being subordinate to the leadership is evident in how the party's president is chosen. Sinn Féin's president is elected each year by all members at the annual conference, but Gerry Adams has been elected unopposed since 1983, and before that Ó Brádaigh was elected unopposed from 1970 to his resignation in 1983. Similarly, while election candidates can be chosen and nominated by party members at constituency conventions, all candidates have to be subsequently approved by a sub-committee of the Party Executive.

As with most political parties, policy is created by a policy committee but it requires approval at the annual party conference before becoming Sinn Féin policy. However, traditionally the Sinn Féin Party Conference accepted policies proposed by the leadership largely uncritically or else they were not given the opportunity to vote on controversial policies which were often removed from discussion and referred to the Party Executive. A British official described the use of this tactic at their 1975 Party Conference where

> the order of business was worked out in advance by a steering committee, which effectively ensured that the more contentious items were not reached. Thus, motions dealing with reactivation of the campaign for withdrawal of British forces in Ireland and 'that powers of decision for election purposes be returned to Sinn Féin', were not taken.[101]

Issues not voted upon were instead left for the Party Executive to decide. A similar tactic was evident at the 1977 Party Conference, where scheduled debates about the tactics to be used in fighting direct elections to the European Parliament and trade union relationships were prevented by Gerry Adams and Niall Fagan (a member of the Sinn Féin executive who would subsequently walk out with Ó Brádaigh over the decision to end abstentionism in 1986) who persuaded the delegates to leave the issue to the discretion of the Party Executive.[102] The British rather scathingly referred to this as 'typical of the dictatorial way in which the *Ard Chomhairle* runs Provisional Sinn Féin'.[103] By the 1980s, leadership dominance of the party was being consolidated even further through organisational changes necessitated by the decision to contest elections. The 1982 annual conference passed a number of changes to the Sinn Féin constitution that essentially increased the power of the central party over regional branches, notably in terms of granting Sinn Féin elected officials *ex officio* membership on all local committees; entrusted Party Executive members to implement and coordinate policy across all Sinn Féin departments; and set up regional conferences to 'gauge grassroots opinion' prior to the national conference.[104] These were deemed necessary to allow greater coordination for the new electoral orientation, but they also had the effect of consolidating the leadership's ability to lead on policy direction at the expense of grass-roots branch members.

Not all decisions could be removed from the grass roots, especially the contentious ones, but those that went to the conference were carefully managed. The three most significant examples of these are the decision to abandon federalism and *Éire Nua*, the decision to end abstentionism in 1986, and the decision to accept the Belfast Agreement and participate in the new Northern Ireland Assembly in 1998. The decision to end federalism, although actually resulting in increased engagement and reformism, was framed and presented as a hardening of republicanism by Adams. He argued that federalism represented a 'sop to unionists', and that 'we must recognise that loyalists are a national political minority whose basis is economic and whose philosophy is neo-fascist, anti-nationalist, and anti-democratic. We cannot, and we should not, ever tolerate, or compromise with loyalism.'[105] Ironically, although abandoning federalism was the start of a process of incremental moderation, it was framed as a way to shore up republicanism and protect it from compromise. When this was combined with the added dimension that the debate over federalism and *Éire Nua* also represented a confrontation between northern republicans looking to take control of the movement from southern republicans, the policy was rejected and 'active republicanism' was adopted.

When it came to ending abstentionism, it was harder to present this as a hardening of republicanism, so instead Adams and his followers emphasised that the changes in direction were strategic and not about compromising or rejecting long-standing goals. Throughout key stages of republicanism's changing direction, both Adams and McGuinness 'drew on their prestige as Provisional militants, the movement's traditions of loyalty, and the weakness of the republican theoretical tradition' to allow the leaders to control the party 'using the ethos of the Army'.[106] Prior to voting on the motion at the party conference, Martin McGuinness, who was seen as a committed militarist by the republican base, gave a speech declaring that war against Britain would 'never, never, never' end until freedom had been achieved even if the party took their seats in the Irish Dáil. This was seen as a defining moment in assuaging grassroots' fears about the changing direction.

A similar tendency was evident in the presentation of the Belfast Agreement for ratification to the party membership. A constructive ambiguity was created around republicanism's commitment to the armed struggle by implementing the strategy known as TUAS, which for some audiences meant Totally UnArmed Strategy while for other audiences it meant the Tactical Use of Armed Struggle.[107] In this context, Adams's key phrase of 'a new phase of the struggle' can be seen as an assertion of ideological continuity for the grass roots, and the leadership frequently gave speeches that 'played to the gallery' of core grassroots supporters by emphasising the radical nature of republicanism and their unapologetic history of violence.[108] Additionally, the leadership's autonomy to make decisions was also enhanced by the high levels of trust granted to them from members, particularly Adams and McGuinness.[109] Finally, many of those more active members who may have been inclined to challenge the direction of the leadership's policy decisions left with the split in the movement in 1986, giving even greater autonomy to the Adams-led leadership.

CONCLUSION

Following the exhaustion and failure of outright rejection, the first foray by republicans into elections was intended to be temporary and focused on the limited remit of furthering the agenda of IRA prisoners. However, early success taught them that electoral interventions could be a useful tactic in meeting republican aims. Widespread support was necessary to generate electoral success and this meant moving beyond the core republican base and seeking the votes of moderate nationalists in Northern Ireland and the Republic of Ireland as well. This generated a number of tensions within republicanism – if they could pursue reforms of the existing system this undermined the need for complete revolution; it recalibrated the emphasis within republican thinking, placing a greater emphasis on short-term aims that did not necessarily entail reunification and less overriding emphasis upon the ideal united Ireland as the immediate goal. It also meant that republicans now needed to align their policies with the preferences of the nationalist electorate if they were to be successful, given their failure to radicalise the preferences of voters. The preferences of the electorate were essentially moderate ones that accepted existing institutions as legitimate sites of authority (particularly in the Republic of Ireland) and who were not wedded overwhelmingly to the need for a territorial expression of an ethnic Irish identity. Crucially, there was also limited support for a campaign of political violence. In this way, republicans were drawn from a process of limited electoral engagement into a more in-depth degree of engagement that entailed accepting the existing institutions, fractionalising their struggle into a series of smaller and more reformist aims, and moving away from singular policies of outright revolution.

Elections served as an important critical juncture that, once the decision to participate was made, delivered increasing returns to republicans by staying on this path, while the costs of turning away from elections were high.[110] A growing electoral mandate strengthened republicanism's political position and leverage and this, in turn, enhanced their importance within the nationalist community and with other actors in the party system. A political mandate was seen as increasingly necessary to achieve a united Ireland rather than relying on militarism and utopian idealism. Once the electoral path was chosen, the costs of leaving it rose. Any turning away from elections would be interpreted by opponents as a failure to obtain a mandate for their military strategy or for their political goals. Additionally, the political future of Northern Ireland was being decided by the British and Irish governments regardless of whether republicans attempted to engage with this process or not. Therefore, they were heavily incentivised to remain on the electoral path and to make it as successful as they could. In this way, electoral participation became steadily embedded within the movement.

It is also important though to consider what moderation did not entail. Participation was strategic and it was an attempt to secure long-stranding republican goals through a new means. It entailed a recalibration of emphasis towards short-term aims, but this did not mean that the long-term goals of a united Ireland and assertions of an alternative claim to sovereignty were weakened. In fact, in order for the leadership to sell the changes to their grass-roots supporters they often had to emphasise these aspects quite strongly. Brendan O'Duffy has argued that the 1980s saw a bi-national sovereignty emerge in the way that Northern Ireland was governed.[111] This indeed may have been the case for some observers, but there was no pluralisation of republicanism's conception of the rightful sovereignty of Ireland as a result of their electoral participation and the policy changes this entailed. The core of their raison d'être has been to undermine the Northern Irish state and establish a united Ireland and this remains undimmed. Today they accept elections as a way to allow them to achieve this goal and agree to abide by the results and outcomes that these elections produce. This was a calculated change in strategy rather than a shift in normative values of the movement where violence and vague utopianism were seen as hindering their political goals while electoral mandates were seen as a potentially valuable asset to achieving them. That is not to say there was no value change within republicanism – after all, they now accept that the existing institutions offer a fair route to realise collective political goals and there has been a shift in values away from revolution towards reform. However, there were limits to the extent of their value change.

NOTES

1. Przeworki and Sprague, *Paper Stones*.
2. Ezrow et al., 'Mean Voter Representation and Partisan Constituency Representation'.
3. Kitschelt, *The Transformation of European Social Democracy*; Kalyvas, *The Rise of Christian Democracy in Europe*; Müller and Strøm, 'Political Parties and Hard Choices'.
4. Przeworski and Sprague, *Paper Stones*.
5. White, *Ruairí Ó Brádaigh*, p. 96.
6. *AP*, September 1971, p. 10.
7. *AP*, 4 February 1973, p. 1.
8. Sinn Féin, *Peace with Justice: Proposals for Peace in a New Federal Ireland*.
9. *Irish Times*, 28 August 1971.
10. Letter from Irish Embassy Dublin to London (Blatherwick to Thorpe), 19 October 1971, FCO 33/1197, NAI.
11. Sinn Féin, *Éire Nua. The Social and Economic Programme of Sinn Féin*, p. 1.
12. Tonge, 'Sinn Féin and the "New Republicanism" in Belfast'.
13. Irish Republican Army, *Freedom Struggle*. This book was banned in Britain and Ireland but a copy is available in Justice 2004/27/7, NAI.
14. Quoted in Taylor, *Provos*, pp. 211–212.
15. See Joe Cahill's speech at Bodenstown in 1971. It is also worth noting that Cahill was one of the Provisional delegates who met with Harold Wilson when he was leader of the opposition Labour Party in 1972, showing that this suspicion of entrusting politically minded figures to guard republicanism was more than just rhetoric.
16. 'Confidential Annex to Cabinet Meeting Minutes, CM(72) 5th Conclusions, Minute 3', 3 February 1972, CAB 128/48, NA; Harold Wilson and Merlyn Rees reached a similar conclusion when they met republicans while leaders of the opposition in 1974. See Rees, *Northern Ireland: A Personal Perspective*.
17. The new year issue of *AP* in January 1972 declared that victory was near for the IRA and this would be the year of triumph. Ironically, similar claims were made in 1973 and 1974 too.
18. Moloney, 'The IRA', p. 20.
19. For example, see the articles written by Adams in the *Republican News* (*RN*) under the pseudonym 'Brownie': 'Active Abstentionism', *RN*, 11 October 1975; 'The Republic: A Reality', *RN* 29 November 1975; 'The National Alternative', *RN*, 3 April 1976; 'A Review of the Situation – Past, Present and Future', *RN*, 14 August 1976.
20. Adams, G., Presidential Address, 1987 Sinn Féin Party Conference.
21. The British government were certainly suspicious that Drumm wrote it himself, doubting that he had the intellectual ability for such a speech. CJ 4/1796, NA.
22. Drumm, J., Bodenstown Commemoration Address, 1977.
23. Adams, *The Politics of Irish Freedom*, p. 64.
24. Moloney, *A Secret History of the IRA*.
25. This is clear from Adams's article in *RN*, 1 May 1976.
26. Przeworski and Sprague, *Paper Stones*, pp. 1–2.
27. For the best overview of the events, see Beresford, *Ten Men Dead*.
28. *AP*, 4 April 1981, p. 12.
29. 'Advice to Taoiseach about MP Owen Carron's request for meeting, 3rd September 1981', DFA 2011/39/1824, NAI. See also the Statement by John Kelly, Minister for Foreign Affairs, to the Dáil on 11 August 1981, DFA 2011/39/1819, NAI.

30. Interview with Danny Morrison.
31. Letter from Seán Mac Stíofáin to *AP*, 3 October 1981.
32. Letter by Thomas Donn, Irish POW, to *AP*, 22 October 1981.
33. *AP*, 18 April 1981, p. 6.
34. *AP*, 5 September 1981, p. 20.
35. *AP*, 5 September 1981, p. 20.
36. Danny Morrison, Bodenstown Commemoration Address, 1981.
37. 'Castle Catholic' referred to nationalists who accepted working through the existing parliamentary structures, derived from Stormont Castle where the Northern Irish parliament met. Republicans typically projected them as making personal gains by taking this position, even though it betrayed the Irish nation.
38. *AP*, 16 May 1981, p. 25.
39. Interview with Alex Attwood.
40. *AP*, 11 July 1981, p. 16.
41. *AP*, 1 August 1981, p. 3.
42. Tonge, 'Sinn Féin and the "New Republicanism" in Belfast', p. 140.
43. Interestingly the British claimed not to be too worried by the initial success of republicans or what this revealed about the preferences of the nationalist electorate, instead seeing it as an outlying occurrence due to unprecedented circumstances. Interview with Robin Butler.
44. Whyte, *Interpreting Northern Ireland*, pp. 67–69.
45. Ibid., p. 80; Coakley, 'National Identity in Northern Ireland'.
46. Hayes and McAllister, 'Sowing Dragon's Teeth' p. 913.
47. Breen, 'Why is Support for Extreme Parties Underestimated by Surveys?.
48. Hayes and McAlllister, 'Sowing Dragon's Teeth', p. 914; Fahey et al., *Conflict and Consensus*.
49. O'Duffy, 'British and Irish Conflict Regulation from Sunningdale to Belfast. Part II'; Todd, 'Institutional Change and Conflict Regulation'.
50. Interview with Ken Bloomfield. Bloomfield also notes that when the secretariat was up and running as part of the provisions of the AIA, he was often the only Northern Irish person in the room, which was mainly populated with officials from Dublin and London. This caused him some discomfort given that the secretariat was concerned with the running of Northern Ireland.
51. Interview with Douglas Hurd. Hurd recounts attempting to brief Molyneux and Enoch Powell under Privy Council rules so that he could reassure them while also ensuring they would not be able to discuss this in public, but Powell refused the briefing (and Molyneux followed his lead) because he wanted to relay any information he found out to his supporters.
52. Interview with David Goodall.
53. Interview with Douglas Hurd.
54. Interview with David Goodall; interview with Douglas Hurd.
55. FitzGerald, *All in a Life*.
56. Interview with Sean Farren; interview with Mark Durkan.
57. O'Huiginn, 'Peace Comes Dropping Slow', p. 143. Interview with Eamonn McKee. Many interviewees from the British side noted with amused frustration the propensity of Irish nationalists and republicans alike to begin negotiations with a history lesson.
58. Interview with Tom King. King's reservations were not over the principle of the AIA and, although he was instinctually unionist, he acknowledged that reform of Northern Ireland and concessions for nationalists were essential. Instead he objected to the way the AIA was negotiated over the heads of local politicians and to some of the procedural details.
59. Interview with Sean Farren; O'Huiginn, 'Peace Comes Dropping Slow', p. 145.
60. Interview with Mark Durkan. Also Tom King noted that US critics of British

policy in Northern Ireland were supportive of the AIA and saw it as a serious and responsible approach to the Troubles.

61. *AP*, 21 November 1985, pp. 8–9.
62. Interview with Martin Mansergh; O'Huiginn, 'Peace Comes Dropping Slow'.
63. 'Report of meeting between Taoiseach and British prime minister', 5 September 1979, TAOIS 2010/19/1646, NAI.
64. *AP*, 6 November 1986, p. 11.
65. *AP*, 7 November 1985, p. 7.
66. *AP*, 27 November 1986, p. 8.
67. *AP*, 30 October 1986, p. 1.
68. For example, Spencer, *From Armed Struggle to Political Struggle*; or Lynn 'Tactic or Principle?'.
69. McIntyre, 'Modern Irish Republicanism', p. 112.
70. Tommy McKearney, former IRA member turned Provisional critic, has outlined the reasons behind the original desire to avoid seeing the conflict as an irredentist one. McKearney, *The Provisional IRA*, p. 96.
71. Interview with Danny Morrison.
72. *AP*, 25 May 1989, p. 3.
73. *AP*, 26 January 1989, p. 1.
74. Evans and Tonge. 'From Abstentionism to Enthusiasm'.
75. Interview with Quentin Thomas. Thomas himself admitted that it was a strange event and it caused the Irish government great consternation that it was even being held. This is certainly the view of O'Huiginn in 'Peace Comes Dropping Slow'.
76. *AP*, 21 March 1996, p. 8.
77. *AP*, 25 April 1996, p. 1.
78. *AP*, 6 June 1996, p. 6.
79. *AP*, 23 April 1998, p. 19.
80. *AP*, 5 June 1997, p. 9.
81. Garry, 'Consociation and its Critics'.
82. Interview with Mark Durkan.
83. One interviewee recalled a joke that said that 'the SDLP used to be known as a party of school teachers, but today they are known as a party of retired school-teachers', to highlight the party's staid image compared to the more dynamic momentum behind Sinn Féin.
84. McAllister, 'The Armalite and Ballot Box'.
85. Evans and Tonge, 'From Abstentionism to Enthusiasm'.
86. Knox, 'Emergence of Power Sharing in Northern Ireland'.
87. Evans and O'Leary, 'Northern Irish Voters and the British-Irish Agreement', p. 89.
88. Barry, *2016 Assembly Election: Transferred Votes*; Barry, *2017 Assembly Election: Transferred Votes*.
89. Evans and Tonge. 'From Abstentionism to Enthusiasm'.
90. Bean, *The New Politics of Sinn Féin*, p. 208.
91. Coakley, 'National Identity in Northern Ireland'.
92. For example, see Mitchel McLaughlin's statement on opposing an Assembly in *AP*, 9 April 1998.
93. O'Huiginn, 'Peace Comes Dropping Slow'; Powell, *Great Hatred, Little Room*.
94. This typical critique came from the letters page of *AP* on 9 April 1998 from a member who called themselves rather presciently 'No Other Law'.
95. *AP*, 14 May 1998, p. 8.
96. *AP*, 10 September 1998, p. 1.
97. *AP*, 10 September 1998, p. 9.
98. Mitchell et al., 'Extremist Outbidding in Ethnic Party Systems is Not Inevitable'.

99. Müller and Strøm, 'Political Parties and Hard Choices'.
100. Moloney, *A Secret History of the IRA*.
101. Letter from R. M. Harris to British Embassy on Sinn Féin Ard Fheis 1975, FCO 87/411, NA.
102. *Hibernia*, October 1977.
103. Letter from Irish Embassy to Whitehall on 1977 Sinn Féin Party Conference (Barrie to Cowper Coles), CJ 4/1796, NA.
104. *AP*, 4 November 1982, p. 5.
105. *AP*, 5 November 1981, p. 6.
106. Bean and Hayes. 'Sinn Féin and the New Republicanism in Ireland', p. 128.
107. Moloney, *A Secret History of the IRA*, p. 423.
108. Ibid.
109. Gormley-Heenan, *Political Leadership and the Northern Ireland Peace Process*.
110. On increasing returns and path dependence, see Pierson, 'Increasing Returns, Path Dependency, and the Study of Politics'.
111. O'Duffy, 'British and Irish Conflict Regulation from Sunningdale to Belfast. Part II'.

4. DEMOCRATISATION AND REINING IN RADICAL REPUBLICANISM

Radical groups often agree to trade in their revolutionary ways in return for democratic reforms which give them a greater stake in power or increased opportunity to gain power. Huntington argued that in return for greater political inclusion radical groups may agree to 'abandon violence and any commitment to revolution, to accept basic social, economic and political institutions ... and to work through elections and parliamentary procedures in order to achieve power and put through their policies'.[1] Revolutionary and ruling elites engage in quid pro quo exchanges which result in the moderation of radicalism in return for increased inclusion.[2] This is not just true of leaders and elites, the mobilised masses may also be willing to limit the demands they make of the state if inclusive gains are won.[3] Incentives and disincentives influence whether such bargains are sought, including the need to stave off a crisis in a regime; pressure from allies to find agreement; material or political gains for the elites; realising the potential rewards of new institutional rules; tackling the grievances and injustices that led to the attempted revolution in the first instance; and whether coexistence has a lower cost than adversarial existence.[4] Additionally, a normative commitment to democratic rule above and beyond a group's immediate strategic interests can also explain why democratic bargains are struck and why groups are willing to compromise and accommodate each other.[5]

Using the concept of democratisation can seem anachronistic in the Northern Ireland context given that Britain is one of the longest-standing democracies in the world. Yet the conflict in Northern Ireland was a conflict over self-determination and contestation over the status of Northern Ireland between two competing nationalisms. For republicanism this was about democratic bargaining where an important part of the peace process was about challenging the democratic character of Northern Ireland. It is possible to identify clear stages in republican strategy that entailed extensive moderation in return for what republicans perceived as the democratisation of political opportunities for nationalists. These stages closely parallel Walter's stages of ending civil wars: deciding to negotiate, striking a mutually agreeable bargain, and implementing the agreed bargain.[6] Initially republicans went through a phase which led them to make the decision to negotiate. This entailed republicans coming into increasing contact with mainstream Irish nationalism and agreeing to make compromises to make themselves 'coalitionable' and build an alliance with these groups. During the actual negotiations republicans compromised their revolutionary positions, in particular their use of violence, in return for institutional and credible guarantees that their goals could be pursued through political channels, facilitated through the power-sharing design. Republican engagement was largely strategic, although given their ademocratic rather than anti-democratic nature, this made it more natural for them to engage. The implementation phase had a distinct meaning for republicans. This was a difficult process whereby republicans removed the last vestiges of their radicalism, especially through decommissioning their weapons, but they did not want to cement the existence of the new institutions created during the peace process forever. Rather republicans aspired to use the peace process to transition to a united Ireland and the implementation phase was about trying to balance accepting the new power-sharing institutions as providing a system of political order but limiting their permanence and only accepting them on condition that they allowed for an opportunity to transition to a united Ireland.

DEMOCRATISING NORTHERN IRELAND OR DEMOCRATISING REPUBLICANISM?

On the surface, the standards of British democracy applied to the governing institutions of Northern Ireland from its foundation in 1921 in the same way as they did to other parts of the UK. Throughout the entire conflict period there were regular inclusive elections which could be freely contested, a competitive party system, and civil and political liberties. But while Northern Ireland may have had a majoritarian variant of a functioning democratic process, only the most optimistic of observers would have described it as a fully functioning and consolidated democratic region. Contestation over the sovereign and democratic status of Northern Ireland was the very core of the problem between two competing nationalisms, and interpretations of Northern Ireland's rightful status directly influenced what the contending parties understood democratisation to entail.[7]

According to the republican viewpoint, Northern Ireland was an inherently flawed political entity established in a manner that violated democratic principles. The partition of Ireland created an artificial unit which denied true Irish self-determination. From this perspective, the only way Northern Ireland could survive as a political entity was by institutionalising discrimination and denying political, social and economic opportunities to the nationalist community. Attempts to challenge the constitutional or institutional arrangements were met with oppression and state violence.[8] Northern Ireland was seen as essentially a neo-colonial project undertaken in the imperial interests of Great Britain and consolidated through the imposition of Westminster-style institutions in order to strengthen the position of the vulnerable majority through the total domination of the minority.[9] Such neo-colonial interpretations of the status of Northern Ireland proliferated throughout the 1960s, placing the root cause of the conflict with Britain's imperial ambitions.[10] Northern Ireland was characterised as a one-party statelet which institutionalised violence in many forms,

> all of which were used for the total coercion of the nationalist community. Institutionalised state discrimination in job allocation and housing, gerrymandered political boundaries, a heavily-armed paramilitary police force with a heavily armed militia, backed up by a wide range of coercive legislation were the tools of state-sponsored violence.[11]

The cumulative result from the republican viewpoint was that working within the British system was inherently compromising and designed to frustrate Irish independence, and therefore the only solution was to use violence and remain outside the system.

For traditional republicanism, unionists were not the problem preventing Irish self-determination. Rather British colonial interference was the real power preventing a united Ireland and it propped up and sustained unionism for its own imperial goals.[12] The main way that Britain ensured its position was through granting the unionist community a 'veto' over the constitutional future of Northern Ireland. This was said to emanate from a combination of the 1920 Government of Ireland Act and the 1949 Northern Ireland Act. The 1920 Act gave Britain complete sovereignty over Northern Ireland while the 1949 Act ensured that there could be no changes to the future status of Northern Ireland without the support of a majority in the Northern Ireland parliament. Given the majoritarian nature of the Northern Irish parliament combined with the unionist majority artificially manufactured by the way the border was designed,[13] this was tantamount to giving unionists a permanent veto over any attempts at constitutional reform by working through the existing system.

In stark contrast, for unionists the only factor that was hampering democracy was the anti-system violence and politics of republicanism, sustained by the Republic of Ireland's irredentist claims, as embedded in Articles 2 and 3 of de Valera's 1937 Constitution. In 1970, unionism was willing to admit that 'a sizeable number of people still do not accept the validity of the State', but the solution did not require institutional, let alone constitutional, reform of Northern Ireland. On the one hand, the Unionist political majority acknowledged that 'Government representatives are in the main seen by Opposition Members as being drawn from a group or class with whom they have little or no affinity' and they even went so far as to state that 'the gap between "them" and "us" must be bridged in some way and if the present attitudes preclude this then some experimentation is necessary'.[14] On the other hand, the suggested policy to bridge this gap was decidedly less than experimental and it entailed inviting the SDLP to form the official opposition within the existing majoritarian parliament. Indeed just weeks before Ted Heath suspended devolved rule and imposed direct rule from Westminster in 1972, Brian Faulkner, the leader of the UUP and prime minister of Northern Ireland, made a defiant statement:

> The Northern Ireland government may be slandered every day of the week as a fascist junta anxious only to beat Catholics into the ground and achieve a military victory. But the fact of the matter is that the elected representatives of the minority have no need to voice their case of their views on the streets, thereby endangering public safety – they have the forum of Parliament and they have an open and pressing invitation from the Government – who, let it not be forgotten, are the democratically elected representatives of the majority, to sit down and reach sensible agreed solutions to our problems.[15]

Implicit in this perspective was the claim that the existing borders of Northern Ireland were the appropriate unit for self-determination and that existing democratic institutions served this process of self-determination well by following the preferences of the majority. Therefore, from the Unionist perspective any peace process was about democratising republicanism to eliminate the IRA threat from Northern Irish politics while still retaining its position within the UK.

So what did democratic bargaining in Northern Ireland actually entail? The lack of a nation-state or an overarching accepted national identity meant that it could never be about building unity behind such an identity. Instead, it was essentially limited to an institution-building process and evoking loyalty to those institutions as methods of delivering the contradictory aspirations of the different parties. It was a process that attempted to move beyond seeing politics in terms of winners and losers and reconciled all parties to accepting the means by which politics should be pursued, even if what constituted the legitimate ends continued to be contested.[16] But this was also about more than building the politics of accommodation through clever institutional design. Democratisation in Northern Ireland not only included a reconstruction of the meaning of democracy and a redesign of the institutions accordingly, it also entailed the removal of anti-system violence and the rejection of revolutionary tactics. In short, it was also a war-to-peace transition. These processes were complementary, whereby changing the dominant practice of democracy in Northern Ireland and republican moderation were mutually reinforcing.

Changing Political Contexts and the Decision to Negotiate

In the late 1980s external factors beyond internal party developments put pressure on republicanism to liberalise its thinking towards negotiating a settlement.

Increasing Nationalist Participation in the Northern Irish Economy

Acemoglu and Robinson argue that stable democratic outcomes are the product of bargains between a small group of elites who wish to preserve the status quo and the leaders of the masses who wish to change the status quo.[17] The likelihood of such bargains being offered or accepted depends upon levels of inequality. They argue that the demand for change comes because the masses are aware of the benefits they will gain from overhauling the status quo, most notably through a redistribution of wealth. Overly high levels of inequality incentivise ruling elites to resist mass pressure for change because they have more to lose (especially if coupled with low costs of repression) while low levels of inequality dampen mass demands for democratisation. Therefore, if there is enough inequality to lead to mass demands for revolution but not enough to incentivise oppression, this then opens the possibility of the ruling elite attempting to strike a bargain with dissenting groups and offer reforms in exchange for abandoning revolution. This process accurately describes what happened in Northern Ireland. Nationalist rates of inequality encouraged demands for revolution from nationalists, which provoked resistance from unionist elites. However, as rates of nationalist economic participation improved and reduced inequality without actually eradicating it, this put pressure upon republicans to enter negotiations and bargain for reforms in return for removing the threat of revolution.

Northern Ireland under the Stormont regime between 1921 and 1972 was characterised by large inequalities between Protestants and Catholics.[18] During this time, Catholics were discriminated against in three main areas. Firstly, there was discrimination in electoral representation through gerrymandering and restrictions of the electoral franchise. For example, nationalists were 'manipulated out of control' of thirteen local councils through changes to the post-1922 electoral rules, including in Londonderry/Derry where nationalists represented 60 per cent of the population.[19] Secondly, there was discrimination in the allocation of public housing in parts of Northern Ireland, notably Fermanagh where although Catholics were a majority of the population they only occupied 568 council houses compared to 1021 Protestant-occupied council houses.[20] Finally, there was extensive discrimination in labour market participation, especially in the public sector. While Catholics were fairly represented in manual and low-skill public sector jobs, they were greatly underrepresented in the ranks of senior professions.[21] In short, high inequality was endemic at the time of the formation of radical republicanism.

Table 4.1 Protestant versus Catholic unemployment rates and Catholic unemployment differentials.

	Protestant unemployment rate	Catholic unemployment rate	Male Catholic unemployment differential
1971 Census	5.5	13.8	2.6
1981 Census	11.4	25.5	2.4
1991 Census	10.7	22.8	2.2
1990 LFS	8.6	16.0	1.8
1991 LFS	7.8	18.4	2.4
1992 LFS	9.1	18.4	2.4
1993 LFS	9.4	18.1	2.1
1994 LFS	8.6	16.1	2.0
1995 LFS	8.1	15.9	2.0
1996 LFS	7.8	12.8	1.6
1997 LFS	5.3	12.2	2.9
1998 LFS	5.4	10.4	2.3

Source: Northern Ireland Census and Northern Ireland Labour Force Survey.

From the outset of the conflict, the British government acknowledged that change was required to include the nationalist minority more fully in all aspects of political and economic life.[22] Successful reforms to remove inequalities were seen as a route to stabilising the region and challenging republican revolutionaries. The British government hoped that 'if [reforms] could contain elements capable of winning a measure of support among moderate Catholics, the IRA might forfeit much of the benevolent neutrality which they enjoyed at the hands of individuals who sympathised with their political aims even while abhorring their methods'.[23] In the early 1970s, following the suspension of the Stormont Parliament, the British government introduced fairer electoral practices and reformed local government.[24] Additionally, under pressure from the British government, the Northern Ireland Housing Executive was established. This in essence took decisions about public housing allocation out of the hands of local elected politicians in an attempt to rein in Unionist politicians favouring Protestants applicants, regardless of levels of need. While these two policies did much to end inequalities in these areas, labour market inequalities proved more intractable.

By the mid-1990s the position of Catholics ameliorated but without actually achieving equality. This challenged republican claims that Northern Ireland was irreformable and revolution was necessary while simultaneously increasing pressure for further reforms to achieve more gains. Catholic unemployment rates throughout the 1970s and 1980s were extremely high, peaking at 25.5 per cent according to the 1981 Census, compared to 11.4 per cent unemployment for Protestants (see Table 4.1). Catholic males were 2.6 times more likely to be unemployed than their Protestant counterparts in 1971 and

Table 4.2 Percentage of Catholics comprising selected employment groups.

	Public sector employment			Private sector employment		
	Managers and professionals	Associate professionals	Lowest skilled groups	Managers and professionals	Associate professionals	Lowest skilled groups
1990	30.8	43.9	38.1	32.2	29.9	38.2
1991	32.6	43.7	38.6	33.3	31.1	39.0
1992	33.4	44.0	38.6	35.3	33.2	39.5
1993	35.9	44.3	40.6	34.5	34.5	39.3
1994	36.8	44.7	41.2	36.3	36.0	40.5
1995	37.3	44.4	41.6	36.7	36.9	40.8
1996	38.2	44.5	42.5	37.4	38.3	40.3
1997	39.0	44.7	42.9	38.0	37.6	41.3
1998	40.1	45.1	43.1	38.8	39.2	41.3

Source: Adapted from Fair Employment Commission for Northern Ireland, *Profile of the Monitored Workforce* (Belfast: Fair Employment Commission for Northern Ireland, 1990–1998). 'Managers and professionals' refers to an average of 'soc 1' and 'soc 2' categories; Associate professionals refers to 'soc 3' and 'Lowest skilled groups' refers to an average of 'soc 8' and 'soc 9'.

2.4 times more likely in 1981. In this context the Westminster government introduced the 1976 Fair Employment Act, making direct discrimination in the workplace illegal. This Act, which was largely self-monitoring and without real regulatory power, was later superseded by the 1989 Fair Employment Act, which made both direct and indirect discrimination illegal and enshrined affirmative action to address labour market inequalities. Although it is debated as to how far changes in labour market employment rates are attributable to this Act or whether they are attributable to a general economic boom in the 1990s,[25] nonetheless the unemployment differential fell from a high of 2.6 in 1971 to 2.0 in the mid-1990s, and even to 1.6 in 1996. Although it is difficult to compare the census data directly to the Labour Force Survey data, it is clear that there was a general decline in rates of Catholic unemployment too.

While there has always been a Catholic middle class in Northern Ireland, this has grown in size and changed in nature since the 1990s. In a study based on male employment categories Breen found that by the mid-1990s, the influence of a man's ethnic group membership in predicting his socio-economic outcomes had declined significantly and that although Protestants still held some advantages over Catholics these had been greatly reduced.[26] In the early 1970s, the Catholic middle class was 'clustered in occupations servicing the Catholic community (teachers, doctors, lawyers, clergy, etc.) with substantial under-representation in business, finance and public administration'.[27] However, as can be seen in Table 4.2, Catholics increased their position in the most senior occupation sectors in both the public and private sectors. During this time Catholics comprised approximately 40 per cent of the population, and between 1990 and 1996 Catholics went from comprising 30.8 per cent of managers and senior professionals to 38 per cent in the public sector and from 32 per cent to 38 per cent in the private sector. These changes were also reinforced by improving Catholic educational attainment. Prior to 1975, Catholic schools significantly underperformed compared to their Protestant state counterparts.[28] After 1975 the position began to improve significantly and, by the 1990s, Catholics were just as likely to have a qualification higher than an 'A level or equivalent', as well as performing comparably in terms of gaining 'A levels or equivalent' and 'O levels or equivalent'.[29] The reforms within the labour market were then making it easier to convert those educational opportunities into employment opportunities.

British government policies that attempted to tackle the economic grievances underpinning the conflict served as a form of preference-shaping within the nationalist electorate as a whole.[30] Socio-economic changes posed a challenge to republicans' claims that Northern Ireland was beyond reform. It is evident that relatively successful reforms to reduce inequalities between Protestants and Catholics were implemented prior to republicans entering formal negotiations. Bean argued a somewhat comparable perspective in that he too observed a change in the economy of Northern Ireland through a restructuring of civil society that precipitated a transformation in republicanism.[31] There was a growing and emerging Catholic middle class with an increased stake in Northern Ireland evident by the early 1990s.

That is not to say that this group wished to maintain the status quo, as clearly many inequalities persisted. Rather, this reduced the appetite for all-out revolution given that the extreme inequalities of the 1921–1972 period were being reined in. Nor is it being argued that changes in the economic structure of Northern Ireland determined that republican elites would enter a bargaining phrase, but rather this created an opportunity to pursue such a strategy. This economic transformation occurred against the backdrop of republicanism's increasing need for votes and against its new found tendency to fractionalise its struggle into short-term electoral-oriented goals. In short, economic changes created an opportunity for elites to pursue a bargain and incentivised them to consider more extensive reforms in exchange for halting revolution.

The Liberalisation of Republicanism through Alliance Building

In a process of democratic bargaining normal interests and alliances between elites are redefined and reshuffled, albeit usually on a temporary basis.[32] Alliances can lead to a change in strategic interests and this, in turn, facilitates striking an agreement. During any successful democratic bargain a united elite needs to emerge prior to institution building to give direction and leadership to the process.[33] It was precisely such alliance building that was at the heart of the second process of liberalisation within republicanism. This process led to Sinn Féin gradually loosening some of their more rigid interpretations of Northern

Ireland and Irish self-determination, culminating in an IRA ceasefire in 1994, and allowing for peace talks.

Within two years of the signing of the AIA in 1985 Sinn Féin was invited by a third party (Fr Alec Reid) to engage in talks with the SDLP. In early 1988 Gerry Adams initially met with John Hume but this was soon widened to a Sinn Féin delegation comprising of Adams, Tom Hartley, Danny Morrison and Mitchel McLaughlin engaged in dialogue with leading members of the SDLP (Hume, Seamus Mallon, Sean Farren and Austin Currie). In addition, Mark Durkan engaged in seconds meetings with members of Sinn Féin to follow up on issues that emerged out of the meetings between Adams and Hume.[34] There was also some contact on a more local level and Alex Attwood reports meeting members of Sinn Féin who were also on Belfast City Council for both parties to get a chance to better understood each other's position.[35] John Hume had previously resisted such requests to meet Sinn Féin but following an interview that Adams gave to *Hotpress*, where Adams referred to the possibility of exploring alternatives to armed struggle, Hume decided to accept the invitation (although not until after the 1987 general election for fear of the meeting leaking and harming their vote share). The motivation for Adams and his colleagues was to test the thinking of constitutional nationalism to see if it really believed what it claimed about the nature of the British presence in Northern Ireland and the role of unionism in Northern Ireland.[36]

In addition, and much more importantly, Sinn Féin were also interested in building a pan-nationalist alliance,[37] or in the words of Martin Mansergh, Albert Reynolds's chief advisor on all things Northern Ireland, a 'democratic nationalist consensus'.[38] Sinn Féin had just released *A Scenario for Peace* (1987), which largely repeated traditional republican policies, and which ended up highlighting to the Sinn Féin leadership how such policies were leading to their political isolation. Tom Hartley stated that:

> the weakness of *A Scenario for Peace* is that we had produced a document which I suppose in republican terms is a 'ground' document. But only republicans read it . . . What we wanted to do was to develop a politic in which we would engage with all the political forces on this island so that it wasn't just republicans talking to republicans.[39]

Therefore, the party's official line to justify entering the talks with the SDLP was their potential to increase Sinn Féin's ability to implement its policy agenda:

> This invitation [to talks] came against a background of persistent attempts by the Dublin and London governments and most of the political parties, including the SDLP, to isolate Sinn Féin completely from the political arena . . . Sinn Féin's view is that the British government needs to be met with a firm, united and unambiguous demand from all Irish nationalist

parties for an end to the unionist veto and for a declaration of a date for withdrawal.[40]

While there was some broad agreement between the two parties, such as that Irish reunification was the ultimate goal and that any proposed solution needed to include the Republic of Ireland, generally the SDLP consistently challenged and refuted many of Sinn Féin's central claims. The main focus for Sinn Féin was on trying to persuade the SDLP that their efforts to reform Northern Ireland were merely propping up British colonial domination of Ireland, that the unionist veto was a bulwark that prevented any constitutional reform, and that Irish self-determination could only be exercised on an all-Irish basis, which reduced unionists to their rightful place as a minority within Ireland.[41] The SDLP delegation asserted that Britain was neutral in Northern Ireland and its only commitment was to implementing a democratic process. Therefore, the best approach to pursuing Irish unity was certainly not armed struggle but attempting to win unionist consent for a political process of extensive constitutional change. The SDLP also argued that unionists no longer had a veto over British policy in Ireland since the implementation of the AIA, but they did have a 'natural veto' as inhabitants of Ireland whose agreement was essential if unity was to be achieved.

The SDLP were very clear that they would be willing to pursue an agreement of broad interests, and this could even include the Irish government, but that this would come with certain conditions:

> The SDLP has no objection and indeed would be willing to work with Sinn Féin or any other party to develop a strategy towards the achievement of agreed common objectives. We would make it clear however that we would be working together on exactly the same terms – using democratic and peaceful methods and without any links or associations with any paramilitary organisations or with support or approval for such activity.[42]

These talks ended without resulting in any immediate agreement between the parties, but the possible incentive of an alliance was established. Sinn Féin now argued that 'the adoption of [a policy demanding Irish reunification] by Sinn Féin, the SDLP and the Dublin government would advance the situation, concentrate everyone's mind, not least the unionists, and put the responsibility where it belongs – with the British government'.[43]

At around the same time, British politicians were attempting to encourage Sinn Féin to accept their neutrality and move towards a process of negotiation. This represented a change in British policy which hitherto had largely followed the Irish lead epitomised by FitzGerald's policy of attempting to marginalise Sinn Féin. Now British officials attempted to enable 'political movement' based on finding an inclusive way to enable Irish republicanism to end its armed struggle and to co-opt the movement.[44] Official talks between the British government and the constitutional parties (known as the Brooke-Mayhew Talks) had largely failed, leaving disgruntlement within all major players. The SDLP were unwilling to commit unless Sinn Féin were part of the process, both because the party believed this was the best way forward and for fear of being outbid by Sinn Féin sitting outside the process. The Unionist parties were still frustrated at the AIA and unwilling to engage unless that was suspended. The Irish government and the SDLP were expecting Labour to be returned to power in 1993 – where Kevin McNamara would most likely become the new Secretary of State and who favoured Irish reunification – so the Irish were trying to hold out for this prospect.[45]

However, behind the scenes engagements were proving much more fruitful. Adams had been in secret talks with British officials since at least 1990 and these largely built on the groundwork laid by Hume-Adams.[46] Through these talks and subsequent official declarations by the British and Irish governments, notably the Downing Street Declaration (DSD) of 1993 and the Frameworks documents of 1995, the British aimed to reassure republicans of their neutrality over the future of Northern Ireland and embed the acceptance of the consent principle by all major parties. The idea was that Sinn Féin could pursue whatever political goals it wished as long as they accepted that any change in the future status of Northern Ireland needed the support of a majority of its population. The DSD represented the clearest recognition yet by the Irish government of this principle of consent and thus a highly coordinated intergovernmental approach was solidifying, albeit both sides accepted that the Irish had a vested interest in the outcome while the British claimed not to have such vested stakes.[47] Significantly, the Secretary of State for Northern Ireland, Peter Brooke, declared in November 1990 that Britain 'had no selfish strategic or economic interest' in Northern Ireland as part of making public reassurances that were being given to republicans in private.[48] The two governments held out the possibility for republicans to be part of a political process provided they gave up armed struggle while simultaneously letting it be known that the process would proceed without them if they did not commit soon.

These new developments were met with an encouraging response from Adams emphasising the importance of the symmetrical relationship between the British and Irish governments as well as implicitly acknowledging how it would be valuable to republicans to build closer relations with the Dublin government. He declared that:

> If the British government is prepared to cooperate with the Dublin government to bring about Irish self-determination . . . then there is a real possibility of progress . . . The Joint Declaration does contain, for the first time ever, a recognition by the British, though heavily qualified, that the Irish people as a whole have the right to self-determination.[49]

Talks between Adams and Hume resumed again in April 1993, and this time they were central to achieving an IRA ceasefire one year later and to Sinn Féin internalising the SDLP position in almost all respects. Sinn Féin was now persuaded that their interests would be best pursued through a pan-national alliance given that the party needed to explore a political process for fear of complete marginalisation. Addressing an internal conference, a senior Sinn Féin leader argued that 'when the leaders of northern nationalism say that there can be no internal settlement, that is a very powerful message', the implication being that it was far more powerful than if Adams had said this on his own from a position of isolation.[50]

Through the resumed talks, Sinn Féin began to shift its position in a way that prepared it for the negotiations to follow in the formal bargaining phase. The idea that interim institutional arrangements in a reformed Northern Ireland were necessary prior to attempting to secure Irish unity by consent became broadly accepted. Tom Hartley attributed this change directly to the alliance-building talks:

> What you have now is that you can't have accommodation without the unionists. You can't have peace in Ireland if the unionists don't have their fingerprints on a settlement. So our thought processes have changed more this last number of years because of that dialogue [with the SDLP]'.[51]

They also began to acknowledge that a British withdrawal would not take place prior to an IRA ceasefire.[52] A pan-nationalist alliance could be used to argue for a strong Irish dimension to any settlement, something that Sinn Féin, the SDLP and the Irish government all agreed upon. The only catch was that before the Irish government and the SDLP would agree to pursue a nationalist consensus position that included Sinn Féin, republicans needed to give up violence.

In August 1994 the IRA announced a complete cessation of military operations and within a week, Adams, Hume and Albert Reynolds, released a joint statement bringing the Irish government formally into the pan-nationalist alliance. Jim McAllister, a former Sinn Féin councillor, placed the loose alliance with the SDLP and the Irish government at the heart of the decision for a ceasefire:

> It is important to remember that the IRA called their cease-fire because they believed the conditions existed for an honest and realistic process to deal with the problems Britain has caused in Ireland ... Republicans have always said that one of the reasons for armed struggle was that those in a position to promote Irish unity and democracy, such as the Dublin government and the SDLP, were sidestepping the issue. They are now proving willing to address the situation and we welcome this.[53]

No longer were republicans the isolated outsiders of absolute radicalism; they were now engaged with other actors within the established political system. While they were certainly still radical in some respects, even after ending violence and outright rejectionism, their radicalism was now defined in relation to that of other actors within the system rather than as a group that was so radical it sat outside the very confines of the system itself.

STRIKING A BARGAIN

Bargains to establish new democratic institutions are typically about 'institutionalising uncertainty' and accepting that 'democracy means that all groups must subject their interests to uncertainty'.[54] Yet Northern Ireland challenges aspects of these understandings, notably just how much was truly negotiable during this phase and the idea that the new democratic institutions could actually institutionalise uncertainty. The need to secure further republican moderation meant that power sharing was pursued, which explicitly attempted to limit the degree of uncertainty in the short term. As many scholars of civil war have argued, power sharing greatly increases the chances of reaching and implementing a settlement by enshrining guarantees that allow radicals to overcome reservations about changing policies.[55] Essentially, guaranteeing republican spoilers a stake in power not only established a credible commitment to reforming the one-party history of Northern Ireland, something that was necessary to overcome what they saw as a history of the unionist veto, but it also allowed republican policy sacrifices to be made by protecting their interests rather than subjecting them to complete uncertainty. In other words, it rendered moderation much more achievable by guaranteeing republicans their stake, in spite of the potential risks that come with democracy. Yet at the same time it was necessary to institutionalise uncertainty over the long-term future of Northern Ireland as republicanism's acceptance was ultimately conditional on viewing this as one stage in a 'stepping stone' process to a united Ireland.

The formal process of striking a bargain ran from the beginning of all-party talks in 1997 until the acceptance of the Belfast Agreement in 1998. At least three transitions were evident: a transition from war to peace, a transition from a majoritarian to a consensus form of democracy, and a reconstruction of the political institutions. Power sharing was not a new British policy, dating at least from the Sunningdale initiative of 1973/1974. Additionally, although options other than power sharing were considered following the failure of Sunningdale, the Belfast Agreement was rooted in earlier agreements like the AIA and the DSD which promoted greater coordination between Britain and Ireland, enshrined the consent principle, and established Irish input into discussions around the constitutional future of Northern Ireland. This helped all parties to the Agreement to be able to compromise knowing that their interests would be protected by a strong institutional legacy.

Soon after the IRA ceasefire in 1994, Sinn Féin issued the policy document

DEMOCRATISATION AND REINING IN RADICAL REPUBLICANISM

Towards a Lasting Peace in Ireland. Alongside their traditional assertions of self-determination, the proposed solutions to the conflict changed markedly. Calls for the immediate departure of Britain were replaced with demands for:

> a British government that makes the ending of partition its policy in Ireland; a Dublin government that has the same policy; cooperation between the London and Dublin governments to bring this about in the shortest possible time with the greatest possible consent and minimizing costs of every kind; that this may be done in cooperation with unionists and northern nationalists.[56]

This was a clear signal from Sinn Féin that it was ready to explore a negotiated settlement, but beginning any talks was to prove difficult. Although the IRA declared a complete ceasefire in August 1994, up until that point there had been an uptick in IRA violence, which the British attributed to the entrenched republican belief that the threat of violence was necessary leverage for any negotiations with the British.[57] Prior to the ceasefire the British had made it clear that after a short period of 'decontamination' preliminary dialogue between the British government and republicans would begin and the government had promised to be highly imaginative in its response, that is a range of options would be on the table if the core tenets of the consent principle were accepted. However, soon after the ceasefire some within John Major's government began to raise concerns that the word 'permanent' had not been used by the IRA. In this context, decommissioning of weapons arose as a proxy to indicate the depth of republican commitment, initially raised by the British and not the Unionists (although they were to take up the issue with vigour later).

This led to delays in starting all-party talks, much to the frustration of the Irish government who recommended that the British simply emphasise the positive and begin talking immediately.[58] While secret talks were actually ongoing between the Conservative government and Irish republicans at this time, they did not result in any progress towards Sinn Féin's inclusion in public negotiations. What explains this delay and the British reservations? The view within Irish circles and within nationalism was that Major's government was reliant on the Unionists for their political survival and thus held hostage. Yet it is not clear that this explains the whole picture, given the tough choices and forceful pushing Major did at other stages regardless of his slim majority. Instead, it was genuine concern that this was purely tactical and republicans could not be trusted. Additionally, there were concerns that David Trimble would lose support from within his own party and that he would be outbid if the process moved too fast.

For Sinn Féin this was a typical British response, overriding the democratically mandated representatives of the nationalist community and erecting new hurdles to prevent republicans from taking a seat at the top table. Therefore in 1996 the IRA brought their ceasefire to an end with a large bomb in London's

Canary Wharf. This was a blow to some British officials who had thought that republicanism had crossed the Rubicon as early as 1993 and could not backslide to the use of violence and entrenched British and unionist suspicions throughout the future of the peace process.[59] Yet republicans made it clear that the return to violence was not a return to unbridled militarism and soon after the explosion Adams baldly stated that Sinn Féin could not abandon the peace negotiations: 'it is simply not good enough to walk away from a peace process which took so long and so much effort to build'. Tony Blair's election in May 1997 and the removal of Major, combined with Bertie Ahern's election in June 1997, helped to reinvigorate the process from the republican perspective. To the relief of the Irish who were frustrated by the unnecessary block,[60] Blair abandoned the need for decommissioning prior to all-party talks provided the IRA reimposed their ceasefire, which they duly did. Talks started, which culminated in the acceptance of the Belfast Agreement by all the major parties, apart from the DUP and the United Kingdom Unionist Party.

The Belfast Agreement was essentially an institution-building document that transformed the traditional form of democracy seen in Northern Ireland to date. The Agreement was explicitly consociational in nature, based on the principles of executive power sharing, proportionality (of the executive, the legislature and public sector positions), equality of the two communities (and others), and enshrining minority vetoes.[61] Interestingly, many of the underlying principles of the Agreement were already in place from earlier intergovernmental agreement between Major and Reynolds and the document embodied many of the features that the SDLP had long argued for.

Some of what would have been thought as the most difficult aspects of the Agreement were less troublesome to address than might have been anticipated. Many of the constitutional and institutional aspects were largely ignored by republicans who had come to accept the constitutional nationalist position but did not want to be seen to be negotiating anything that recognised partition. Strand One of the negotiations covered the status of Northern Ireland within the UK. This was largely negotiated by the SDLP and the UUP as republicans chose not to engage with this strand (although they initially tried to resist the idea of any Northern Irish Assembly but soon abandoned this and then left the negotiations to others), implicitly accepting the need for a power-sharing assembly but refusing to be seen to negotiate this. Strand Two concerned the relationship between the Republic of Ireland and Northern Ireland. Although this was of central importance to republicans and their strategy hinged upon creating strong North-South institutions, this strand was largely negotiated by the Irish government. The Republic of Ireland agreed to amend its constitutional claim and, interestingly, a working group led by Martin Mansergh on the Irish side and John Chilcot on the British side had previously developed an acceptable formula for what would replace Articles 2 and 3 of the Irish constitution.[62] The finalised North-South institutions were more limited in scope than republicans would have liked, but republicans were aware of the need to concede on this strand to unionists in order to secure a deal, and republicans won the revocation of Section 75 of the Government of Ireland Act (1920), an important symbolic gesture for them, in return.[63] Strand Three focused on the relationship between the UK and the Republic of Ireland, establishing a British-Irish council as a counterweight to the North South Ministerial Council (NSMC).

Rather than focusing on the formal strands, republican negotiators were much more interested in issues of core salience to their base that would allow them to sell the Agreement as a victory for nationalists. This meant pushing hard for the release of republican prisoners as early as possible (republicans wanted them released within one year, Blair wanted it within three years, so they compromised on within two years), an overhaul of policing in Northern Ireland, and enshrining the European Convention on Human Rights into Northern Irish law as well as establishing a Human Rights Commission.[64] In addition, they succeeded in delaying a final ruling on decommissioning until a later date, and instead the Agreement committed all parties to do all within their power to deliver decommissioning within two years – a vague phrasing that was to come back to haunt the implementation phase.

The Agreement helped to moderate republicanism by providing it with guarantees and subsequently interlocking its fortunes with that of the Agreement. The shift towards a consensual form of democracy was about challenging the unionist veto and the idea of indivisible sovereignty operated by central Westminster decree. Ending majoritarian rule became synonymous for republicans with moving closer to a united Ireland. This led to the seemingly unthinkable position just fifteen years earlier that republicans now saw the establishment of consensual institutions within a devolved Northern Ireland as somewhat of a victory. An editorial in *An Phoblacht* declared:

> [Unionist] desire for an internal settlement with a devolved administration comes from their wish to restore majority rule, that is, unionist domination, in the Six Counties. But the British, under the pressure of Irish nationalists, have now firmly enshrined into their political project for the Six Counties the principle of power-sharing in some shape or form.[65]

While campaigning for an endorsement of the Agreement, Adams argued that:

> it is the notion of being top dog which sustains unionist supremacy. We are dealing here with justice issues, cultural rights, political rights, economic rights and national rights. We are also dealing with the reality of removing the reason from elements within unionism for their very existence as unionists. Because if the union does not guarantee their top dog position, then they can have no more loyalty than I do.[66]

As such, seeing consensus democracy as a step towards a united Ireland embodied a very particular understanding of unionist interests. In return republicans acquiesced to the need to gain the consent of a majority of inhabitants of Northern Ireland to secede from the Union. Similarly, Gerry Kelly emphasised that 'The Good Friday Agreement is a contract between opponents; not an agreement between friends' as a further way to emphasise republicanism's reasoning for accepting the deal.[67]

Fundamental for republicans was the North-South dimension of the Agreement, which emerged as their main hope for building momentum towards a united Ireland. Republicans argued that securing Irish input into the Northern Irish executive was a great victory and prevented portraying the conflict in Northern Ireland as an internal issue. Maximising the Irish dimension, it was hoped, would lead to closer links on an all-Ireland basis which would provide the foundation for ultimate reunification. Sinn Féin's Party Executive argued that 'the [Agreement] is not a political settlement. When set in the context of our strategy, tactics and goals, the [Agreement] is a basis for further progress and advance of our struggle. It is another staging post on the road to a peace settlement'.[68] It is in this context that electoral success in the Republic of Ireland became as central to the republican vision as electoral gains in the North. Sinn Féin, as the only political party competing in both jurisdictions in Ireland, could convincingly claim an all-Ireland dynamic was in place if they rose to executive power in both Northern Ireland and the Republic of Ireland.

Once again this was a process of accepting the reformed institutions as a system of rule but it was not about accepting the legitimacy of that rule. The ruling institutions were agreed on condition they provided a route for republicans to realise their alterative claim to sovereignty. Securing full acceptance may have meant providing guarantees in the short term but it also meant removing guarantees about the future of Northern Ireland and introducing uncertainty in the long term. The future of Northern Ireland was now subject to popular majority referendum. Such an approach appealed to republicans who always had their own majoritarian streak, typically arguing that unionists should be treated as a minority in a majoritarian system of all-Ireland democracy. Bourke sees an irony in the fact that ultimately the constitutional fate of Northern Ireland is now decided by majority vote through a referendum of its inhabitants. The core problem facing Northern Ireland in the 1970s is still present today, namely a majoritarian political process that has the capacity to alienate a very sizeable group, only this time it could potentially be some future nationalist majority imposing its will upon a unionist minority to become part of a united Ireland.[69] Arthur Aughey sees more immediate problems in the Agreement's attempt to solve the competing sovereignty claims. He argues that the fundamental tension between each community's aspirations was overcome by imposition and appeasement, which only served to undermine the transformative power of the negotiated settlement in the eyes of the unionist community.[70] However, any suggestion that anything other than accommodation of the opposing community's right to their aspirations could be built into the peace settlement seems implausible. Uncertainty had to lie at the heart of the Agreement as this is the essence of democracy. Power sharing tried to limit this uncertainty and did so in the short term, but Northern Ireland's long-term future needed to be thrust into doubt in order to secure republican acquiescence.

What emerged as the most intractable issues for republicanism, namely the military aspects such as decommissioning and reform of the police force in Northern Ireland, were not finalised in the Belfast Agreement but deliberately left to be dealt with by independent commissions in the consolidation phase. This meant that republicanism's moderation in the transition phase was ambivalent. There was significant moderation in terms of ending violence permanently, agreeing to participate in the institutions of Northern Ireland under British sovereignty, accepting the need for unionist consent to achieve a united Ireland, and acquiescing to abide by the outcomes of this process. However, the symbolic legacy of their radicalism remained undimmed. Republicans prevaricated over decommissioning, continued to point out the ongoing existence of the IRA, refused to apologise for or distance themselves from the legacy of armed struggle and continued to use their physical threat in the political arena, albeit in a diminished form. Thus by the end of the transition phase republicans were accused simultaneously of still being radicals in disguise by their unionist opponents and of being overly compromising and traitors to a united Ireland by disillusioned former comrades. Indeed a relatively small number of these comrades split from the provisional movement in protest at accepting the Belfast Agreement, adding to those dissidents who left with Ó Brádaigh in 1986 in protest at ending abstentionism.[71]

Yet from the position of hindsight it is clear how this transition phase locked republicanism into a certain path that meant that many of these ambivalences had to be resolved in the consolidation phase. This was summed up by one republican activist in a note of resigned acceptance:

> we appear to be on a road of stepping stones to a united Éire, a path which some object to. This path was not chosen recently, but by the Irish traitors in 1921. Much as some may dislike this road, there appears to be no going back. This is the road we are on, and we may as well follow it.[72]

IMPLEMENTATION AND THE PARTIAL CONSOLIDATION OF
REPUBLICAN MODERATION

Republicans engaged in the bargaining phase in a strategic and limited fashion, but this was unsustainable if the Agreement was to be implemented fully. Republican interests were now closely tied up with the successful operation of the Agreement in order to achieve their aspirations of a transitional route to Irish unity. The implementation phase became about tackling many of the militant aspects of republican radicalism that had been postponed. Republicans needed to demonstrate a clear commitment to the moderate path to show that they had more than a shallow affiliation with the new democratic system of order. Central to this process was a change in their relationships with other political actors, especially Unionists to whom Sinn Féin now needed to make itself coalitionable in order to establish functioning power sharing. At the same time, republicans were only willing to consolidate the new Northern Ireland to a limited extent. They committed themselves to consolidating the functioning democratic institutions, but they could never consolidate Northern Ireland as a political unit itself for fear of giving it a degree of permanence or legitimacy.

Understanding this process requires examining what precisely is meant by consolidation in the Northern Ireland context. Schedler suggests that there is a continuum of 'democraticness', with highly authoritarian systems on one end of the contiuum, moving through to electoral democracies, then to liberal democracies, and finally to advanced liberal democracies at the other end of the continuum.[73] He argues that where a regime is placed on this continuum will dictate what a process of democratic consolidation entails. For example, an electoral democracy is more democratic than an authoritarian regime and it holds regular clean and competitive elections. However, it sometimes fails to uphold political and civil freedoms essential for a liberal democracy. Therefore, in electoral democracies, democratic consolidation is about preventing a deterioration back to a more authoritarian incarnation and instead pushing for the liberalisation of the polity. In contrast, liberal democracies have all the components of a strong and healthy democracy in both procedure and spirit and consolidation in this case is about preventing slippage back to an electoral democracy.

Republicans understood their efforts in the peace process as an attempt to push Northern Ireland from an electoral democracy to a liberal democracy. They wished to move beyond the formal holding of free and fair elections to a situation that was more focused on ensuring the equality of civil, social and political rights for Northern Irish nationalists. However, it is not entirely clear that they would ever want Northern Ireland to become an advanced liberal democracy as this implies that it is long-established and embedded. While the lack of regression would be welcome to republicans, the idea of Northern Ireland becoming long-established would not be compatible with their transitional vision. In contrast, unionists understood the peace process as attempting to eliminate the anti-system violence and behaviour of the IRA and Sinn Féin in order to secure the state within the UK and push it towards becoming an advanced liberal democracy. So unionists saw their role both as a form of 'negative consolidation' by getting all groups to accept democracy as the only game in town, and 'positive consolidation' by changing Irish nationalist attitudes towards accepting the legitimacy of Northern Ireland.[74] However, republicans may have seen it as a form of negative consolidation in terms of removing the state's violence and discriminatory policies, but it is also clear they would only want a limited degree of positive consolidation.

This can be seen as another example from republicanism that highlights

Lamounier's distinction between acquiescence and legitimacy in democ-ratisation.[75] Republican's acquiesced to the new institutional arrangements and agreed to participate within them. Unionists read this as endorsing the legitimacy of Northern Ireland and celebrated this recognition (and many disillusioned former republicans despaired at the recognition). However, for republicans this was about participating purely in order to transform Northern Ireland into something that would be acceptable to them in the long term – a united Ireland. They saw their participation as bestowing no normative legiti-macy upon the institutions or the territory of Northern Ireland as it is currently constituted.

Attempting to implement the Belfast Agreement's new institutions in 1999 threw sharp relief upon republicanism's ongoing radicalism. Unionists were strongly insistent on the need to disband the IRA and on the decommissioning of its weapons. Although no longer engaging in violence against the British state, ongoing IRA activity remained. The IRA was used to enforce the Belfast Agreement in nationalist areas; it continued to act as a policing body in local communities including engaging in punishment attacks for lawbreakers; IRA volunteers undertook the largest bank robbery in the history of the British and Irish states; the IRA broke into the special branch headquarters; and three volunteers were arrested in Colombia training FARC guerrillas. As late as 2002, the IRA and Sinn Féin were accused of running a 'spy-ring' in the new Northern Irish Assembly. In this context, IRA decommissioning became of central importance to Unionists who refused to share power with Sinn Féin before this was completed.

Explanations for republican prevarication were varied, depending on who was explaining. For republicans, retaining their weapons was about preventing the trap down the road from the British and unionists, whom they mistrusted. Republicans needed to retain their weapons because once they gave them up Britain, being the more powerful state, might begin to encroach upon their deal. Republicans also saw militarism as being at the core of the movement from its foundation, making it harder to step away from. For example, imme-diately after embracing elections and becoming the new president of Sinn Féin, Gerry Adams felt the need to reassure the republican base that armed struggle was still central to his approach, stating that 'there are those who tell us that the British Government will not be moved by armed struggle . . . The history of Ireland and British colonial involvement throughout the world tells us that they will not be moved by anything else.'[76] Even after the first ceasefire in 1994, in response to a shout from the crowd calling to 'bring back the IRA', Adams responded 'they haven't gone away, you know'.[77] For unionism, this was simply republicans hoping to retain negotiating leverage as long as pos-sible by holding a gun to the head of the negotiations. For the governments, they were not unsurprised by republican prevarication and there was certainly awareness that this was in part about negotiating leverage, but they also saw it as an inability of Adams and McGuinness at this time to take the whole movement with them and the need to avoid splits within republicanism.[78] Another factor was that the British were more worried about developments within the unionist bloc at this time and were immediately focused on David Trimble's waning power. Republicans too may well have seen the changing electoral dynamic and began to hold out for a deal with the DUP rather than making a hasty deal with a dying UUP.[79]

Decommissioning soon rose to crisis levels, threatening to derail the implementation of the Agreement entirely. The Unionists initially attempted to coerce republicans into decommissioning by evicting Sinn Féin from the Assembly, a measure that required cross-community support not forthcoming from the SDLP, and so they suspended Sinn Féin from the NSMC instead. However, when decommissioning was still not forthcoming and with Unionists threatening to bring down the Assembly, the British government stepped in and suspended the Assembly. This happened on four occasions between 2000 and 2007, twice only for twenty-four hours but also for almost five years between 2002 and 2007. The initial suspension was undertaken rather unilaterally by Peter Mandelson, then Secretary of State, much to the chagrin of Irish officials who believed the crisis was best resolved by enforcing the terms of the Agreement rather than suspending power sharing. Republicans were not too happy with the suspension, nor the way it was imposed by Mandelson either. They railed against the decision, declaring that:

> The legislation which has been passed this week permits the Secretary of State to rule by decree – he can suspend the Assembly now, tomorrow, next week or whenever he wants to, at any time in the future. Those with a vote count for nothing . . . Morally it should be that Sinn Féin is [in the Assembly] by absolute right of its electoral mandate, but the British Government have ensured that it is not. To wilfully deny this mandate and bring down the Assembly by disgraceful parliamentary machination may in some perverted way be legal, but it is not moral.[80]

This moment probably represents a low in British-Irish relations during the peace process phase, but later suspensions were used more tactically and were more closely coordinated with the Irish government.

Given the depth of republicanism's commitment to its weapons, which they held on to long after making significant movement in a range of other policy areas, how was this eventually overcome? Although the formal design of the power-sharing institutions guaranteed Sinn Féin a stake in executive power, informally they still needed to make themselves an acceptable partner for the Unionists to be willing to work with them. Sinn Féin was not 'coalitionable' as long as the IRA retained its weapons and republicans fell short of the 'total and absolute commitment to exclusively democratic and peaceful means of resolving differences' as enshrined in the Agreement. The republican political strategy hinged upon making the new Northern Irish institutions work, with a clear alignment of the self-interest of the revolutionaries with the interests of the peace process. This was most obviously the case in their desire to use the NSMC to generate a path to Irish unity, but the successful implementation of the Belfast Agreement also directly impacted on Sinn Féin's electoral performance. Gerry Adams acknowledged that 'the success of this process will not only be judged on what structures emerge from it but on how the lives of people from day to day are improved'.[81] For republicans to realise any impact on people's lives, this required devolved power sharing rather than direct rule from Westminster.

The governments too began to change their strategy in an effort to finalise implementation.[82] In 2002 Tony Blair gave a speech during which he declared that the peace process was at a 'turning point' and that 'we cannot carry on with the IRA half in, half out of this process. Not just because it isn't right any more. It won't work anymore.'[83] Ambiguity was no longer a friend of the peace process.[84] Although there was some initial and partial decommissioning during this time, full decommissioning was not completed until 2005. Britain shifted its focus to bringing in the DUP rather than propping up David Trimble,[85] and republicanism now considered this a more viable partner for a future power-sharing deal.

In this context, the republican leadership slowly moved towards a position of agreeing to decommission but did so while trying to exploit this bargaining power. Republicans insisted that decommissioning could only occur within the wider context of the 'demilitarisation' of Northern Ireland as a whole and this necessitated the scaling back of the British Army and reform of existing policing in Northern Ireland. Additionally, the process had become internationalised with brokers to oversee it and by 2005 the choreography for decommissioning was agreed by republicans, the DUP and the two governments. Decommissioning was completed in 2005 with an IRA statement that 'our decisions have been taken to advance our republican and democratic objectives, including our goal of a united Ireland'.[86] However, the real impetus for this decision was clearly the need to strengthen the institutional framework and for republicans to gain greater access to using these institutions to further their goals.

Putting the possibility of a return to violence beyond their reach opened up the possibility of implementing the final aspect of the Agreement – restoring the power-sharing institutions and the devolution of policing and justice to a Northern Irish government that included republicans. Nationalism (both constitutional and republican) had a historic mistrust of policing in Northern Ireland. Since 1921, the devolved police force, the Royal Ulster Constabulary (RUC), was the equivalent of a paramilitary police force under the political control of a Protestant one-party state.[87] The sectarian nature of the RUC became even clearer for republicans from 1970 onwards and it was republican orthodoxy that the RUC were 'routinely involved in the torture and ill-treatment of nationalists'.[88] As McGarry and O'Leary argued, 'the absence of police legitimacy has been importantly connected with the absence of political legitimacy for Northern Ireland: nationalists have found the RUC unacceptable because it has been associated with and has defended unacceptable political arrangements'.[89] Yet the republican strategy necessitated removing the fact that nationalists were being ruled by policing powers exercised by a sovereign British government whose authority they rejected.

Once again faced with the reality that unionists would not share power without Sinn Féin endorsing a Northern Irish police force, and under increasing pressure from the British, Irish and US governments, Sinn Féin shifted position to demonstrate a stronger commitment to a reformed Northern Ireland. Peter Hain led with a strategy of restricting the allowances and payments for all elected officials and civil servants associated with the Northern Ireland Assembly unless power was restored – a policy that was more aimed at the DUP than Sinn Féin. He also embarked upon passing social policies around water charges and shrinking the number of local councils – policies that were deeply unpopular with local politicians and to whom he said that they could take over such policies if they would only agree to restore power.[90] In this way, both parties had an incentive to restore the institutions as soon as possible.[91]

In spite of a number of concerns by both Sinn Féin and the SDLP that the Patten Commission's recommendations on reforming the policing of Northern Ireland were not being fully implemented by the British government,[92] at a special conference in 2007 Sinn Féin members overwhelmingly voted to support policing in Northern Ireland and Sinn Féin took its place on the Northern Ireland Policing Board. The devolution of policing was later finalised with the Hillsborough Castle Agreement of 2010. Following elections in March 2007, Sinn Féin emerged as the largest nationalist party and the historically 'hardline' DUP as the largest unionist party. A power-sharing executive was agreed and Sinn Féin's Martin McGuinness became deputy First Minister. This was seen by many commentators as the extremists emerging to dominate Northern Irish politics, but the reality was that republicans were already a moderate actor by this stage, forsaking revolution, accepting participation and pursuing reforms within the confines of the status quo.

The final test of republicanism during the consolidation phase was its response to dissident terrorism – essentially former comrades-in-arms who rejected moderation in favour of armed struggle until Irish reunification is realised. Their evolving response can be seen as moving from a strategic commitment to the peace process to a deeper commitment as their responsibilities towards the governance of Northern Ireland increased. Their shallow and minimalist commitment was unsustainable to gain the policy goals they pursued and therefore deeper commitments to the moderate path needed to be displayed. The first real test of republicanism's new direction from dissident terrorists came with the Omagh bombing in August 1998. Planted by the Real IRA in an effort to disrupt the peace process, the bomb killed twenty-nine people. Clear condemnations of the bombing followed from both Adams and

McGuinness, but Sinn Féin also refused to cooperate with the investigation because it was led by the RUC. Frampton argues that Sinn Féin's response was to condemn the attack as an attack on the peace process and as a strategic failure, but not to offer a moral condemnation of the act.[93] Tony Blair too expected a stronger statement from Sinn Féin in the wake of the attack, such as declaring an end to the IRA.[94]

After the endorsement of the St Andrews Agreement and the ensuing devolution of policing and justice powers, Sinn Féin was now one of a group of parties tasked with defending Northern Ireland from the violent anti-system threat. For example, following the assassination of a Catholic policeman by former members of the Provisional IRA in 2011 (again in the town of Omagh), Martin McGuinness as deputy First Minister was a leader in the devolved government involved in using the resources of the state to attempt to arrest and prosecute the attackers. As late as 2012 an important tool used against dissident terrorists was non-jury courts.[95] Sinn Féin previously described such courts as 'contrary to normal standards of justice and for which – in the current situation [post-Belfast Agreement] – there remains no façade of justification'.[96] Yet now Sinn Féin was a member of the government which wielded these courts against their former comrades and new enemies. When tested, republican leaders in government aligned themselves with the Northern Irish institutions over the principles and violent tactics of their former comrades. In their evolving response to dissident terrorism and the shift from passive condemnation to active suppression of those who pursued the same tactic and interpretations of the conflict as republicans themselves pursued some time earlier, it is clear to see a commitment to the subordination of militarism in favour of securing Northern Ireland and its institutions.

It was at this level of showing clear commitments to the new institutions that the consolidation of republican moderation was undertaken, and it was not about changing their values or ethnic goals. There were limits to the extent to which republicans would ever tolerate alternative conceptions of the 'rightful' sovereignty of Northern Ireland. Governing institutions were accepted as a route to solving conflict, but Northern Ireland remained part of an unfinished nation-building project with an air of inevitability towards its final resting place as part of a united Ireland. As an ethno-nationalist party it is hard to imagine how it could be any other way. Certain beliefs and values were inherent to their ethno-national nature and may have been subject to dilution but not to eradication. Means changed but ends had a large degree of fixity in this case. The moderate shift in tactics was about exploring alternative ways to realise the desired territorial conception of Irish nationalism and not about a rejection of armed struggle as a right. Republicans remained unapologetic for their hitherto armed struggle which they saw as necessary, and the salience of their militarism was evident from the fact that this dimension was much slower to moderate than their acceptance of intermediate constitutional stages to Irish unity.

CONCLUSION

Democratisation in Northern Ireland is atypical given the anomalous nature of the political unit. Northern Ireland had two competing sovereignty claims, and the very fact of its existence is called into question by republicans. This was not just a case of two competing claims for control over access to executive power; it was much more fundamental than this. It was competing claims over the sovereign basis of Northern Ireland and whether the institutions governing it should reflect its transitional nature or should reflect its nature as a normalised part of the UK.

Republican moderation through democratic bargaining was again a path-dependent process of increasing returns. Following the political and economic liberalisations of the late 1980s, republicans were heavily incentivised to pursue a negotiated reformist agenda. This was reinforced by their electoral participation because the republican vote shares were now aligned to an increasingly prosperous Catholic nationalist population. Once republicans engaged in striking a negotiated peace deal their interests rapidly became entangled with the survival and fate of the Belfast Agreement. The power-sharing institutions and the institutional guarantees these created – alongside rendering the long-term future of Northern Ireland within the Union uncertain – gave republicans the confidence to alter strategies knowing that their interests would be protected. In the implementation phase, republicans were incentivised to remove all ongoing anti-system behaviour and instil democracy as the only acceptable method of pursuing their goals because a gradual transition to a united Ireland had been accepted in the course of bargaining over the Belfast Agreement. Therefore, republicans needed to promote and support the new institutions over the vestiges of their revolutionary history. Thus, further moderation was exacted. Deviations from the new path were met with the suspension of the Northern Irish Assembly and the marginalisation of republicanism.

Moderation was a process facilitated by the changing relationships between republicans and other political actors. They began as absolute outsiders, distant from any relationship with other actors due to their use of violence and revolution. However, each phase brought them into closer contact with other political groups. In the course of the bargaining they moved themselves from a position of absolute radicalism to a position of relative radicalism. They were no longer absolutely outside the system, but following their ceasefire they were now able to define themselves as radical in relation to the nationalist party they competed against within the same system. Similarly when entering the power-sharing executive, Sinn Féin needed to reposition itself from a party that was historically outside the system and beyond acceptability to unionist politicians to one that was a coalitionable partner. Again this entailed a shift from absolute to relational radicalism. Crucially though, maintaining a position of relational radicalism was impossible for Sinn Féin as the implementation process demanded clearer commitments to the moderate path, and even its relational radicalism dimmed over time. However, republican consolidation was never about consolidating Northern Ireland as a durable and stable political unit. Indeed, its legitimacy, in terms of any normative commitment to its existence, continued to be denied. Instead, consolidation was about securing the functioning of a new set of institutions that republicans aspired to use to transition to a united Ireland. For republicans, the reformed Northern Ireland was inherently transitional, one step on an inevitable and historically determined road to reunification.

Notes

1. Huntington, *The Third Wave*, p. 170.
2. Di Palma, *To Craft Democracies*.
3. Bermeo, 'Myths of Moderation'.
4. Di Palma, *To Craft Democracies*, p. 30; O'Donnell et al., *Transitions from Authoritarian Rule*; Linz and Stepan. *The Problems of Democratic Transition and Consolidation*.
5. Mainwaring, 'Transitions to Democracy and Democratic Consolidation'.
6. Walter, *Committing to Peace*.
7. Bourke, *Peace in Ireland*; McGarry and O'Leary, *Explaining Northern Ireland*.
8. Farrell, *Northern Ireland: The Orange State*; Clifford, *Northern Ireland: What is it?* Neither Farrell nor Clifford was ever a member of Sinn Féin or the IRA but they shared the republican analysis.
9. Sinn Féin, *Freedom*.
10. McGarry and O'Leary, *Explaining Northern Ireland*, chapter 2.
11. Sinn Féin, *The Sinn Féin/SDLP Talks*, p. 6. Its one-party nature was evident from the fact that between 1921 and 1972 the UUP composed the entire Cabinet and only one Cabinet appointment in this time was not a Protestant.
12. Sinn Féin, *A Scenario for Peace*.
13. Laffan, *The Partition of Ireland*.
14. 'Government Policy on the Minority', FIN/30/P/20 1970, PRONI.
15. 'Statement by Prime Minister (Mr Brian Faulkner) at Stormont on Tuesday 7th March 1972', PRONI.
16. Aughey, *The Politics of Northern Ireland*.
17. Acemoglu and Robinson, *The Economic Origins of Dictatorship and Democracy*.
18. It should be noted that whether or not inequalities were the product of (direct and indirect) discrimination is a debated topic in the literate, with some arguing that Catholics' subordinate position stemmed from larger family sizes and their refusal to participate in some areas of public employment, especially in the security forces. See, for example, Compton, *The Contemporary Population of Northern Ireland and Population Related Issues*.
19. Whyte, 'How Much Discrimination was there Under the Unionist Regime, 1921–68?'.
20. Ibid.
21. Ibid.
22. 'Cabinet Confidential Annex CM(71) 46th Conclusions, Minute 3', 9 September 1971, CAB 128/48/5, NA.
23. 'Confidential Annex CM(72) 13th Conclusions', Thursday 7 March 1972, CAB 128/48/5, NA.
24. Smith and Chambers, *Inequality in Northern Ireland*.
25. Muttarak et al., 'Does Affirmative Action Work?'.
26. Breen, 'Class Inequality and Social Mobility in Northern Ireland', p. 396.

27. Osborne, 'Progressing the Equality Agenda in Northern Ireland', p. 343.
28. Whyte, 'How Much Discrimination was there Under the Unionist Regime, 1921–68?'.
29. Labour Force Survey, *Religion Report*.
30. For a discussion of how governments attempt to shape the preferences of an electorate to their own advantage, see Dunleavy, *Democracy, Bureaucracy and Public Choice*, pp. 112–144.
31. Bean, *The New Politics of Sinn Féin*.
32. Di Palma, *To Craft Democracies*.
33. Higley and Burton, *Elite Foundations of Liberal Democracy*.
34. Interview with Mark Durkan.
35. Interview with Alex Attwood.
36. Interview with Mark Durkan.
37. It should be noted that the SDLP vehemently rejected the idea that this should be considered an alliance and saw nothing formal enough between the parties to merit this label. Interview with Sean Farren.
38. Interview with Martin Mansergh.
39. Quoted in Taylor, *Provos*, pp. 302–303.
40. Sinn Féin, *The Sinn Féin/SDLP Talks*.
41. Ibid.
42. Quoted in ibid.
43. Murray and Tonge, *Sinn Féin and the SDLP*, p. 170.
44. Interview with William Fitall; interview with Quentin Thomas.
45. Interview with William Fitall; interview with Sean Farren.
46. Sinn Féin, *Setting the Record Straight*.
47. Interview with Quentin Thomas; interview with Martin Mansergh. It was certainly not always clear that the Irish accepted British claims to neutrality to quite the extent that Britain asserted it was neutral. See also O'Huiginn 'Peace Comes Dropping Slow' for how times during John Major's tenure were viewed as an example of where Britain was far from neutral.
48. Brooke, P., *Speech at Whitbread Restaurant*, London, 9 November 1990.
49. *AP*, 6 January 1994, p. 5.
50. *AP*, 5 October 1995, p. 7.
51. Quoted in Taylor, *Provos*, p. 303.
52. Sinn Féin, *Towards a Lasting Peace in Ireland*.
53. *AP*, 9 February 1995, p. 10. Ironically in spite of this endorsement, McAllister was soon to leave Sinn Féin in protest at the removal of the IRA from Northern Irish politics.
54. Przeworski, 'Some Problems in the Study of the Transition to Democracy', p. 58.
55. Hoddie and Hartzell, *Strengthening Peace in Post-Civil War States*; Walter, *Committing to Peace*.
56. Sinn Féin, *Towards a Lasting Peace in Ireland*, section 5.
57. Interview with William Fitall.
58. Interview with Quentin Thomas.
59. Interview with William Fitall.
60. Interview with Eamonn McKee.
61. O'Leary, 'The Nature of the Agreement'.
62. Interview with John Chilcot.
63. Kerr, *Imposing Power-Sharing*, p. 94.
64. Murray and Tonge, *Sinn Féin and the SDLP*, pp. 213–239.
65. *AP*, 2 February 1995, p. 7.
66. *AP*, 29 January 1998, p. 9.
67. *AP*, 15 April 1999, pp. 10–11.
68. *AP*, 30 April 1998, p. 12.

69. Bourke, *Peace in Ireland*.
70. Aughey, 'The Art and Effect of Political Lying', p. 14.
71. See Frampton, *The Legion of the Rearguard*; Sanders, *Inside the IRA*.
72. *AP*, 30 April 1998, p. 12.
73. Schedler, 'What is Democratic Consolidation?'.
74. Negative consolidation is the removal of anti-democratic behaviour while positive consolidation is more concerned with a change in beliefs. See Pridham, 'The International Context of Democratic Consolidation'.
75. Quoted in Przeworski, 'Some Problems in the Study of the Transition to Democracy', p. 51.
76. Adams, G., Presidential Address, Sinn Féin Ard Fheis, 1983.
77. *AP*, 17 August 1995, p. 11.
78. Interview with Joe Pilling; interview with Bill Jeffrey; interview with Jonathan Phillips; interview with Eamonn McKee.
79. Interview with Joe Pilling; interview with Peter Hain.
80. *AP*, 10 February 2000, p. 2.
81. *AP*, 5 February 1998, p. 1.
82. Bill Jeffrey is unsure if there was anything coherent enough to be called a 'strategy' in the British government at the time, but rather it was about implementing the Agreement and responding to the challenges that arose as necessary.
83. Blair, T., 'The full text of Tony Blair's speech in Belfast', *The Guardian*, 17 October 2002 <http://www.theguardian.com/politics/2002/oct/17/northernireland.devolution>.
84. Interview with Jonathan Phillips; interview with Eamonn McKee.
85. Interview with Jonathan Phillips.
86. 'IRA Statement in Full' 28 July 2005, *BBC News Online* <http://news.bbc.co.uk/1/hi/northern_ireland/4724599.stm> (last accessed 21 September 2016).
87. Sinn Féin, *Policing in Transition*.
88. Sinn Féin, *A Police Service for a New Future*.
89. McGarry and O'Leary, *Policing Northern Ireland*, p. 41.
90. Interview with Peter Hain.
91. In addition, Blair and Ahern made it known they would be leaving office soon and wanted power sharing restored before they departed.
92. Interview with Alex Attwood. See Independent Commission on Policing for Northern Ireland, *A New Beginning: Policing in Northern Ireland*.
93. Frampton, *The Legion of the Rearguard*, pp. 249–250.
94. Powell, *Great Hatred, Little Room*, p. 139.
95. 'Seven People Face Terrorism Charges in Northern Ireland', *The Guardian*, 19 May 2012.
96. Sinn Féin, *Policing in Transition*.

5. THE US AND BROKERING REPUBLICAN MODERATION

In order for moderation through institutional inclusion to take full hold, it was necessary for the US to act as a powerful external broker throughout the negotiations of the Belfast Agreement and during the consolidation of republican moderation. Just as consociational theory needed to be tailored for the ethnonational context by acknowledging the role of international actors,[1] similarly the moderation of republicanism required a powerful external broker. Like many external interventions,[2] it was short and targeted, not of relevance in the early stages of republican moderation and only mattered during the formal peace process phase and its implementation.

The role of the US in enabling republican moderation through institutional contact was very specific. It provided a series of credible guarantees to republicans that their interests would be protected and given fair representation when entering a bargain with the more powerful British state. As Walter argues:

> the greatest challenge [during negotiations to end a civil war] is to design a treaty that convinces the combatants to shed their partisan armies and surrender conquered territory even though such steps will increase their vulnerability and limit their ability to enforce the treaty's other terms. When groups obtain third party guarantees for the treacherous demobilization period that follows the signing of an agreement . . . they will implement the settlement.[3]

In this way, an international intervention can help overcome the reluctance of adversaries to commit to moderation where there is a history of hostility engendering suspicion of the adversaries' motives. The US provided a series of incentives and disincentives that encouraged republicanism to increase their engagement with the peace process.[4] Combined, these factors led to greater republican inclusion within the ruling institutions. What is more, although certain sections of Irish-America flirted with promoting radical republican views in the 1970s, by the time the US government embarked upon its role as guarantor it had firmly embraced a constitutional nationalist understanding of how the conflict should be resolved. That is not to say that it was an active promoter of Irish unity, but given that it accepted Irish unity as a legitimate political aspiration it strongly promoted that this needed to be pursued through the principle of consent and certainly not through armed struggle. Therefore, if republicans wished to avail themselves of the US as a broker and guarantor, they once again needed to make themselves coalitionable to the US and accept an exclusively constitutional path.

Although there can be little doubt that the initial impetus for the moderation of radical republicanism was rooted in the domestic context, this international dimension was crucial in speeding up and consolidating the process. This interpretation is highly compatible with explanations of the international dimension to democratisation, which emphasises the twin factors of leverage and linkage.[5] Leverage refers to the democratising pressures that a powerful Western government can exert over a group, such as using economic and political incentives, putative sanctions and diplomatic pressure. Linkage refers to the extent of an authoritarian group's ties to the US, the EU and Western-dominated multilateral institutions. These include economic, geopolitical, social, communication and transnational civil society links, which serve to heighten the salience of democratic norms, increase the possibility of an international response to violating such norms and create domestic constituencies with a stake in adhering to democratic norms. Interestingly, Levitsky and Way argue that geographical proximity is the most important factor in establishing linkages, but in the Northern Irish case, the geographical distance of the US was compensated for by the shared sense of historical identity and the potential for Northern Ireland to serve as a successful example of a new foreign policy direction for the US.

US Policy and Northern Ireland During the Cold War

During the Cold War period, the US generally refused to engage in any policy that would jeopardise their relationship with Britain. De Valera had already learnt this lesson much to his disappointment as early as the Paris Peace Conference in 1919 when President Wilson refused to support Ireland's bid for self-determination for fear of upsetting his British allies, in spite of the Irish case fitting with Wilsonian principles.[6] The US position was one that expressed sympathy with Irish nationalists but recognised the issue as a domestic one within Britain's sovereignty. Led by advice from the State Department about how to best serve US economic and strategic interests, US policy publicly supported the British policy of the day.[7]

That is not to say that this was an uneventful time in US–Northern Irish relations and a range of Irish-American lobby groups and some key political figures tried to shape a more activist US policy – efforts that were largely unsuccessful.

What is also observable within this period is a rise in the role of domestic constitutional nationalists, most notably John Hume but also members of the Irish Embassy, to counter political sympathy for radical republicanism in the Irish-American diaspora. Indeed, by the end of the Cold War, constitutional nationalism was embedded in Irish-American thinking as the only legitimate route to pursue a united Ireland. This is not to say that the US actively pursued a policy of Irish reunification, but, rather, to the extent that they saw Irish reunification as a legitimate goal to be pursued by some actors within Ireland then this had to be done peacefully and without recourse to violence. Thus by the time America became more interventionist under Clinton, it was already clearly established that such an intervention would not tolerate violent republicanism and that it would only tolerate an Irish nationalist position that worked through democratic institutions to gain consent for unification. There was no scope for Sinn Féin to shape the nature of the US intervention in a radical direction and instead republicans needed to frame themselves within a constitutional approach to appease US interests.

From the outset of the Troubles, all parties to the conflict believed that the US could have an important influence over the direction and framing of the conflict. Given that almost 44 million Americans at this time described themselves as having Irish ancestry, they also had a strong interest in the region.[8] It was with this in mind that in 1969 the Irish government petitioned the US to support a proposal to dispatch UN peacekeeping troops immediately to Northern Ireland and endorse the reunification of Ireland as the only acceptable solution to the emerging violence. The US government's reply was to express sympathy but emphasise that it would not intervene in an affair that they accepted as the remit of another sovereign state:

> The Government of the United States is deeply distressed by the human suffering that has resulted from the recent events in that area. Nevertheless, the Government of the United States has no appropriate basis to intervene with regard to the domestic political situation or civil disturbances in other sovereign countries.[9]

It may have been clear in advance to Jack Lynch, the Irish Taoiseach at the time, that such an approach would be unsuccessful,[10] but nonetheless this indicated the potential influence the US government was seen as possessing. Indeed following a visit by Tip O'Neill and others to Ireland in 1979, Jack Lynch stated that 'the influence of the United States with the British Government was enormous and we would hope that the United States would indicate to the United Kingdom that positive moves would have to be made'.[11] Although Northern Ireland was occasionally raised in Congress, it was clear that it did not fit in with US foreign policy goals and Lynch's calls for intervention fell on deaf ears. This sympathetic but detached stance was to remain in place throughout the Cold War era.

Yet the lack of intervention at the most senior political level of the president and the State Department did not mean that the US as a whole was completely uninterested in events. By the end of the decade a number of non-governmental organisations had arisen in urban centres across the US that were to prove a crucial resource for republicans, in some cases in terms of providing finance and weapons and in other cases in terms of providing equally important moral sustenance.[12] The most prominent of these was the Irish Northern Aid Committee (Noraid), established in New York in 1970 by the anti-Treaty Civil War veteran Michael Flannery. Initially its membership was dominated by Irish-born individuals who had emigrated to the US and it was not until the 1980s that US-born members exceeded its Irish-born membership. Noraid presented itself as a group focused on fund-raising for the republican charity, *An Cumann Cabhrach* (The Welfare Branch), which provided welfare and support for the families of republican prisoners. In reality, however, the group was widely seen as channelling money to the purchase of arms. Although self-reported figures for such a group should be treated with caution, they are indicative of the group's importance to republicanism: Noraid sent almost US$6 million to Ireland between 1970 and 1986.[13] The fund-raising potential of Noraid was directly related to key events in Northern Ireland, and so 'Noraid declared remittances of $312,700 for the six months following Bloody Sunday [in January 1972], significantly higher than the $121,722 it raised the following year.'[14] Similarly, it raised almost US$500,000 in the first half of 1981 following the start of the hunger strike, raising more in three months than it did in most years.[15]

Noraid was not solely for financial benefit, although clearly this was its most important role. It also provided morale and ideological support for the use of violence, typically rooted in romantic visions of the Easter Rising and the War of Independence. The Irish government saw this as another important front on which they needed to battle violent republicanism. Seán Donlon, Ireland's Ambassador to the United States, argued in 1979 that 'a great deal of support for the IRA has drifted away in the North and they needed to point somewhere else for the moral basis of their campaign. The obvious place to look was Irish-Americans'.[16] This is not to imply that Noraid and the republican movement were always in perfect harmony and operating as a single organisation. A potentially divisive issue between the two was the socialism advocated by the Northern republican leadership which had very limited appeal to the conservative working-class base of Irish-Americans. It was in this context that Gerry Adams was forced to deny there was any Marxist element within Sinn Féin for fear of hampering the fund-raising potential offered by Irish-America.

Another important group at this time was the Irish National Caucus (INC) established in 1974 specifically to lobby Congress. As a lobby group, the INC went to great lengths to distance itself from supporting political violence and emphasised that none of the money it raised was sent back to Ireland, albeit INC members retained a decidedly republican interpretation of the conflict.[17] At the behest of the INC, the Ad Hoc Congressional Committee for Irish Affairs was established in 1977. This Committee was chaired by Mario Biaggi who, although without a direct connection with Ireland himself, was a Representative for New York with important political connections to Irish-America. In 1979 the Ad Hoc Committee was crucial in introducing a suspension in sales of handguns to the RUC, a decision that was met with expressions of deep regret within Britain. The decision followed an investigation by an English judge, Harry Bennett, into allegations of mistreatment of prisoners by the RUC at Castlereagh interrogation centre, and his conclusion that some injuries experienced by prisoners 'were inflicted by someone other than the prisoner himself'.[18] In this political climate the Ad Hoc Committee successfully pressured the White House into the suspension because there were no guarantees the weapons would not be used indiscriminately against nationalists.[19]

Its other major success was the momentum it managed to build behind the MacBride Principles, which ultimately led to Britain passing the Fair Employment Act (1989) in response to this pressure.[20] In 1984, Seán MacBride, former anti-Treaty leader, former Minister for External Affairs in the Irish government and, at the time, the Chairman of the INC in the Republic of Ireland, lent his name to a set of fair-employment principles designed to promote a code of conduct for US firms operating in Northern Ireland. By 1987 these principles had been endorsed by trade union federations as well as by state legislatures in Massachusetts, New York, New Jersey, Connecticut and Rhode Island. Eventually, after thirteen state legislatures had adopted this legislation, in 1996 these were adopted at the federal level. This was significant because it implied that the British government was either not trusted to tackle, or not capable of tackling, discrimination against Catholics and additional legislation was actually required.

Yet Irish-America was not homogenously supportive of the radical republican position and within ten years of the start of the conflict groups like Noraid and the INC were largely sidelined in favour of constitutional nationalist approaches. Although there were waves of sympathy for republicans during the hunger strikes, in general by the early 1980s Irish-America, especially at the political elite level, had consolidated their opinion behind a non-violent and reformist position. Much of the reason why this moderate consensus emerged was down to the mobilisation of domestic Irish actors, including successive Irish governments, who lobbied hard to rein in potential support for radicalism.[21] John Hume was crucial here.[22] Hume's motivation in engaging the US stemmed from the collapse of the Sunningdale Agreement in 1974, which convinced him that 'a purely internal solution would not succeed and that in an intimidatory culture constitutional nationalism was not strong enough on its own right to win its case through reason'.[23] Although Sunningdale was not a purely internal solution in that it envisaged a role for the Irish government in Northern Ireland through a Council of Ireland, its collapse under Unionist dissent and the failure of Britain to push the unionist community towards a united Ireland were key problems from Hume's perspective. In light of this earlier setback he worked under the assumption that drawing in powerful external allies, notably the US government and key actors within the Irish-American diaspora, would increase the pressure on Britain to force Unionism towards a settlement that could ultimately bring a united Ireland closer.[24]

Beginning in 1972, Hume steadily built a close relationship with Ted Kennedy and Hume's framing and proposed solutions to the conflict were soon evident in the public statements of Kennedy. Kennedy, along with Senator Daniel Patrick Moynihan, the Speaker of the House, Tip O'Neill and Governor Hugh Carey of New York, formed a group known as the 'Four Horsemen'. Although Kennedy had flirted with more radical positions in the early 1970s, such as proposing a resolution to the Senate in support of British withdrawal from Northern Ireland in October 1971, and although Tip O'Neill was a key influence in passing legislation suspending the sale of handguns to the RUC, as the decade progressed these leading figures harmonised around a clear SDLP position. On St Patrick's Day 1977, the Four Horsemen released a statement condemning republican violence in Northern Ireland; later that year Kennedy praised the contribution of Ulster-Scots to America; and in August 1977 the Four Horsemen met with President Jimmy Carter and persuaded him to release a statement condemning violence, expressing support for a peaceful settlement that included the Republic of Ireland and promising financial support from the US in the event of a negotiated settlement – a statement warmly welcomed by Irish Taoiseach Jack Lynch.[25]

This should not be mistaken for a shift in US policy towards Northern Ireland, which remained aligned behind a clear non-interventionist stance and supportive of Britain, and Carter's statement sank with little effect.[26] However, it does indicate that once the decision to become more interventionist was made by Clinton fifteen years later, individuals who were subsequently to emerge as key actors within Irish-America in the political and business world were already largely committed to a constitutional nationalist position that embodied the SDLP interpretation of the conflict and its solutions. Thus, there was no scope for republicans to radicalise Irish-America but rather they needed to make themselves coalitionable to gain the benefits of being able to align themselves with these powerful interests. When the Clinton government became more interventionist the parameters of what was an acceptable policy to pursue were already set – namely, non-violence, a resolution that included the Irish government and the pursuit of Irish unity through consent.

CLINTON'S INTERVENTION AND THE 'SQUEEZING' OF REPUBLICANISM

As Sinn Féin moved towards the possibility of negotiating a settlement and undertaking significant shifts in many of their policy positions, there were fundamental issues of mistrust on all sides. From the republican perspective, the US government acted as a third-party guarantor of the peace process and helped republicans to overcome commitment problems by offering credible guarantees that its interests would be protected even after demilitarisation. The US-appointed special envoy, former Senator George Mitchell, saw his role as enabling the parties to overcome mistrust and strike a deal, and in his role of chairing the talks that led to the Belfast Agreement he was able to make gains that neither government could secure.[27] However, given the Clinton administration's relatively sympathetic view of the difficulties facing Adams and McGuinness from outflanking and dissidents, the US government was content not to push the IRA too strongly on decommissioning and this issue remained unresolved by the end of Clinton's and Mitchell's tenure. This was to prove the greatest obstacle to implementing the peace process and it was finally solved when George W. Bush's envoy took over, who was more willing to coerce republicans on this issue. The US were central to solving the thorny decommissioning issue, not necessarily in terms of making the deals, which were done by British and Irish officials, but they were central in incentivising and pressurising republicans to take those deals.[28]

During the Cold War the US was locked into an intimate security partnership with Britain and jeopardising this by intervening in Northern Ireland was close to unthinkable.[29] Thus the ending of the Cold War freed the US to become more interventionist, a stance which Clinton pursued under his liberal interventionist doctrine. Some in Britain initially saw the US intervention as an attempt by Clinton to shore-up support within the Irish-American electorate, with Michael Mates, a minister for state in the NIO, deriding it as 'cynical playing to the green Irish vote'.[30] Yet such an interpretation does not really ring true. Admittedly almost 20 per cent of Americans described themselves as of Irish origin, but many of these were Ulster-Scots who may have resented or been unimpressed by a US intervention. It is also not clear that this policy was even a vote winning policy,[31] and Clinton himself famously described his electoral fortunes as hanging on economic policies ('it's the economy, stupid') rather than foreign policy towards a relatively unimportant territory in Europe.

Instead, the US intervention in Northern Ireland is more compatible with Downs and Stedman's argument that major powers primarily engage in foreign interventions for their own strategic gains.[32] Indeed, 'at the heart of Clinton's Irish initiatives lay the desire to establish, in conditions which did not risk the loss of American lives, internationalist precedents for American peace promotion'.[33] This was particularly important given the poor record of Clinton's administration in foreign policy in the first year of his tenure as president following notable criticism over US policy in Somalia and Rwanda. Clinton was able to use a successful settlement in Northern Ireland to shape the role of the US in other conflicts in a post-Cold War era and add credibility to American interventions elsewhere, as well as resonating with his personally held liberal interventionist belief system. As Clinton himself at the time stated:

> I think sometimes we are too reluctant to engage ourselves in a positive
> way because of our long-standing special relationship with Great Britain

and also because it seemed such a thorny problem. But I have a very strong feeling that in the aftermath of the Cold War, we need a governing rationale for our engagement in the world, not just in Northern Ireland.[34]

In the course of his presidential election campaign, Clinton promised to appoint a peace envoy to Northern Ireland and grant Gerry Adams a visa to the US if elected. A group of Irish-Americans formed to put their support behind Clinton and to pressure him to follow through on these pledges, naming themselves Americans for a New Irish Agenda (ANIA). This group was comprised of Irish-American entrepreneurs who were an established part of corporate America with strong political connections. They described themselves as 'Irish-American corporate people' taking the 'issue out of bars and into the boardrooms' and they were committed to a peaceful resolution of the conflict in Northern Ireland.[35] Although in the first six months following his election Clinton failed to appoint a peace envoy or grant Adams a visa as he struggled to developed a cogent overseas strategy, following the breakthrough signing of the DSD by the British and Irish governments in December 1993, this soon changed. Clinton proved very open to taking advice from the Irish government and, at their request, he declined to appoint a peace envoy to allay Irish fears that this would disrupt their own behind-the-scenes negotiations.[36]

Other important US players were looking to be more proactive in the search for peace rather than just restricting themselves to act as a guarantor and broker, as the US government necessarily had to. Bruce Morrison was a former congressman with a long-standing interest in Irish affairs who, along with a delegation comprising Chuck Feeney,[37] Bill Flynn and Niall O'Dowd, embarked on a fact-finding mission to Northern Ireland in September 1993.[38] The reality of the trip was that Morrison met with several leading republicans (as well as Unionists and loyalists, although the DUP refused to meet him and decried him as a 'troublemaker' and 'meddler')[39] in an effort to persuade them to move towards a ceasefire by offering them legitimacy and access to influence. The potential that Morrison held for republicans was the close links he had to the Clinton administration and his influence in keeping Northern Ireland on the agenda with policy-makers in the US. In addition, Morrison held out the promise of an economic boom if peace could be secured, declaring on the eve of the mission that 'we view the issue in both its political and economic aspects. You can't have one without the other. It is foolish to believe we can have economic development without political progress.'[40]

A sign of the importance of Morrison's visit, and by extension the role of Irish-America in extracting concessions from republicanism, was that the IRA imposed a clandestine ceasefire for its duration.[41] The ceasefire mattered for two reasons. It made it clear that Irish-America was behind the inclusion of Sinn Féin in any peace negotiations and it allowed Sinn Féin to prove to the two governments that they could impose a ceasefire with grass-roots republican support should the leadership request one. During the visit, Morrison stepped up his public calls for Clinton to appoint an official peace envoy, something widely sought after by republicans. Morrison himself used the notion of Major's increasing reliance on Unionist MPs as proof that British neutrality was not possible and therefore the US needed to offer oversight of any peace talks.[42] It was no coincidence that it was soon after another Irish-American delegation visited again in 1994 that the IRA finally declared what was to become their lasting ceasefire. Morrison had been steadily building pressure on republicans to enact their long-touted ceasefire, such as criticising an IRA bombing in October 1993 for giving the US delegation 'a bigger mountain to climb' and stating that it made it more difficult for Clinton to get involved.[43]

At the same time, members of the ANIA continued to lobby for a visa for Gerry Adams. In December 1993, Clinton granted Adams a 48-hour visa ostensibly to attend a conference organised by Bill Flynn in his capacity as chairman of the National Committee on American Foreign Policy. The visa was granted under pressure from the Irish-American lobby, including Senators Kennedy and Moynihan, who hoped it would strengthen Adams's standing both internationally and within the IRA in his efforts to engage in a peace process. According to Adams, the granting of the visa brought forward the IRA ceasefire by about one year, presumably by convincing the hawks in the republican movement that the peaceful path delivered real results.[44] In the following years, Adams was granted further visas and in 1995 he was allowed to fund-raise for Sinn Féin, a factor which helped to divert money away from Noraid.[45] There was also the promise of an economic peace dividend of inward investment through an International Fund (in line with such promises, by 2011 around 20 per cent of private sector jobs in Northern Ireland were linked to US companies and their subsidiaries).[46]

The decision to become more interventionist, as signalled by the granting of the visa to Adams, was a deeply contested one within the administration at the time.[47] Foreign policy was traditionally heavily influenced by the State Department, which strongly prioritised the interests of the British government given their important strategic partnership with the US in the realms of economic and foreign affairs. Knowing that granting Adams a visa would upset the British, along with deep concerns about legitimising a man closely associated with an ongoing terrorist organisation, the State Department strongly disagreed with granting the visa. In contrast, Clinton's close inner circle of policy advisors on Northern Ireland, namely Tony Lake, Nancy Soderberg and Trina Vargo, along with important figures like Edward Kennedy and the Irish-American lobby and the Irish government, all supported granting the visa in the anticipation that it could act as a conduit to enmesh the senior republican leadership in politics and reinforce their drift towards seeking an exclusively peaceful solution. While Clinton ultimately granted the visa, thus bypassing the State Department, there was certainly some scepticism and constructive doubts around the role of the US intervention.

The granting of the visa served an important purpose in the moderation of republicanism. From George Mitchell's perspective, 'it validated Adams and gave him access to the world stage', helping to make him an acceptable person to engage with in a process of negotiation.[48] As Kerr argues, 'someone had to legitimise Adams on the international stage, and it certainly could not have been Major'.[49] What is more, the visa acted simultaneously as an incentive to moderate and a disincentive to resist moderation. Cox argues that 'it gave republicans a glimpse of new vistas which might be made available to them if they changed course'.[50] The lure of this incentive was clear when Mitchel McLaughlin reassured grass-roots republicans by stating that 'Sinn Féin now, through our president Gerry Adams, has direct access to the corridors of power in Washington.'[51] Yet at the same time, the threat of removing these gains acted as leverage over the republican movement. 'By letting Irish republicans know that it had friends in high places who it could easily lose if it failed to deliver, it put further pressure upon them to call off the violence.'[52] MacGinty sums this position up with a quote from the Irish premier's press secretary about why they supported the granting of the visa to Adams in the first instance:

> Sinn Féin will pay a price for going to Capitol Hill. A lot of powerful people went out on a limb for Adams. If he doesn't deliver, they'll have him back in the house with the steel shutters [Sinn Féin headquarters, Falls Road Belfast] so fast his feet won't touch the ground. We're slowly putting the squeeze on them, pulling them in, boxing them in, cutting off their lines of retreat.[53]

Although the British government was aggrieved at the granting of the visa,[54] with John Major famously refusing to take Clinton's phone calls for five days, this derived from disgruntlement that London no longer held sway over US policy as much as it derived from the actual granting of the visa itself. There was also a general air of caution within the British government towards US interventions. This was not just related to the allegedly negative personal dynamics between Major and Clinton, and it extended into Blair's time in office too. The British government tended to view the US as pro-nationalist, even if they were not pro-republican, and therefore British officials fretted about the destabilising effect of a US intervention upon the unionist community and the delicate nascent peace process.

In contrast, republicans widely welcomed the move, reassured that the US would help address the asymmetry in their negotiations with Britain.[55] The US's role in part became about giving republicans confidence so that they could end violence and accept Britain at its word without fretting that it was a colonial master's plot to demilitarise a problematic insurgency before returning to the status quo. This was a genuine concern for republicans, with Adams arguing that a crucial factor in delays over decommissioning was 'the depth of insecurity for nationalists living in the North', given the large presence of the British army, the partisan history of the RUC, and the presence of loyalist paramilitaries.[56]

Clinton had demonstrated to republicans and nationalists that the US administration would no longer unquestioningly act in the interests of the British. But his administration still needed to gain the acceptance of both the British and, most importantly, the Unionist negotiators who viewed them as potentially highly sympathetic to Irish nationalism. Therefore, in order for the US to fulfil a role as an external broker in the Northern Irish peace process, it was necessary that it acted in a scrupulously neutral fashion to win acceptance from Britain and Unionism. One significant way such neutrality was demonstrated to Unionism was the clarity and firmness with which the US government stated its belief that for those seeking Irish unity, only unity through consent could be seen as a legitimate route. Additionally, Tony Lake strove to be seen as fair and even-handed within the confines of Clinton's policy, reaching out to Unionists and the British immediately after attempting to draw republicans into the peace process.[57] Indeed so successful was the US administration at establishing the neutrality of its interests that by 1994 David Trimble, future leader of the UUP, stated after a meeting with the Vice President Al Gore,

> they made it absolutely clear that they have no formula for the political way forward, that they want to help in what way they can the political process and that it is up to the two governments and the parties in Northern Ireland to determine the political way forward.[58]

As such, the US became acceptable to all parties – it came to be seen as a broker who could help deliver republicanism and get it to endorse the principle of consent by the British and Unionists, and it continued to be seen as a powerful ally who could provide key benefits and counterbalance potential British perfidy by republicans. In this way, British suspicion of US involvement changed markedly and under both Major's and Blair's administrations there wasn't a 'glimmer of light' between the two positions, albeit US involvement was seen as more effective on some occasions than on others.[59]

The depth of mutual mistrust and suspicion was clear as soon as negotiations were attempted, as was the US's role in stabilising republicanism's commitment. The role of the US government and Irish-America was notably important in extracting what was to become the lasting IRA ceasefire and in giving momentum to the initial negotiations in very difficult circumstances. Prior to the IRA declaring the August 1994 ceasefire, Adams stated that he received commitments from visiting US businessmen, including that they would 'act as guarantors insofar as they could, and do their best to get the US government to act as guarantors, so that any agreements entered into by the governments were adhered to'.[60] Bruce Morrison was one of those providing these guarantees and he later noted that Sinn Féin 'wanted somebody they knew could speak with authority to the White House and speak back to them', describing assurances from the White House as 'absolutely indispensable' to securing an IRA ceasefire: 'I was able to lay out for the White House what was needed and the necessary assurances were given. I communicated in writing and orally these things, and there was a process in the White House that gave back assurances sufficient to do the deed.'[61]

Even after the declaration of the ceasefire, there was still much mistrust between the main internal parties that hampered progress. Once the IRA declared a ceasefire, the issue of the permanency of this ceasefire came to the fore. Unionist leaders were in the position of neither wanting to, nor being able to, negotiate with Sinn Féin representatives, let alone share government with them, while the IRA retained its arms. John Major was publicly sympathetic to the Unionist position, even if British officials rejected the idea that this altered their negotiating stance.[62] Adding to the complications, Major was reliant on Unionist members of parliament to pass some key votes at Westminster, undermining his claims to neutrality in the eyes of republicans.

Republicans were insistent that they could only put their weapons beyond use as part of a broader strategy to demilitarise the whole conflict, including scaling back or removing the British military apparatus. Adams declared that demands to symbolically begin disarming prior to a political settlement were tantamount to 'a gesture which would symbolize an IRA surrender' and that 'Sinn Féin cannot, will not, involve itself in a futile exercise to bring about an IRA surrender.'[63] For republicans,

> on one level, [decommissioning] was simply a propagandist ploy by the British government to "humiliate" the IRA, on another, the precondition of decommissioning was simply "the ambush up the road", an attempt to protract the process of "decontamination" of Sinn Féin by a government for whom "negotiation is war by another means".[64]

Republicans believed that 'the armed struggle prevented a settlement on British terms',[65] and therefore it was difficult for them to abandon this. They also feared being left vulnerable to attack if they decommissioned. *An Phoblacht* argued that 'given the experience of the past, when a virtually defenceless nationalist community in the north was attacked by loyalists and the militarised RUC, it is unrealistic to expect that community to disarm unilaterally'.[66] For republicans, decommissioning could only occur as part of the negotiated settlement, not prior to its negotiation and they suggested that an independent third party would help in this situation.[67]

Amidst this rapidly entrenching position of mutual mistrust, Clinton appointed George Mitchell as a peace envoy to Northern Ireland in December 1994. His role in this process is somewhat disputed – some British officials claim that his appointment was mainly accepted as a way of preventing more direct intervention by Clinton himself while simultaneously co-opting Mitchell to the British position.[68] Such a perspective exclusively sees the talks through a British prism, where the challenge was to get republicans to give up violence and accept the constitutional status quo. However, for republicans Mitchell's appointment was much more of a signal that Britain would not be allowed to dictate the talks in the interests of Unionism.

Initially Mitchell's position focused on encouraging investment and economic development, but it rapidly expanded into much more than this. In one of his first tasks, Mitchell chaired the International Body of Decommissioning, tasked with finding a way to resolve the contrasting positions between republicans on the one side and the British government and unionists on the other. The Commission's report concluded that paramilitary groups should not decommission arms prior to all-party talks but rather some decommissioning should occur during the substantive negotiations. Mitchell expressed his surprise that the British government seemed to assume that his report would agree with them and recommend decommissioning prior to beginning negotiations,[69] and his ultimate recommendation of parallel decommissioning was reassuring to republicans of the independence of US interests and their willingness to defy British interests.[70] John Major largely rejected this idea, suggesting instead that an elected Forum for Political Dialogue be established as a conduit into multi-party talks, largely to give Unionists political cover prior to direct talks with Sinn Féin.[71] The IRA responded by ending its ceasefire in February 1996, although it has been argued that there were plans to end the ceasefire within grass-roots republican circles prior to the publication of Mitchell's report.[72] Renewed violence remained until Tony Blair's landslide electoral victory in the British general election of 1997 introduced fresh impetus into the peace process. Mo Mowlam, the new Secretary of State for Northern Ireland, announced that 'decommissioning is secondary to actually getting people into talks'.[73] Alongside this, the US government placed increased pressure upon republicans to accept British reassurances about negotiations,[74] paving the way for a renewal of the IRA ceasefire in August 1997 and for Sinn Féin to enter all-party talks. To further consolidate US reassurances to accept negotiations with Britain in good faith, Mitchell was appointed to chair the talks.

The shape of the Belfast Agreement was largely already in place prior to negotiations and the outstanding aspects were actually negotiated by the British and Irish governments rather than Mitchell, although Mitchell was important in gaining consensus over the relations between Ireland and Northern Ireland.[75] Yet even if the parameters of the settlement were already in place, the presence of Mitchell in the chair helped extract republican consent through confidence building in a way that the British government alone could not achieve. Jonathan Powell, Tony Blair's Chief of Staff and lead negotiator for the British, suggested that Mitchell could achieve progress given his status as an independent and international broker.[76] US guarantees were again crucial for republicans at the stage when they were required to accept the final Agreement, just as they had been when republicans were considering their first ceasefire. Late into the final night of negotiations and prior to agreeing to take the document to their grass roots for approval, Adams described a crucial phone call with Bill Clinton:

> I told [Clinton] that I thought we had the basis of an agreement, but a lot depended on how the British delivered on its commitments . . . I told the President that if we were to see this agreement delivered, then he had to ensure that the British didn't pull out of their commitments. I also pointed up the hard reality that the unionists had yet to engage with us. I told him my fear was that once negotiations were over, pressure would be off the Brits and the UUP . . . Bill Clinton understood this. He was prepared to do all he could to guarantee any agreement.[77]

This same ability was on display in the implementation phase of the Belfast Agreement. In the year following the historical agreement, little progress was being made and a devolved assembly was yet to be established, with the Unionists still hesitant to enter government with Sinn Féin prior to decommissioning. The British and Irish governments attempted but failed to break the deadlock when they suggested a timetable for the establishment of a Northern Irish Assembly in a manner that was indexed to decommissioning. Again this proposal was rejected by the parties in Northern Ireland, leading to the two governments inviting Mitchell to return and undertake a one-year review in an effort to move the process forward. Republicans continued to reject the need to decommission prior to Sinn Féin entering a devolved executive and they viewed decommissioning as an issue used by Unionists to disguise the fact that they just didn't want to share power with Irish nationalists. As such, republicans blamed the Independent International Commission on Decommissioning (IICD),[78] established in 1997 prior to the Belfast Agreement to handle decommissioning, for allowing the issue to be dominated by partisan interests.

For republicans it was the failure to strengthen the position of international third parties that threatened the process by allowing it to become dominated by domestic actors they did not trust. Mitchell's review proposed the solution of establishing a devolved Assembly immediately and to aim to complete decommissioning by April 2000. As an indicator of good faith he requested paramilitary organisations to appoint a representative to liaise with the IICD. Republicans accepted this offer and by December 1999, the Northern Ireland Executive was established and Sinn Féin held the health and education portfolios while the IRA still retained its arms.

The Clinton administration was again important in this implementation phase when the British government was attempting to limit the reforms of the RUC to less than those recommended by their own independent Patten Commission.[79] The Blair government, and Peter Mandelson as Secretary for State of Northern Ireland, felt the need to tone down the recommendations made by the Commission in order the bolster the vulnerable position of David Trimble within his UUP, but this came at the cost of further undermining the trust that republicans had in British governments to implement the Belfast Agreement in full.[80] In this situation, both the Clinton administration and the Irish government were crucial in pressuring the British to implement Patten's recommendations in full, and prevent what was seen by republicans as British attempts to renege.[81] Here again was evidence that the US intervention under Clinton had a profound effect upon republicanism in terms of its willingness and ability to commit to the new institutions. It acted as a stabilising force, reassuring republicans that a fair long-term macro-democratic settlement with relatively low risks would be secured along with redressing some of their grievances.

Yet there were limits to what Mitchell and Clinton could achieve and by the time their tenure came to an end in early 2001 the Northern Irish Assembly was highly vulnerable (having already been suspended once), and full decommissioning remained the biggest obstacle to the peace process. Clinton and Mitchell had succeeded in internationalising decommissioning and the IICD was broadly accepted as the appropriate channel to achieve decommissioning, but there was little substantial movement forthcoming on this. Here, again, was clear evidence that the final and most radically salient aspect of republicanism was its militarism, and decommissioning was difficult to tackle.

BUSH AND THE IMPOSITION OF REPUBLICAN DECOMMISSIONING

By the time of the election of George W. Bush in 2000, the scope for US intervention had greatly dwindled. The IRA and other paramilitaries were on ceasefires which were looking increasingly permanent, the Belfast Agreement was in place and the principles of power-sharing had been endorsed. However, decommissioning and the permanent disbandment of the IRA were the outstanding issues that were threatening to destabilise the peace process, and this is where the new administration's efforts were to focus. In general, Northern Ireland was a lower priority for Bush than for his predecessor, but that did not imply that he was disengaged. Indeed it would be a mistake to think of Bush as having a radically different policy to Clinton towards Northern Ireland. Both Clinton and Bush were firmly on the side of bringing republicans to a position of exclusively using peaceful politics and both deployed envoys with a view to coerce and pressure change. However, there can be little doubt that the peace process was less of a priority for Bush (there was also less scope for US engagement) and that he was less willing to upset the British government given the importance of this alliance in the context of the Iraq War. Therefore, this phase of US involvement became less about acting as a guarantor to reassure republicans and more about using coercion and moral pressure to remove republicanism's military capability permanently.

Although the Northern Irish Assembly was in place at the start of 2001 it was living a precarious existence, as would be evidenced by two 24-hour suspensions that were imposed in August and September of that year. The UUP under Trimble continued to struggle to share power with Sinn Féin without IRA decommissioning. Although on 6 May the previous year the IRA had released a statement saying that 'the IRA leadership will initiate a process that will completely and verifiably put IRA arms beyond use', this was yet to happen. Jonathan Powell noted that a recurring theme of his negotiations with republicans throughout this phase was repeated evasions by Sinn Féin and the IRA over precise phrasing that they were committed to decommissioning.[82] The British government's efforts to offer concessions on the demilitarisation of Northern Ireland as a whole failed to move the IRA. Irish negotiators too had little breakthrough on this issue and at one point an IRA representative threw a bullet across the negotiating table at an Irish official, declaring that this was the only decommissioning they would see.[83]

When Bush assumed office in 2001 he appointed Richard Haass to serve as his Special Envoy in Northern Ireland. Haass immediately emphasised a change in direction by signalling that he believed the solution to Northern Ireland's outstanding tension was primarily something to be tackled by the British and Irish governments and that the solution did not lie in Washington.[84] A return to the policy of non-intervention looked likely, especially given that Northern Irish policy was relocated from the White House back to the State Department. Although there was a clear change in direction, non-intervention never really materialised for two reasons. Firstly, Haass continued to assert an interest in the peace process, primarily to promote the Bush administration's internationalism and to be associated with a successful peace process on the world stage. Secondly, the key events of the arrest of three IRA men in Colombia and the attacks of 9/11 2001 gave the US a huge desire to impose decommissioning in line with their wider goals in the 'war on terror'. There is a danger of overstating the significance of events in 2001 for decommissioning. After all, full decommissioning did not come until 2005, some four years after these 'crucial' events. Also, clearly, whether the attacks of 9/11 happened or not, the US was committed to support the process of decommissioning. Yet nor should these events be ignored entirely and they undoubtedly shifted the discourse for some of the key players.

On 11 August 2001, three members of the IRA were arrested in Colombia for travelling using false passports and charged with training FARC guerrillas in mortar bombing techniques. This event massively eroded sympathy for republicans both within the US political elite and within their new allies in corporate Irish-America and 'the discovery of the "Colombia Three" rattled Congress and the Bush administration. Both signalled their anger with the republican movement by calling for congressional hearings into the matter.'[85] Bill Flynn called on the IRA to disarm immediately in the aftermath of the arrests. Jim Gibney, a senior Sinn Féin strategist, noted its effect upon republicanism, stating that 'There is no doubt that Colombia was very damaging to Sinn Féin in the United States . . . and a lot of work has been done by Sinn Féin representatives in the United States to try and deal with the fallout from that.'[86]

A more wide-reaching event was the attack on the World Trade Centre exactly one month later. After the experience of a very large-scale terrorist event in one of the heartlands of what was hitherto their Irish-American support base, more forceful emphasis was placed by the US envoy upon decommissioning. The new Northern Irish peace envoy, Richard Haass, changed the tone of his engagement from one of cajoling to one of outright pressure on republicans.[87] He threated to withdraw fund-raising visas from Sinn Féin officials in the future and this was backed up by Bill Flynn who threatened the withdrawal of donations from corporate US. Schmitt argues that the effects of the 9/11 attacks were that they cut off the ability of republicans to return to violence because any such moves would alienate their international supporters and they would rapidly lose the political capital they accumulated through entering the peace process seven years earlier.[88] Demands for immediate IRA decommissioning were now receiving a more sympathetic hearing within the US government and this created an opportunity to increase the pressure on republicans to put their arms permanently beyond use. Jonathan Powell also argued to republicans that 9/11 rendered their form of terrorism obsolete, having been superseded by a more high profile and threatening variety.[89]

With their scope for delay and prevarication greatly reduced, just six weeks later the IRA engaged in its first tentative acts of decommissioning and further decommissioning was to follow in March 2002. However, soon stalling and failure to complete the process was to resurface. In 2003 Haass left his post in disagreement with Bush over the direction of the war on terror and he was replaced by Mitchell Reiss who increased the pressure on republicans to finalise decommissioning. Reiss stated that he saw his role as eliciting a change of policy stance from Sinn Féin towards endorsing the police service and completing decommissioning in full, and he used the influence of Irish-America and governmental pressure to achieve this.[90] Following the largest bank robbery in the history of the state by the IRA and the killing of Robert McCartney in a pub brawl by a senior IRA leader and subsequent witness intimidation by IRA members, republicans came under hitherto unseen levels of US pressure. Reiss continued to increase the pressure during Adams's visit to the US on St Patrick's Day in 2005. During this trip, 'wherever Adams went in Washington, he faced bipartisan opprobrium' including from former allies.[91] Adams was not invited to the White House, Ted Kennedy and George Bush refused to meet him, and previously supportive Irish-American groups denounced republicans for their ongoing links to violence. Additionally, Sinn Féin members were now being denied fund-raising visas.[92] A senior political figure in the US noted that members of Congress were no longer willing to go out on a limb for republicans: 'Ten years ago we could have got 20 congressmen and half a dozen senators from both parties to sign a letter to the president . . . Today we'd have trouble getting one.'[93]

The threat of the withdrawal of US support and recognition soon focused republican minds. The following month, after returning to Ireland and with

Westminster and local elections looming, Adams called for the IRA to engage in purely political and democratic activity. In July 2005 the IRA announced that it had 'formally ordered an end to the armed campaign ... All IRA units have been ordered to dump arms ... The IRA leadership has also authorised our representative to engage with the IICD to complete the process to verifiably put its arms beyond use.' Decommissioning of IRA weapons was complete by September that year, paving the way for a withdrawal of US interests in the peace process, which were already waning by this stage anyway.

CONCLUSION

Ending entrenched civil wars often requires international actors acting as brokers and guarantors. In this respect the moderation of ethno-national radical groups needs to include an examination of the international dimension. That is not to say that moderation originated in the international context and domestic circumstances in Britain and Ireland were the initial drivers of this process. However, the international context was a crucial facilitator for completing moderation. This is not just about bringing in a new external actor to bargain with republicans, although this was certainly part of it. It was also about the US being perceived by republicans as guaranteeing their interests while also being an acceptable broker to the Unionists and the British too. This was a process of underpinning a stable and predictable basis to the new institutions in Northern Ireland that reduced the risks for republicans to commit to a peace process. Over time, incentivising leverages turned to more pressurising leverages, and the threat of withdrawal of US support and the exercise of moral condemnation came to the fore to secure decommissioning. The linkages between republicans and the US were crucial to ensuring that these leverages were effective, and these links stemmed from a strong and active diaspora and sense of shared history on the republican side, and a sense that Northern Ireland could be used as a model of effective foreign policy interventions on the US side.[94]

This brings us back to an important overarching question: what was the nature of the republican moderation generated by this causal factor? The role of the international intervention was much more limited in time and scope than that of elections and democratic bargaining. The effects of US engagement were more akin to de-radicalisation than moderation, by which I mean a short-term process specifically focused on removing the use of violence rather than the longer-term and gradualist processes already examined. The US intervention certainly encouraged participation, but many of the incentives and the momentum towards participation were already in place in the domestic context. George Mitchell was not necessarily involved in negotiating the actual content of the Belfast Agreement given that the broad parameters of the internal strand had been in place for a long time. Rather the role of the US was about eliciting negative moderation – the removal of anti-system violence and revolution. Again it did not necessarily entail positive moderation – a total change in the values or beliefs of republicans. In order to secure the support of the US as a guarantor, republicanism needed to make itself coalitionable. For the US this required eliminating the armed struggle and accepting the consent principle – in other words, the same position as that espoused by the British and Irish governments. What it did not require was a change in value or attitudes towards a united Ireland. Many in Irish-America were sympathetic to the pursuit of a united Ireland and did not demand that republicans should give up their core goals or change their position on the legitimacy of Northern Ireland. As such, moderation was about the elimination of violence but not concerned with changing values.

NOTES

1. McGarry and O'Leary argue that consociational theory needs to be modified for the ethno-national context by looking to the external dimensions of the state. McGarry and O'Leary. 'Consociation and its Critics'. Kerr, *Imposing Power-Sharing*, does just this.
2. Walter, *Committing to Peace*.
3. Ibid., p. 3.
4. Lynch, *Turf War*; Thompson, *American Policy and Northern Ireland*, pp. 71–96; Cochrane, 'Irish-America, the End of the IRA's Armed Struggle and the Utility of "Soft Power"'; Arthur, *Special Relationships*, pp. 132–159; Wilson, *Irish America and the Ulster Conflict*, pp. 106–140.
5. Levitsky and Way, 'International Linkage and Democratization'; Levitsky and Way, 'Linkage versus Leverage'.
6. Kissane, *The Politics of the Irish Civil War*, p. 45.
7. Lynch, *Turf War*, chapter 2.
8. This number comes from the 1980 Census and it includes Irish Americans of both Catholic and Protestant ancestry. It is worth noting that these two groups had 'separate experiences of immigration [that] led to a loss of visibility on the part of the Ulster-Scots and an exaggerated sense of political importance among those of a Catholic background'. Arthur, *Special Relationships*, p. 136.
9. Minutes of a Meeting at the State Department, 26 August 1969 between Dr O'hEideain (Chargé d'Affaires, Ireland), Mr Lawton (Third Secretary, Ireland), Mr Springsteen (Deputy Assistant Secretary for European Affairs, USA) and Mr Goldstein (Irish Country Officer, USA), DFA 2006/44/406, NAI.
10. Sanders, *Inside the IRA*, p. 105.
11. 'Visit of US Congressional Delegation, 19th April 1979', TAOIS 2010/19/1646, NAI.
12. See Dumbrell, 'The United States and the Northern Irish Conflict 1969–94', for a full overview of these groups and their goals.
13. Guelke, 'The United States, Irish Americans and the Northern Ireland Peace Process', p. 522.
14. Sanders, *Inside the IRA*, p. 112.
15. Ibid., p. 169.
16. *The Evening Press*, 24 September 1979.
17. Guelke, 'The United States, Irish Americans and the Northern Ireland Peace Process', p. 525.
18. Committee of Inquiry into Police Interrogation Procedures in Northern Ireland, *Report of the Committee of Inquiry into Police Interrogation Procedures in Northern Ireland*.

19. Thompson, *American Policy and Northern Ireland*, pp. 86–87.
20. It should be noted that various British officials and ministers caution against over-estimating the influence of US pressure at this time, arguing that internal change was underway anyway. Interview with Douglas Hurd; interview with Robin Butler.
21. MacGinty, 'American Influences on the Northern Irish Peace Process'.
22. Both British and Irish officials acknowledge the efforts of John Hume in shaping US opinion during this time. Interview with Martin Mansergh; interview with Robin Butler.
23. Interview with Mark Durkan; Arthur, *Special Relationships*, pp. 138–139.
24. Interview with Mark Durkan.
25. 'Visit of US Congressional Delegation 19 April 1979, Tip O'Neill, Joseph McDade, Thomas Foley', NAI Taois 2010/19/1646.
26. Lynch, *Turf War*, p. 21. Indeed Lynch comprehensively dismisses explanations that see a steady drift towards more US intervention during this time and which culminate in Clinton's interventionism, instead arguing that Clinton represented much more of a sharp break with policy to date.
27. 'Mitchell confident settlement can be reached in "good faith" negotiations', *Irish Times*, 30 May 1997; Mitchell, *Making Peace*, p. 37.
28. Interview with Jonathan Phillips.
29. Cox, 'Bringing in the "International"'.
30. Quoted in Dumbrell, 'The New American Connection', p. 358.
31. Guelke, 'The United States, Irish Americans and the Northern Ireland Peace Process', argues that there is no evidence that Irish issues had anything other than a marginal impact on electoral outcomes in the US (p. 535).
32. Downs and Steadman, 'Evaluation Issues in Peace Implementation'.
33. Dumbrell, 'The New American Connection', p. 358.
34. Quoted in O'Clery, *The Greening of the White House*, p. 8.
35. Quoted in Arthur, *Special Relationships*, p. 157.
36. 'Reynolds to discuss fact-finding mission to NI with Clinton', *Irish Times*, 10 March 1993, p. 1.
37. Feeney, who made his fortune through duty-free shops at airports, became a huge asset for a post-ceasefire Sinn Féin, easily becoming the party's biggest US donor. By 2015 he had given the party almost US$800,000. 'Top US donors to Sinn Féin', *Irish Times*, 5 March 2015, p. 4.
38. A rather flattering account of Morrison's contribution is given in a book written by his friend, Penn Rhodeen, *Peacerunner*.
39. 'Irish American group will meet Sinn Féin leaders', *Irish Times*, 8 September 1993, p. 1.
40. 'Visiting US group to discuss "constructive role" on North', *Irish Times*, 6 September 1993, p. 5.
41. 'Morrison's talks led to lull in IRA action', *Irish Times*, 13 September 1993, p. 1. A previous clandestine ceasefire had been attempted in March 1993 for a visit by Bill Flynn but this failed to hold.
42. 'Pressure for Clinton to act on NI envoy grows', *Irish Times*, 24 August 1993, p. 3.
43. 'Irish American leaders say bombing is a major set-back to goals', *Irish Times*, 26 October 1993, p. 8.
44. O'Clery, *The Greening of the White House*, p. 168.
45. Dumbrell, 'The New American Connection', pp. 358–359.
46. Ibid., p. 359.
47. 'Irish Americans in power struggle over NI policy', *Irish Times*, 15 March 1993, p. 4; Lynch, *Turf War*.
48. Mitchell, *Making Peace*, p. 113.
49. Kerr, *Imposing Power-Sharing*. See also Clancy, *Peace Without Consensus*, p. 64.

50. Cox, 'Bringing in the "International"', p. 687.
51. *AP*, 31 August 1995, pp. 12–13.
52. Cox, 'Bringing in the "International"', p. 687.
53. MacGinty, 'American Influences on the Northern Irish Peace Process'.
54. Jonathan Powell, in *Great Hatred, Little Room*, notes how he was working in the US Embassy at the time and, like Major, against the decision but with hindsight saw the value in granting the visa.
55. *AP*, 21 September 1995.
56. Adams, *Hope and History*, p. 214.
57. O'Clery, *The Greening of the White House*, p. 134.
58. Ibid., p. 161.
59. Interview with Joe Pilling.
60. Adams, *Hope and History*, p. 176.
61. 'President's man played pivotal role in setting up ceasefire', *Irish Times*, 4 August 1997. Bruce Morrison, however, rejected the use of the term 'guarantor' preferring the phrases 'friend of the process' and 'supporter of a just settlement'.
62. Interview with John Chilcot; interview with Quentin Thomas.
63. *Irish Times*, 14 June 1995.
64. Brown and Hauswedell, *Burying the Hatchet*, p. 20.
65. *AP*, 2 March 1995, p. 5.
66. *AP*, 27 October 1994, p. 6.
67. Sinn Féin, *Submission to the Mitchell Commission*.
68. Mitchell, *Making Peace*, p. 77.
69. Ibid., p. 30; Powell, *Great Hatred, Little Room*, p. 83.
70. Adams, *Hope and History*, p. 154.
71. Interview with Quentin Thomas.
72. Bew et al., *Talking to Terorists*, p. 137.
73. 'Decommissioning secondary to inclusive talks – Mowlam', *Irish Times*, 10 May 1997.
74. Clancy, *Peace Without Consensus*, p. 73.
75. Ibid., p. 180.
76. Powell, *Great Hatred, Little Room*, p. 156.
77. Adams, *Hope and History*, p. 363. Mitchell, *Making Peace*, p. 178, also cites the importance of this phone call in eliciting republican support, as well as phone calls to other participants in the final stages of the negotiations.
78. The IICD was established in 1997 as part of the negotiations for the Belfast Agreement and attempted to internationalise the issue of decommissioning to help in its resolution. It was chaired by the retired Canadian general, John de Chastelain, and also included the Finn Tauno Nieminen and the American Donald Johnson.
79. Independent Commission on Policing for Northern Ireland, *A New Beginning: Policing in Northern Ireland*.
80. As noted in the previous chapter, the SDLP and Irish government also grew frustrated with the British stance on implementing the Patten Commission. Interview with Alex Attwood.
81. 'Adams accuses Mandelson of emasculating Patten recommendations', *Irish Times*, 11 July 2000; 'Government has not gutted RUC reform bill says Mandelson', *The Guardian*, 15 November 2000.
82. Powell, *Great Hatred, Little Room*, passim.
83. Interview with Eamonn McKee.
84. Clancy, *Peace Without Consensus*, p. 114.
85. Ibid.
86. Quoted in Frampton, *The Legion of the Rearguard*, p. 148.
87. 'Picking up the baton of Mitchell', *Irish Times*, 26 March 2004. This article sug-

gests that 'fairly well attested legend has it that [Haass] berated Gerry Adams and Martin McGuinness, and that first "act" of decommissioning soon followed'.

88. Schmitt, 'The US War on Terrorism and its Impact on the Politics of Accommodation in Northern Ireland'.
89. Powell, *Great Hatred, Little Room*, pp. 202 and 310.
90. Reiss, *Negotiating with Evil*, pp. 36 and 67.
91. Clancy, *Peace Without Consensus*, p. 150.
92. 'Adams faces task in US of restoring faith in Sinn Féin', *Irish Times*, 12 March 2005; 'Senator Kennedy refuses to meet Adams', *Irish Times*, 14 March 2005.
93. 'The end of the affair', *Irish Times*, 12 March 2005.
94. America's interest in using Northern Ireland as a successful example of their brokering ability is evident from Clinton's reluctance to return to Northern Ireland during the crisis on decommissioning, and he only came on condition that he (mistakenly) thought progress was being made. See Powell, *Great Hatred, Little Room*, p. 182.

6. BRITISH POLICY TOWARDS IRISH REPUBLICANISM

The emphasis so far has been upon how sustained inclusion within a set of credible institutions incentivised and extracted republican moderation. This raises the necessary question of what was the role of the British state in this process, given that it largely defined the space in which political competition occurred. Many existing studies assume that British policy contributed to republican moderation by co-opting republicans and sucking them in to mainstream politics.[1] This may have been part of their final strategy in the formal peace process, but British policy across the long-term conflict as a whole was certainly not this coherent or clearly focused around the goal of co-option. In fact, even during the formal peace process John Chilcot rejected the idea that the British were seeking to enmesh republicans, stating instead that it was about finding a way forward for both sides.[2] It has also been argued that the process of dialogue itself and the way the British crafted this was crucial.[3] But such emphases neglect the wider context in which dialogue occurred and the long-term nature of republican moderation, which began long before the formal talks that led to the peace process.

A better understanding of British policy is to appreciate how it enabled republican moderation through two key conditions. Firstly, it focused on creating a credible institutional framework for political competition in Northern Ireland that reduced the risks of participation for all sides. Secondly, British policy was highly tolerant of the emergence of Irish republicanism as a political force and did not seek to suppress it, even while imposing very robust anti-terrorist legislation against the IRA. A credible institutional framework and tolerance of republicanism as a political force allowed republicans to commit to a moderate path knowing that the institutional framework offered a genuine opportunity to exercise power without inherently favouring one side over the other in advance. In other words, British policy enabled moderation through inclusion to occur and it is doubtful that decisions to moderate by republican elites at critical junctures would have become binding in the absence of these factors.

Yet it would be a mistake to think tolerance and building strong institutions was always a clear plan by British policy-makers. British policy was often messy and contradictory, developing in response to the proclivities of different prime ministers and secretaries of state and without a clear direction, especially in the 1970s and first half of the 1980s. Although there appeared to be some consistencies in British policy and bipartisanship across governments, this masks important divergences both between and within the major parties in the 1970s.[4] Any seeming continuities actually derived from British policy becoming locked in place due to an inability to pursue any other option rather than because there was consistency across successive governments. However, with the signing of the AIA in 1985, even though this was undertaken for different reasons by the variety of actors who negotiated it, successive British and Irish governments began to cohere around building strong intergovernmental relationships and later returned to a policy of power sharing (and this time a model of power sharing that included republicans in the process). As the intergovernmental relationship developed and strengthened, strong institution building followed and republicans were able to emerge within mainstream politics.

A STRONG AND CREDIBLE INSTITUTIONAL FRAMEWORK

Northern Ireland was an anomalous political entity in many respects, which both sustained republicanism's discontent and enabled its moderation. For the vast majority of its existence since 1921, Northern Ireland was rejected as a legitimate site of political authority by a sizeable minority of its population. The notion that Northern Ireland could be a fair democracy, certainly prior to the 1970s, was rejected by Irish nationalists. Instead Northern Ireland and its institutions were seen as inherently biased and unable to provide a basis for equitable political competition. In fact, the Northern Irish political unit between 1921 and 1972 was highly compatible with Hartzell et al.'s definition of a weak state, which is a state 'dominated by a single group or coalition of groups [that] acts aggressively towards out-group interests, exploiting and repressing their politically disadvantaged peoples, [and] combines the hardness of military and police strength with the softness of political illegitimacy'.[5] This is not to claim that Northern Ireland was a state, but it is to show the degree of fragility in its devolved governing institutions.

One of the main challenges to be overcome in the process of transforming revolutionaries into stakeholders is low levels of trust towards the ruling status quo. This inhibits the willingness of radical groups to work through existing institutions and engenders a reluctance to commit to peaceful politics for fear that the institutions will be inherently biased against the pursuit of their goals. Credible institutional guarantees, and power sharing in particular, enable minority groups to overcome mistrust and commit to a peace process.[6]

It is within this context that the importance of British policy towards strengthening the role of impartial and ultimately inclusive institutions mattered. It allowed republicans to accept political institutions as an alternative route to pursue their goals and it brought them into contact with their moderating impact. While it may have been clear to all sides that strengthening institutions to overcome grievances within the nationalist community was necessary, the 1970s and early 1980s saw little actual achievement in this direction by either the Conservative or Labour Parties. It was not until the AIA in 1985 that more coherent policies around strengthening institutions in cooperation with the Republic of Ireland emerged. Indeed this was what ultimately set Northern Ireland apart from many other sites of ethno-national conflict. Where other conflicts suffer from a weak set of political institutions combined with poor socio-economic outcomes, Northern Ireland had the long history of British democracy behind it and, although suffering from significant inequalities and relative poverty compared to other parts of the UK, it was clearly a 'First World' country.

Confused British Policy and the Lack of Direction, 1972–1984

The first decade of British policy towards the conflict in Northern Ireland was confused. It sought to create greater opportunities for nationalists and embedded tolerance of Sinn Féin, but this was combined with attempts to marginalise republicanism and almost exclusively relying on military engagement rather than political initiatives (with the exception of Sunningdale, of course). It was clear to the British from the very start of direct rule in 1972 that they needed to provide more political opportunity for nationalists and that resolution would require reconciling the UK's relationship with Ireland. In spite of this awareness, following the collapse of the initial effort at power sharing through the Sunningdale Agreement, no real political initiatives were attempted or pursued. There were also some clear differences between the Labour Party and the Conservative Party over how to manage Northern Ireland. To the extent that British policy appeared consistent during this time, this is because general policy principles became locked in place and, following the collapse of Sunningdale, no Westminster government had the political capital or desire to offer anything different. Therefore, although aware of the need for meaningful institutional reform, this did not actually occur until the mid-1980s.

Following the imposition of direct rule, Edward Heath's government clearly believed that profound institutional change and constitutional engineering were necessary to render Northern Ireland's politics acceptable to disgruntled and newly mobilised Irish nationalists. A Cabinet memorandum in March 1972 acknowledged that 'the normal Westminster system will continue for many years to come to provide automatic Unionist majorities. If we are to ensure minority participation we must therefore depart from our accepted systems'.[7] Additionally, reconciling a historically tense relationship with the Republic of Ireland was seen as necessary, both to make Northern Ireland more acceptable to nationalists and to get the Republic of Ireland to act in a 'responsible' way towards the issue. In an internal policy memo briefing, William Whitelaw, the first Secretary of State for Northern Ireland, argued that,

> whether, in the end, arrangements for the internal government of Northern Ireland are made on devolutionary or on integrationist lines, we are wholly persuaded that no settlement will 'stick' for more than a brief period if it does not tackle the fundamental and underlying problem of the relationship between the United Kingdom and Ireland.[8]

British conflict management policy was initially framed around the Sunningdale Agreement's attempt at power sharing in 1973/4 conceived under Ted Heath and Willie Whitelaw, and reluctantly continued under the subsequent Labour government of Harold Wilson and his Secretary of State, Merlyn Rees. Irish republicans were excluded from this process due to their links with ongoing violence and their perceived unwillingness to compromise on their demand for British withdrawal. Nonetheless, Sunningdale represented a recognition of the distinct preferences of Irish nationalists and that these should be accommodated in the design of political institutions. Sunningdale cast tentative doubt upon the permanence of Northern Ireland within the Union, with Ted Heath stating as early as November 1971 that 'if at some future date the people of Northern Ireland want unification and express that desire in the appropriate constitutional manner, I do not believe the British government would stand in the way'.[9]

Sunningdale sought to strengthen ruling institutions by providing guarantees to moderate nationalism in the devolved government of Northern Ireland. The aspiration was that this would dislodge any support within the general population for the more extreme elements of republicanism and republicanism would ultimately wither as people accepted constitutional politics and reformism as the way forward. The initiative never came close to realising this goal, instead getting bogged down in sectarianism. However, it did set the path in which British policy was to become settled for the rest of the 1970s – half-heartedly pursing devolutionary reforms to encourage greater nationalist participation but without pushing too far for fear of upsetting Unionists and destabilising the territory even further. That is not to say that Sunningdale was a complete failure. At the very least it should be noted that when Major and Blair were to eventually return to power sharing as an option in the 1990s, power sharing was not a completely new beginning given that the idea had already been explored in this context and many of the key players were familiar with its foundation.[10]

When Sunningdale collapsed within less than a year, with it collapsed any possibility for government-led progress in the aftermath that followed. The reasons for the failure of Sunningdale are well covered elsewhere and are most notably attributed to Unionist intransigence and scepticism towards an Irish dimension.[11] For the new Labour government in 1974 that inherited

Sunningdale from its Conservative predecessors, its collapse derived from pushing an Irish dimension upon a unionist population that was simply not willing to accept this.[12] In this way, Sunningdale's failure also brought an end to the possibility of Anglo-Irish cooperation (this possibility was not to be seriously revived until the AIA more than ten years later).[13] For John Hume, the root cause of the collapse was not Unionist intransigence, which after all was to be expected, but the lack of political will shown by Wilson and Rees in the face of adversity, and Labour's generally lukewarm stance towards the initiative.[14] Labour's limited enthusiasm towards Sunningdale was evident from the outset when Wilson threw what could only be described euphemistically as his 'full support' behind the government's initiative. He declared in a debate:

> If, as appears likely, the Government's initiative [Sunningdale proposals] contains some elements which are worthy of support, the House should give our full support and, even if we consider the package as a whole totally and perhaps bitterly inadequate, we should then seek to build on what is good.[15]

When the party came to power, Labour focused more on how it was 'bitterly inadequate' rather than ever genuinely attempting to 'build on what is good'.

In the ten years which followed Sunningdale's failure, governments of neither hue offered any particularly imaginative options to tackle the conflict going forward. For the rest of the 1970s, neither Wilson's nor Callaghan's administrations had the will or the political capital to undertake any initiative to solve the conflict.[16] Both Wilson and Callaghan indicated preferences for pursuing significantly different policies towards Northern Ireland but simply failed to do so when they were in office.[17] Wilson considered fairly radical options including granting Northern Ireland dominion status and even withdrawal.[18] However, the furthest either idea got was a Cabinet committee discussion, which duly rejected the possibility. Callaghan, after retiring as prime minister, indicated that he thought a structured British withdrawal might have been worth considering,[19] but while in office he repeatedly asserted that it was an internal issue and wanted the people of Northern Ireland to resolve it. In fact, the boldest government policies during this time were the rather obvious and tame options of pursuing some (ultimately limited) reforms to the economy and public services.

Wilson and Callaghan's policy instead was containment of the conflict and pursuing the military defeat of the IRA. Merlyn Rees entered a truce and negotiations with the IRA in 1975, but never with any sincere commitment. Instead his goal was to drag out the ceasefire as long as possible to run down the IRA's capacity. Rees's successor under Callaghan, Roy Mason, introduced the policies of criminalisation, Ulsterisation and normalisation in an effort to displace responsibility away from the British army over to the Ulster Defence Regiment (UDR) and the RUC and to engage the IRA militarily. Mason also sent the SAS into Northern Ireland. So hardline were his security policies that it was an area in which Margaret Thatcher failed to outbid Labour in the 1979 general election campaign.[20] For O'Leary, Rees's and Mason's policies ultimately backfired, helping to build sympathy for Sinn Féin and threatening the position of the SDLP, as well as undermining the idea that Britain was really the neutral arbiter it claimed to be.[21]

The most notable reason for this atrophy in British policy was a lack of political capital by Wilson or Callaghan to undertake new initiatives, but their lack of interest and failure of imagination should also not be dismissed. Harold Wilson had a governing majority of just three seats, which Callaghan was to inherit and lose after some key by-election defeats. Callaghan spent most of his premiership fighting for his political survival while facing a severe recession and coping with seismic events such as the 'winter of discontent'. He then became reliant on UUP MPs to survive as a government. Following the collapse of a pact with the Liberal Party, Callaghan needed UUP MPs to abstain so he could survive a vote of no confidence in 1978. In return for Unionist support he granted Northern Ireland an additional five seats in the Westminster Parliament (all of which were won by the UUP at the 1983 election when they first came into effect), leading to accusations that he was pursuing an integrationist agenda. Such accusations were ultimately costly to Callaghan when in 1979 he lost another vote of no confidence by just one vote, with SDLP leader Gerry Fitt and Fermanagh and South Tyrone independent nationalist MP Frank Maguire both abstaining from voting with the government in protest at Callaghan's policies towards Northern Ireland.[22]

Following the collapse of Callaghan's government and the election of Margaret Thatcher in 1979, initially it looked like British policy towards Northern Ireland would continue to drift as it had throughout the 1970s. Having won the election with a manifesto that promised greater integration of Northern Ireland with Westminster, a policy influenced by Airey Neave and Enoch Powell, integration was never pursued in reality.[23] Instead Thatcher focused on Northern Ireland as a security issue, and defeating the threat of terrorism from the IRA was her main goal in the region. Her first two secretaries of state, Humphrey Atkins and Jim Prior, both pursued some form of devolution but to very little effect. In reality little changed between 1979 and 1984, with a general aspiration for institutional reform in place, but containment of the conflict and security issues taking precedence.

What is more, the Labour Party distanced itself from any shared sense of cohesive British government policy at this time. Under the persuasion of Kevin McNamara, who was to become the shadow Secretary of State for Northern Ireland in 1987, and against the backdrop of the hunger strikes and the rise of the radical left to rule the Labour Party, the party began to adopt notably pro-Irish unity policies. McNamara was somewhat of an outsider within his own party in terms of his enthusiasm for a united Ireland and it was certainly not the undisputed party line.[24] Nonetheless, at the 1981 Party Conference the party agreed to adopt a motion committing it to campaign actively for Irish unity. It also questioned the ongoing use of the Emergency Powers Bill by the Thatcher government. The 1983 manifesto criticised the Unionist 'veto' (adopting republican language in the process), albeit while simultaneously committing to the need for consent, and in 1989 it produced a document entitled 'Towards a United Ireland'. Indeed, it was suggested that part of the reason for the collapse of progress in the peace process under Major some years later was that the Dublin government was holding out for the election of Labour and McNamara, who it thought would be much more sympathetic to their position.[25]

Clearly this was not an age of bipartisanship and nor were initiatives being pursued with any sense of purpose or achievement. But there was an understanding within both sides that institutional reform was required to solve the Troubles. This understanding largely ran in the background of British policy throughout the 1970s. It was not meaningfully pursued because Labour preferred containment following the collapse of Sunningdale, even if their real preferences were for something bolder, and Thatcher's priority was security. However, this was to change with the AIA, which was to open the space where meaningful strengthening of the institutions could be pursued and when British policy actually became more coherent and made some progress.[26]

Strengthening the Institutions and Intergovernmental Cooperation, 1985–1998

The most important development in terms of strengthening the institutional framework to govern Northern Ireland, and which had a profound effect upon republicanism's future moderation, was the AIA. This represented a shift in British policy which showed a willingness to confront and override Unionist wishes, a commitment to closer intergovernmental cooperation, and it enabled the SDLP to argue with republicans that their interpretation of the causes of conflict was mistaken and therefore revolutionary violence was not justified (see Chapter 4). It also represented a change in Irish policy, with the Irish adopting a more inclusive approach to solving the conflict rather than a confrontational one, even if FitzGerald was still intent on marginalising Sinn Féin at this point in time. The net result was the laying of a foundation for a strong and stable institutional framework that allowed nationalists to pursue their goals through the existing system, confident that they would not be systematically disadvantaged – something that could not be said about earlier incarnations of the ruling institutions in Northern Ireland.

The consequences for long-term peace were almost completely unintended by many key actors. Thatcher rarely showed a sustained interest in the management and reform of Northern Ireland and civil servants and Secretaries of State for Northern Ireland were rarely closely examined or followed by the Cabinet.[27] This provided a large degree of freedom to pursue policies that would not be accepted by Thatcher in other parts of the UK. This is not to say that violence and terrorism in Northern Ireland were not an extremely high priority and of great concern to Thatcher, which of course they were, but rather that the day-to-day administration and non-military policies were of much lesser interest. For example, Jim Prior essentially ran Northern Ireland on the basis of Keynesian economic principles at a time when the government was imposing full-bodied monetarism throughout the rest of the UK.[28] Douglas Hurd stated that each time he discussed Northern Ireland with Thatcher he had to go back over all previous discussions as she typically failed to remember or show much interest in Northern Irish issues beyond security.[29] John Chilcot also noted the freedom of working in the NIO to try different policy initiatives given the distance (both geographically and politically) from Whitehall.[30]

Under these working conditions, an informal approach by Dermot Nally to David Goodall that greater intergovernmental coordination should be considered was sanctioned by Thatcher, starting a process that was to culminate in the AIA. The British negotiated the AIA in an effort to extract additional security cooperation from the Republic of Ireland to strengthen their efforts to defeat the IRA. To achieve this they were willing to make concessions around Irish input but without conceding any sovereignty.[31] Garret FitzGerald entered negotiations hoping to bolster constitutional nationalism by gaining concessions from the British to show that Northern Ireland could be reformed, thus marginalising the political rise of revolutionary Sinn Féin.[32] In other words, the Irish saw the AIA as a way to challenge the British narrative of the conflict as a security issue and hoped to make it more a political issue, while ironically Thatcher signed the AIA hoping to increase security.[33] Thatcher very reluctantly signed and soon regretted this endorsement, especially following the resignation of her close advisor Ian Gow in protest and complaints from her close ally and now UUP MP Enoch Powell. What is more, she never believed that the Irish implemented security cooperation to the extent that they should.[34] The Irish government, on the other hand, realised increased support for constitutional nationalism and the SDLP in the short term and, in an unanticipated development, incentivised Sinn Féin to accept constitutional nationalist positions to counter their political marginalisation.[35]

The AIA had many important institutional dimensions that facilitated republican moderation. It opened up a space which allowed Irish advisory input into the running of Northern Ireland (something Douglas Hurd, Secretary of State for Northern Ireland during most of the negotiations, claimed they already had on a de facto basis anyway),[36] thus realigning the British and Irish relationship away from its historically negative roots.[37] It recognised that Britain would allow Northern Ireland to secede if this was the majority will of its inhabitants, something that Britain was happy to recognise in return for Irish recognition of the need to gain the consent of the unionist population for any change in the status of Northern Ireland. This was relatively easy for Britain to concede, according to Robin Butler, Cabinet Secretary at the time, as such a policy was in line with Britain's long-standing approach to self-determination towards its former colonies.[38] It demonstrated to republicans that reform of Northern Ireland was possible and that the political future of Northern Ireland was being decided by the two governments, regardless of whether republicans or other spoilers engaged with the process or not, increasing the fear of their marginalisation. In addition, the AIA was imposed against the will of Unionist politicians, showing that the British government was willing to defy their intransigence and was not slavishly tethered to Unionism's interests.

The momentum of the AIA was to subside once it was up and running. Thatcher lost interest in the initiative somewhat, especially when it failed to realise the security gains she anticipated. Tom King, who succeeded Douglas Hurd as Secretary of State, sustained the largely security emphasis within British policy, especially in light of the personal vitriol he suffered at the hands of Unionism. Indeed many within the Conservative Party continued to advocate security-based solutions to the conflict throughout the rest of the 1980s and into the 1990s. Most notably, former Prime Minister Ted Heath as late as 1994 continued to advocate security-based solutions to the conflict from the backbenches. Much as in the early 1970s, he called for political reforms that strengthened the position of nationalists in the hope of marginalising republicanism's appeal combined with more intense counter-insurgency and security measures.[39] Meanwhile Thatcher's final Secretaries of State, Peter Brooke and Paddy Mayhew, attempted again to establish devolved government, but little progress was made and Mayhew was content with emphasising security. *Plus ça change* for much of the Conservative Party, it would seem.

FitzGerald, meanwhile, lost the next Irish general election and was replaced by Charles Haughey, who had failed to embrace the AIA while in opposition but proved pragmatic enough to work with it once in power.[40] Yet his ascent to power also brought with it a shift in Irish policy, and Haughey ultimately largely bypassed the AIA in his quest for a breakthrough in Northern Ireland. The shift in Irish policy was in a very different direction to the standard British policy to date, instead exploring ways to reach out and include Irish republicanism in a peace process. A liaison role was assumed by his trusted advisor Martin Mansergh, who was to maintain this over the next two decades for Albert Reynolds and Bertie Ahern.[41] The Irish government then, in coordination with the SDLP and the Hume/Adams talks, became more intent on outreach to republicanism and working to bring it into a political process. Increased intergovernmental cooperation between Ireland and Britain then allowed Fianna Fáil to try to steer both governments' efforts in a more inclusive and coordinated direction (initially with the DSD, then the Framework Documents and finally the Belfast Agreement). It was against this backdrop of Irish policy arguing that republicans should be included in any settlement that British policy became more coherent.

The next major push for formal institutional reform by the British came with the peace process. Much of the peace process entailed designing institutions that lowered the risks for republicans to change their path away from violence to peaceful politics. Britain needed to make its position to republicans credible when it asserted that the future of Northern Ireland was potentially uncertain and that secession would be facilitated if this was the majority will of the people of Northern Ireland. Making this claim credible was particularly important given republican mistrust of the British state, which inhibited republican willingness to commit to a new moderate path. The 1975/1976 IRA ceasefire had entered republican folklore as almost leading to its demise due to disingenuous British tactics of dragging out the ceasefire to hallow out the IRA's capacity. British perfidiousness was also seen in Thatcher's intransigence over the hunger strikes and Major's demands over decommissioning. Equally on the British side there was much mistrust around republicans and the sincerity of their ceasefire given the reluctance to decommission and evasiveness over the future of the IRA.[42] Under these conditions, British assertions that they had no selfish strategic or economic interest in Northern Ireland were given institutional manifestation by guaranteeing a voice for nationalists and recognising the legitimacy of the pursuit of a united Ireland so long as this was done peacefully.

The institutional design of the Belfast Agreement was about providing such guarantees to overcome mistrust and creating incentives that locked actors within non-violent politics.[43] It restated Britain's willingness to facilitate secession and this was granted in return for republicans accepting the need to gain the consent of the unionist community. The use of proportional representation and the single transferable vote created a very open electoral system that inhibited domination by any single party or community, while awarding executive positions in proportion to the percentage of votes secured. As such, this design encouraged parties to maximise their vote share. Ongoing British sovereignty over Northern Ireland was counterbalanced with the NSMC. Additional powers and responsibilities were devolved as the Agreement stabilised, something republicans sought so that they could remove as much decision-making as possible from Westminster. Indeed, the British were surprised at the lack of contestation over the internal institutions within republicanism, which was much more interested in the North-South dimension and the release of prisoners.[44] The collective effect of the new institutions was to lower risks for republicans and incentivise them to abandon their greatest leverage, namely the armed struggle, and to pursue their goals through the reformed institutions instead. Adopting this set of institutional designs was comparatively easy for Britain compared to other participants, given that Britain insisted it was neutral in the process and, as long as the consent principal was accepted, they had little distance to move.[45]

With hindsight, British policy can be seen as steadily removing weaknesses from the historical institutional arrangements that governed Northern Ireland prior to direct rule and instead coalescing around the goal of providing increased political opportunity for the nationalist minority. British policy was also intent upon strengthening the working relationship with the Republic of Ireland, although what the nature of that relationship should be evolved within British policy from one primarily based around security cooperation to one more based around shared political responsibility. British policy was about providing an institutional framework that lowered the risks of participation for nationalists and that was accepted as credible by the minority. This created a space into which republicanism was confident enough to move without fearing that the institutions would systematically work against them, and this ensured increasing levels of political inclusion and, as a consequence, increasing moderation. British policy seemed to make the most progress in this direction when the lead was taken by officials seconded from Whitehall to work in the NIO rather than relying on local officials. Famously, Ken Bloomfield believed he had been cut out of the process of negotiating the AIA due to Whitehall's lack of trust.[46] However, such an interpretation seems a little paranoid. Rather, to the extent that officials from outside Northern Ireland made more progress this was not because local civil servants could not be trusted but rather that they were too close to make the hard choices that would affect the communities in which they lived.[47] Once again, the geographical and political distance of Westminster from Northern Ireland allowed for important policy innovations.

BRITISH TOLERANCE FOR THE POLITICISATION OF IRISH REPUBLICANISM

The other important dimension of British policy throughout the conflict period was a high degree of tolerance towards the politicisation of Sinn Féin and the political goals of republicanism. This allowed Irish republicanism to emerge in the political arena without having to sacrifice its core goals.[48] There are two broad models of responses by democratic governments to anti-system threats, although intermediate positions between the two are often sought in practice. A tolerant and accommodating approach prioritises freedom of expression and assumes that greater political inclusion of extremists in democratic processes will lead to their moderation. In contrast, intolerant and suppressive approaches use more repressive legislative measures on the grounds that it is necessary to protect the substantive values of democracy, which are often challenged by anti-system groups.[49] When it comes to separatist anti-system threats, states are typically reluctant to make concessions, such as adopting policies of group recognition or territorial decentralisation, for fear that this may ultimately empower separatist groups.[50]

Yet, unusually when compared to how other states respond to separatist threats, the British state granted policies of cultural recognition to Irish nationalists, it sought to decentralise power and promoted power sharing, it allowed Sinn Féin to emerge as the leading political force for Irish nationalism, and it even agreed to facilitate the secession of Northern Ireland should that be the majority decision of the people living there. This tolerance of Sinn Féin and its political goals is quite distinct from how the British government responded to the IRA, which was met with some of the strongest anti-terrorist legislation in the democratic world, demonstrating that responses to violent threats and responses to political threats need to be separated.[51] Without this political tolerance Irish republicans would not have moderated in the way that they did.

In 1973, Willie Whitelaw, the Conservative Secretary of State for Northern Ireland, instructed civil servants to draw up legislation considering the possibility of de-proscribing Sinn Féin, legislation that was ultimately passed by his Labour successor Merlyn Rees. The reasons given for this move were varied, depending on the audience. The most pragmatic reason offered was that prosecutions of republicans generally came from membership of the IRA, which would remain proscribed, rather than membership of Sinn Féin, and as such it was unnecessarily illiberal legislation. Other reasons included that it would show the public how little support republicans had if they were allowed to run in elections, or else show that they were fearful to put their policies to a public mandate if they did not run. However, the most common reason offered to fellow parliamentarians in Westminster was that offered by Merlyn Rees when he declared that:

> in my view there are signs on both extreme wings there are people who, although at one time committed to violence, would now like to find a way back to political activity. [De-proscription] is the counterpart of our action against those who use violence.[52]

This degree of tolerance of Sinn Féin soon became an embedded British policy that was not reversed even when the IRA was at its most belligerent. This is another classic example of British policy becoming locked in place in the 1970s, even though there is no clear or singular overarching goal underpinning it. In 1978, when Jim Callaghan and Roy Mason were solely focusing on containing the conflict and boosting the security powers to deal with the IRA threat, re-proscription was mooted but this was cautioned against by the Attorney General's office which argued strongly that 'there is political advantage in leaving Provisional Sinn Féin unproscribed'.[53] Even when Sinn Féin's emergence threatened established politics and was destabilising Northern Ireland, the British government largely maintained its tolerance, albeit while continuing to try to isolate Sinn Féin from popular support. When republicans emerged with such force into the electoral arena in 1981 in both the UK and Ireland, this initially caused concern within some quarters that it represented a radicalisation of formerly moderate Catholics. In a briefing letter to Margaret Thatcher in June 1981, the NIO wrote that:

> We have tended to regard the involvement of the Provisionals in political activity as a development to be encouraged. But it is a development that requires a response from Government, as their terrorist activities receive a response. There is a very general agreement that the Catholic

community has been disturbed by the hunger strikers' deaths, that it blames Government, that there is a degree of alienation and that the Provisionals are getting more support. Unless their political exploitation of the hunger strike situation – and the resulting recrudescence of support for the Provisional IRA – can be countered, then the Provisionals 'going political' can succeed where their terrorist activity has failed.[54]

One suggested response by the NIO was the re-proscription of Sinn Féin, along with the possibility of introducing an oath of allegiance for elected officials to the British monarch – a suggestion that was to be ignored by Whitehall.[55]

   The Irish government also expressed concern about what the election of radical Sinn Féin candidates implied and in a letter from Garret FitzGerald to Margaret Thatcher urging her to do more to end the hunger strike, he wrote 'this is a development which directly threatens the stability of our state through the intrusion of interests which would never have been lent such formal authority but for the propaganda effects of the confrontation in the Maze'.[56] This somewhat panicked response from the Irish government fitted in with British interpretations that while Irish republicans posed a considerable terrorist threat to UK security, they posed a much greater existential threat to the very core of the Irish political system, which after all had its roots in the Free State.[57] The electoral challenge of Sinn Féin was especially worrying to the establishment in Ireland because of its permissive electoral system and, in 1981, two elected hunger striking prisoners prevented Charles Haughey from being able to form a majority government and placed them in a crucial position, if only they had taken up their seats.[58]

   Yet even amidst this pressure, the Westminster government refused to squeeze the political space in which republicans were competing. Thatcher's time as prime minister is certainly not synonymous with compromise with republicanism. Her intransigence towards republicanism and her military approach is well documented and is most clearly epitomised by her response to the hunger strike. Alongside adopting a primarily military response, it also included imposing a broadcasting ban (under pressure to follow the lead of Conor Cruise O'Brien who had imposed such a ban in Ireland back in 1976) and forcing local councillors to take an oath rejecting violence. Nonetheless, tolerance for the political dimension of Irish republicanism remained. Instead of hastily banning Sinn Féin, the Thatcher government saw the success following the hunger strikes as the product of a fairly unique set of circumstances rather than a signal of the radicalisation of the electorate.[59] This is not to claim that Thatcher welcomed Sinn Féin's emergence into the electoral arena, and the dominant British approach remained trying to defeat the IRA militarily, but nor did the government adopt politically suppressive measures even at the height of the dual political-military Armalite and ballot box approach. The stands in stark contrast to other cases, such as the regular bans of Kurdish nationalist parties in Turkey or the banning of Herri Batasuna in Spain.

British tolerance was also evident in their acceptance of the pursuit of a united Ireland. Ted Heath had already indicated as early as 1971 that he could not envisage standing in the way of a united Ireland if this was the majority will of the inhabitants. However, early phrasings of this idea were perhaps more about enshrining the Unionist veto – by asserting that the status of Northern Ireland would not be altered without the consent of the majority – than they were about giving hope to nationalists. It was only later that the flip side of this, namely that secession was possible if the majority consented, was positively framed in a way that was alluring to nationalists. The AIA, while recognising that presently the majority wished to remain in the Union, also included the commitment that 'if in the future a majority of the people of Northern Ireland clearly wish for and formally consent to the establishment of a united Ireland, [both governments] will introduce and support in the respective Parliaments legislation to give effect to that wish'.[60] Within a couple of years Peter Brooke's declaration that Britain had 'no selfish strategic or economic interest' in Northern Ireland followed.[61] Both of these claims were reasserted in the key documents of the peace process, including the DSD, the Framework Documents and the Belfast Agreement.

Tolerance was further evident in British approaches to the disbandment of the IRA. While strongly insisting that decommissioning of weapons needed to occur and that republicans needed to demonstrate that their ceasefire was permanent, neither Major's nor Blair's governments sought to extract a concession from the IRA that the historical use of armed struggle was unnecessary nor did they demand an apology for past acts of violence. Indeed, the British and Irish governments allowed the IRA to continue as an organisation after it had decommissioned its weapons. It was accepted that an IRA which was not a military threat was preferable to its eradication, which may have created a power vacuum into which dissident republicans could have emerged.[62] This remained the case even though the IRA was linked to forty-five deaths following the first ceasefire in 1994.[63]

There were important temporary periods during which British tolerance of republicanism was restricted and this was generally associated with the reliance of the government of the day on UUP MPs for its political survival or to pass key legislation. James Callaghan pursued greater integration of Northern Ireland rather than accommodation when he became reliant on Unionist MPs for his political survival. During the peace process John Major unwaveringly (and for many unnecessarily) demanded IRA decommissioning prior to engaging in talks with Sinn Féin, something that was seen by the Irish government as deriving from his reliance on UUP MPs to pass key votes related to the EU given his slim majority and rebellious backbenchers.[64] Yet even under these conditions this really only impacted on short-term policy stances. Longer-term policies of tolerating Sinn Féin remained.

Given that British governments have been largely tolerant throughout the entire period of British rule from 1972 onwards, this raises the question of why Britain was not more accommodating from an earlier stage. Britain's response to Sinn Féin's anti-system threat was firmly in the tolerant camp from the outset of the conflict, even while simultaneously implementing strong anti-terrorist legislation against the IRA. However, this was initially a largely ineffective policy because tolerance was combined with exclusionary efforts to isolate republicans from political processes and an inability to build strong institutions, a confusingly mixed strategy that O'Duffy argues was one of the worst state strategies that could be pursued.[65] Throughout the 1970s and 1980s, Sinn Féin was tolerated but was certainly not included in any political initiatives. In the Sunningdale period, and under Wilson and Callaghan, republicans were perceived as too militant for negotiations.[66] Similarly, Thatcher may have made limited concessions to Irish nationalists and accepted the political goal of a united Ireland if won through consent, but she certainly did not accept that she should include or negotiate with republicans (it is pretty certain that republicans would not have been willing to negotiate with her either). The concessions of the AIA were made in order to increase the military effort to defeat the IRA and not out of some effort to entice Sinn Féin into greater participation. In other words, for the first two decades of the conflict, policies of tolerance sat alongside policies of exclusion and marginalising republicanism from the political life of Northern Ireland. This meant that accommodation was never possible nor was it rational for Sinn Féin to trade off militancy for greater participation. It was only when tolerance was combined with inclusion and attempts to broker peace, initially under Major and then subsequently under Blair, that a fully accommodating strategy was implemented.

How British Policy was Possible

If democratic governments facing a separatist threat must deliberate over whether to accommodate but risk further empowering separatists, or fail to accommodate but risk being perceived as suppressive, then the British response is unusual in its high degree of accommodation. Although there are a minority of cases of democratic states that have pursued some form of accommodation, with Canada, India and the former Czechoslovakia all offering varying degrees of recognition to their minority separatists, the British response to republicanism is certainly the most notable case of recent accommodation. The literature on state responses to secessionist demands struggles to offer an adequate explanation to the question of why such extensive accommodation was pursued in this case. Existing explanations tend to focus on economic and security reasons. States are less likely to accommodate if a disputed region is of high economic value, high symbolic value or of key strategic importance.[67] Governments are also less likely to seek accommodation if they fear this will set a precedent for other separatist groups within the state.[68] On the other hand, states are more likely to seek accommodation if they are democratic,[69] or if a separatist group is internally divided in the hope this will pull the group apart,[70] or if there is a mutually hurting military stalemate.[71] Although indeed Northern Ireland was of low strategic and economic value by the 1990s and was even a drain on resources, Britain sought accommodation in spite of the fact that this potentially set a precedent for the future of Scotland within the Union and claims that there was a stalemate in place are robustly disputed.[72]

An important set of domestic conditions enabled Britain's response and successive British governments were highly tolerant of Sinn Féin because they had nothing to lose by tolerating them in the short term. The political autonomy of successive British governments from the territory of Northern Ireland allowed them to commit to the secession of Northern Ireland and electoral support in Northern Ireland was generally not crucial to the survival of the government of the day, allowing them to pursue potentially unpopular policies.

Throughout the conflict period, Westminster was rarely reliant upon the outcome of votes in Northern Ireland. None of the major parties had any meaningful electoral presence there. The Labour Party refused to compete in Northern Ireland, even going so far as to reject applications from potential members from Northern Ireland.[73] Although there was a Northern Irish Labour Party until 1987, it was not an official affiliate of the British Labour Party and thus members had no voting rights over Labour Party policy and it was entirely irrelevant in Westminster elections. Similarly, the SDLP had some close informal links with the Labour Party, but certainly no official relationship (most clearly demonstrated by Gerry Fitt's refusal to support James Callaghan when he lost a vote of no confidence by one vote in 1979).

The Conservative Party did not compete in elections in Northern Ireland until 1986 and has never won more than 6 per cent of the vote in any election. Although affiliated with the UUP, and certainly many Conservative Party members and MPs have sympathy for unionism, this relationship too was strained, especially after Ted Heath's decision to implement direct rule against Unionist wishes in 1972. Indeed after Heath made his decision to implement direct rule, the UUP withdrew itself from the Conservative whip in spite of hitherto voting with the Conservatives since 1921. In addition, Northern Ireland was rarely mentioned by the main Westminster political parties during electoral campaigns and manifestos.[74] The topic was of extremely low political salience to the point where the government of the day did not need to heed or follow public opinion on the issue. Indeed the highest electoral salience ever given to Northern Ireland was in 1995 when 8 per cent of respondents identified it as the most important electoral issue, but generally it has been as low as between 1 to 3 per cent.[75]

The indirect impact of Northern Irish parties on the electoral fortunes of Westminster parties has also been low, although not entirely absent. Northern Irish parties have only had the possibility of influencing the survival of a Westminster government on three occasions. In 1974, Ted Heath approached Harry West, leader of the UUP, about taking the Conservative Party whip in a coalition government with the Liberal Party. However, when the Conservatives and Liberals were unable to strike a deal this option collapsed, and Harold Wilson's Labour Party came to power instead. In October 1974, Wilson's slim majority of two, which Callaghan inherited in 1976, opened up the possibility of Unionist influence which resulted in a restriction of the policy that the Labour Party could pursue in Northern Ireland. Again in 1992, although John Major began with a majority of ten, by the end of his term this had been eroded through eight by-election defeats for the Conservatives. This, combined with some unruly backbenchers, allowed for Unionist influence. However, the general tendency has clearly been for Northern Ireland to be marginal to the political fortunes of Westminster governments.

Additionally, Northern Irish issues were never fully integrated into the policies or agenda of Westminster governments. This can be traced back to the nature of the UK as a Union state rather than a unitary state.[76] Within the UK, each of the constituent nations was integrated into the political centre to a different degree. Wales was conquered by England and underwent close to complete assimilation, although some cultural nationalism remains. Scotland consensually entered the Union through the 1707 Act of Union, which allowed it to preserve a separate political and cultural identity from England. In contrast, Ireland was a case of failed conquest and incomplete nation building. This meant that it was never fully integrated into the political centre nor seen as an integral part of the Union in the way that the other constituent nations were integrated. Aughey and Gormely Heenan argue that Northern Ireland was always a case of the politics of Great Britain *and* Northern Ireland, with the emphasis on Northern Ireland being distinct from the rest of Great Britain.[77] Similarly, Dixon has argued that British policy towards Northern Ireland was shaped by the belief that Northern Ireland was different to the rest of the UK and therefore different policies were required than would be acceptable in the rest of the Union.[78] British policy in Northern Ireland was required to secure the support and cooperation of the Republic of Ireland and other international opinion, which heavily incentivised reducing nationalist alienation and promoting a stable political settlement. Under these conditions, policies of building institutional strength and pursuing the tolerance of Irish republicanism were possible.

CONCLUSION

British policy did not extract republican moderation through conscious long-term strategies of interplay and co-option, although strategic interplay was undoubtedly important at various points in negotiations. Rather, British policy enabled republican moderation by supplying a political space into which republicans could move while still pursuing their ethno-national politics. In order to gain the acquiescence of republicans to pursue a more moderate path, it was necessary that British policy created a credible set of institutions. These institutions needed to lower the risks republicans perceived in their decision to move away from their trusted strategy of armed struggle and to abide by the outcomes of democratic politics instead. This was achieved through the guarantees of power sharing and reassurances by the British that republicans could continue to pursue their long-term ethno-national goals.

In this way, republicans increased their inclusion and engagement with democratic institutions, which in turn were demanding ever-increasing moderate concessions. British and Irish policy by the mid- to late 1980s ensured that there existed a principled pathway by which republicans could change strategy while still retaining their core reason for existence. In other words, strategic moderation became possible when republican demands for a new avenue to pursue their goals were met with the supply of a clear political space by British policy. The emergence of such a path was not necessarily intentional, as is clear from the initial combination of a policy of tolerance towards Sinn Féin with a policy of marginalisation by both governments – a confusingly mixed and inept strategy. But due to the unanticipated consequences of the AIA and subsequent reforms of political institutions, a new framework eventually emerged which ensured that the republican leadership's desire for a path to moderation was met with British supply of an acceptable and principled route.

NOTES

1. Bean, *The New Politics of Sinn Féin*; McIntyre 'Modern Irish Republicanism'.
2. Spencer, 'Negotiations and Positions: An Interview with Sir John Chilcot', p. 90; some interviewees described Quentin Thomas as the first person who pursued a clear strategy of attempting to co-opt republicans, but he himself rejected this idea (interview with Bill Jeffrey; interview with Quentin Thomas).
3. Powell, *Great Hatred, Little Room*.
4. See Dixon 'British Policy Towards Northern Ireland', for an argument that British policy was consistent and bi-partisan.
5. Hartzell et al., 'Stabilizing the Peace after Civil War', p. 185.
6. Steadman, 'Spoiler Problems in Peace Processes'; Hartzell and Hoddie. *Crafting Peace*; Mattest and Savun, 'Fostering Peace after Civil War'; Hoddie and Hartzell, *Strengthening Peace in Post-Civil War States*.
7. 'Cabinet Memorandum by the Secretary of State for the Home Department', 3 March 1972, CAB 129/162/1, NA.
8. 'Political Settlement: The "Irish Dimension"', 8 September 1972, PRONI.
9. Northern Ireland Office, *The Future of Northern Ireland*, part II, section 39.
10. Kissane, *New Beginnings*, chapter 5.
11. Kerr, *The Destructors*.
12. Rees, *Northern Ireland. A Personal Perspective*.
13. O'Duffy, 'British and Irish Conflict Regulation from Sunningdale to Belfast. Part I'; O'Leary, 'The Labour Government and Northern Ireland, 1974–9'.
14. 'SDLP showed a particular contempt for Merlyn Rees', *Irish Times*, 4 January 2005.
15. Hansard Record, HC 20 March 1972, vol. 833, col. 1083.
16. Interview with Tom McNally.
17. O'Leary, 'The Labour Government and Northern Ireland, 1974–9'.
18. Interview with Bernard Donoughue; Kerr, *The Destructors*.

19. O'Leary, 'The Labour Government and Northern Ireland, 1974–9', p. 198.
20. Interview with Tom McNally.
21. O'Leary, 'The Labour Government and Northern Ireland, 1974–9'.
22. Famously, Frank Maguire travelled from Northern Ireland to Westminster in order to abstain in person!
23. David Goodall emphasised the need to distinguish between Thatcher's policy preferences and those of the rest of the government and civil service, which often won out in the long term.
24. Interestingly, in 2010 Sinn Féin organised a conference in London about the inevitability of Irish self-determination, at which McNamara gave a speech. It was also attended by Jeremy Corbyn and Ken Livingstone and positively reported by Seumus Milne in his *Guardian* column, showing how the traditional left came to power in Labour about twenty years too late to be of any real benefit to republicans!
25. Interview with William Fitall.
26. O'Duffy, 'British and Irish Conflict Regulation from Sunningdale to Belfast. Part II'.
27. Interviews with Jim Prior, Douglas Hurd and John Chilcot.
28. Interview with Jim Prior. He recounted a story of Thatcher visiting Northern Ireland by helicopter and her noting with surprise that the quality of the roads was very high, leading her to complain about the level of infrastructural investment by Prior in the region.
29. Interview with Douglas Hurd.
30. Interview with John Chilcot.
31. Interview with David Goodall; interview with Douglas Hurd.
32. FitzGerald, *All in a Life*.
33. Interview with Eamonn McKee.
34. For a typical reflection of the British government's view that the Irish government was not avid enough in fulfilling its duties, see the cable from the US Embassy in London to Washington, 'Northern Ireland – Controlling the Violence', 9 August 1988, *US Cable Leak* <https://wikileaks.org/plusd/cables/88LONDON16998_a.html>. This drew on conversations and intelligence from within the British government.
35. The SDLP, although closely liaising with the Irish government, rejected the idea that constitutional nationalism needed a crutch either ideologically or electorally, but accepted that FitzGerald saw it in those terms. Interviews with Sean Farron and Mark Durkan.
36. Interview with Douglas Hurd.
37. Todd, 'Institutional Change and Conflict Regulation'.
38. Interview with Robin Butler.
39. Heath, 'Outflank the IRA bombers', *The Times*, 10 June 1993, p. 16.
40. Interiew with Martin Mansergh.
41. It was made clear to Mansergh that he would be fulfilling this role in his capacity as an advisor to Fianna Fáil, a political party, and not as an advisor to the Irish government.
42. Powell, *Great Hatred, Little Room*.
43. O'Leary, 'The Nature of the Agreement'.
44. Powell, *Great Hatred, Little Room*; interview with Quentin Thomas.
45. Interview with Quentin Thomas. Post-AIA, British claims to neutrality were a lot more resilient to close scrutiny than in the 1970s when such claims rang a little hollow.
46. Interview with Ken Bloomfield, and it is also discussed in his books. London's response to Bloomfield at the time was to say that it suited them to keep Bloomfield separate from the process so that Unionists would still talk to him after the deal

was struck even when Unionist politicians refused to talk to any other British official in protest.

47. Interview with Jonathan Phillips.
48. Whiting, 'Moderation without Change'.
49. Rummens and Abts, 'Defending Democracy'; Capoccia, *Defending Democracy. Reactions to Extremism in Interwar Europe.*
50. Brancati, 'Decentralization: Fuelling the Fire or Dampening the Flames of Ethnic Conflict and Secessionism'; Erk and Anderson, 'The Paradox of Federalism'; Walter, 'Building Reputation'.
51. Müller, 'Militant Democracy'.
52. Hansard HC Debate, 4 April 1974, vol. 871, col. 1476.
53. 'Proscription of Provisional Sinn Féin and Others', 26 October 1978, CJ 4/2374, NA.
54. 'The Provisionals – Political Activity'. Memo Forwarded to the Prime Minister 16 June 1981. PREM 19/505, NA.
55. 'Sinn Féin: "Policy Group on Non-Violence Declarations", 1985–1987', CENT/3/76A, PRONI.
56. 'Letter from the Taoiseach to the British Prime Minister, 10 July 1981', DFA 2011/39/1824, NAI.
57. Interview with Quentin Thomas; Spencer, 'Negotiations and Positions: An Interview with Sir John Chilcot'.
58. It should be noted that Haughey never perceived Sinn Féin to be electoral threat and Martin Mansergh argues that it did not become an electoral threat until possibly in the 2000s when Bertie Ahern was in power. Interview with Martin Mansergh.
59. Interview with Robin Butler; interview with Jim Prior.
60. Anglo-Irish Agreement 1985, Article 1 (c).
61. Brooke, 'Speech at Whitbread', London, 9 November 1990.
62. 'Michael McDowell: Abolition of Provisional IRA was never on the cards', *Irish Times*, 26 August 2015. Jonathan Phillips acknowledged that both governments saw merits in the ongoing existence of the IRA in helping to keep order as the armed struggle was wound down and stressed the challenge of attempting to prove that the organisation was disbanded which undermined the viability of pursuing this. But the British and Irish were both highly intent on eradicating its military and criminal capability.
63. 'IRA linked to 45 violent post-ceasefire deaths', *Belfast Telegraph*, 31 August 2015.
64. Interview with Martin Mansergh; Quentin Thomas spoke of the disquiet that Major's political position raised within some circles of Irish officials during the peace talks, although Thomas rejected the idea that electoral interests were the reasons for Major's hard stance on decommissioning.
65. O'Duffy, 'British and Irish Conflict Regulation from Sunningdale to Belfast. Part I'.
66. Interview with Bernard Donoughue, although the reality of this view has been challenged by Ó Dochartaigh, 'The Longest Negotiation'.
67. Diehl, *A Road Map to War*; Toft, *The Geography of Ethnic Conflict*.
68. Walter, 'Building Reputation'.
69. Ibid.
70. Cunningham, 'Divide and Conquer or Divide and Concede'.
71. Zartman, 'The Timing of Peace Initiatives'.
72. Tonge et al., 'So Why Did the Guns Fall Silent?'.
73. Roberts, 'Sound Stupidity: The British Party System and the Northern Ireland Question'.
74. McGarry and O'Leary, *Explaining Northern Ireland*, pp. 115–119.
75. Trumbore, 'Electoral Politics as Domestic Ratification in International Negotiations'.

76. Bogdanor, *Devolution in the United Kingdom*.
77. Aughey and Gormley-Heenan. 'The Anglo-Irish Agreement'.
78. Dixon, 'British Policy Towards Northern Ireland', p. 364.

7. CONCLUSION

There is very little that Irish republicans, the Irish government and the British government all agree on when it comes to the conflict in Northern Ireland. Yet one thing around which there is a rare degree of unity is that all three groups see the onset of a military stalemate as the driving force behind the transformation of Irish republicanism. If anything, what is remarkable is the overall level of ready acceptance of this idea by senior government officials and leading republicans.[1] The assumption is that republicans tried to achieve their goals through violence for twenty-five years more or less, but when both the British army and the IRA realised neither was close to defeating the other, negotiating positions were re-evaluated and a dignified route out of violence was crafted. Framing the resolution of the conflict in these terms pushes the negotiation process and the nature of dialogue to centre stage in the transition to non-violence.[2] It also implicitly embraces an understanding of republicanism's transition as binary in nature, going from a radical group to a largely moderate one with little grey area in between.

This book sees the process of republican moderation differently, both in terms of the causal drivers of the process and in terms of what it understands moderation to mean. Instead of seeing moderation as a decision taken on the basis of an appraisal of the military capacity of the IRA, the decision to moderate has been placed within its wider political context. Moderation occurred as a result of sustained and increasing inclusion within a set of stable democratic institutions. This was a path-dependent process of increasing returns that locked republicans behind the choice of increased engagement and participation and which heavily incentivised removing radicalism.

From this perspective, moderation is much more of a gradual and long-term process that dates back to initial engagements with elections at the start of the 1980s. It was not a simple dichotomous shift from radical to moderate, but rather it was a multi-layered process with some aspects of republicanism changing at a different pace than others and some aspects remaining continuous and changing little. It is only through a careful disaggregation of the transformation that it becomes clear that the first aspect to moderate was an acceptance of increased participation and engagement with existing institutions, while the militant dimensions and use of armed struggle were much slower and harder to change. Meanwhile the belief in an alternative claim to sovereignty and the rejection of the legitimacy of British rule never really dimmed at all, but were instead pushed to the long term.

The way in which increased inclusion extracted moderation is noteworthy. Initial engagement with electoral institutions was intended to be a purely strategic and instrumental adoption of a new tactic that would complement their revolutionary fervour, not undermine it. Yet as has been seen time and again in many other contexts, working through liberal democratic institutions simply does not allow for revolution. The very act of participation itself can be considered the beginning of moderation as it represented the abandonment of outright rejection and parallel states. But no matter how ambivalent, sceptical or determined republican leaders were to avoid getting seduced by elections or letting them compromise the movement's radical edge, this was simply impossible if they wanted to avoid complete electoral marginalisation.

Once the decision to try and win support from voters was made, even while simultaneously rejecting the sovereign legitimacy of the parliaments which those elections were seeking to fill, compromises to their radicalism were required. Republicans found that they needed to reach out to supporters beyond their core, groups which had decidedly moderate preferences and did not demand immediate territorial reunification as the sole route to constitutional progress. Republicans also had to concern themselves with improving the immediate social and economic conditions facing potential voters if they wanted to win their vote. Of course, republicans could claim, for example, that unemployment was the combined result of British neo-colonialism (not hugely plausible) and institutionalised discrimination (much more plausible), but ultimately tackling everyday socio-economic issues meant pursuing reformism. This undermined claims that only revolutionary action could lead to true democracy. In this way, elections gradually broke down republicanism's radicalism, forced it to commit to moderation, and encouraged this in some policy areas more than others.

Having already moderated somewhat, albeit not in its use of violence, this readied republicanism to engage in a long process of negotiating over the design of democracy in the future of Northern Ireland. This process enmeshed republicans further in liberal democratic institutions, extracting more moderate concessions and, most notably, bringing an end to their use of violence. Elite bargaining over democracy required building loose and temporary alliances to pursue shared nationalist goals. Republicans had to make themselves coalitionable to potential partners and change their outright confrontational relationships with other actors. The specific designs of the power-sharing institutions and the Single Transferable Vote (STV) electoral system further consolidated their moderation.

Although moderation was the product of sustained institutional contact, it would be a mistake to think of British policy as consciously planning to co-opt republicanism into ever-greater contact with state institutions. Explanations which focus primarily on interplay and exchange theory give British policy an omniscience and sense of purpose that in reality it simply lacked. Perhaps by the time of Major's negotiations with republicanism some British officials began to think about how to draw in republicans, but even this interpretation is rejected by some British officials. Instead moderation began much earlier in the 1980s at a time when British policy was confused, disjointed and internally contested by different viewpoints within the government. If anything, the Irish government under Charles Haughey was much quicker to explore the need to include Sinn Féin in negotiations than the British. Instead Britain's policy success lay in its tolerance and its commitment to creating strong institutions, and this approach only began to show any gains towards republicanism when Britain combined tolerance with inclusion under Major, rather than running the confusing strategy of tolerance with the goal of excluding or marginalising republicanism, as was the case in earlier governments. In other words, Britain responded to developments within republicanism that emerged out of institutional inclusion, rather than proactively shaping those developments through stalemate and interplay as is often assumed.

The other factor which was crucial in delivering republican moderation was the role of the US, which acted as a powerful external guarantor and international actor. The US government was crucial in that it reinforced moderation through institutional inclusion by providing reassurance to republican elites that their interests would be protected and any peace agreement would be implemented fairly. This was crucial because of the asymmetry in power between republicans and the British state, especially given republican mistrust of the Westminster government in general and the suspicion that British claims to neutrality were rather shallow (with Major's reliance on Unionist MPs used as evidence to support the republican suspicion). Alongside this, significant incentives around economic investment and access to political influence cemented the process. In short, a powerful external actor reinforced moderating trends and became a key player in delivering moderation through institutional inclusion.

So what is offered here is a pathway to moderation that places institutional inclusion at its core. Inclusion provided republicans with incentives to moderate and this was reciprocated by British policy that opened a political space into which republicans could move. This entailed diverting the tactics used from violent contestation to political contestation but not their goals. The implications of this for other cases are discussed further below, but first it is worth considering how this change in strategy influenced the way republicans pursued their ultimate goal of a united Ireland.

The Republican Strategy in Action

A crucial claim made by the Adams/McGuinness leadership is that while republicans changed their tactics they did not change their goals or interpretation of the conflict. Given that moderation is multi-layered, the values and beliefs of republicanism were able to remain constant while the behavioural level of tactics and strategy underwent dramatic change. Here the case of Irish republicans differs somewhat from other cases of moderation through institutional inclusion. Studies of non-separatist radical groups, notably Islamists, argue that moderation is not complete unless it includes both behavioural and ideological change.[3] However, ideological moderation was not necessary in the case of republicanism because, like many other ethno-national groups, nothing in its ideology is inherently anti-democratic. Making an alternative claim to sovereignty, as long as it is pursued democratically, does not clash with notions of political pluralism. Although the use of violence was embedded in republicanism, this sat alongside a commitment to democracy, rendering the group ademocratic rather than anti-democratic. Forsaking the use of violence as a tactic was enough to make the group compatible with the principles of liberal democracy and therefore behavioural change alone was sufficient to render the group moderate.

A degree of ongoing continuity in beliefs and goals is clear from the many speeches and policy stances adopted by republicanism, especially during the tricky phase when the party agreed to abide by the principles of the Belfast Agreement. The aspiration for unification remained but was pushed to a long-term project. Central to the republican claim that the movement is still committed to a united Ireland is its assertion that the Belfast Agreement is a purely transitional accord, something that will gradually lead to a united Ireland. The belief is that the Agreement will achieve this by creating a fairer playing field for republicans to pursue consent to secede from the UK and be absorbed into the Republic of Ireland. There is no reason to doubt the sincerity of Adams's and McGuinness's desire to use the Belfast Agreement in this way or to think that either of them adopted this stance purely as rhetoric to placate disgruntled grass-roots members and prevent factionalism.[4] However, it is worth exploring how realistic such an aspiration is and what exactly Sinn Féin in power has done to achieve it.

So what have republicans have done since the peace process to advance a united Ireland? The short answer is 'remarkably little', or certainly very little of tangible substance has been achieved. Although there has been much bombast from republicans about the pursuit of a united Ireland ('we are all mandated to work by peaceful and democratic means to bring about the unity of Ireland. We in Sinn Féin hold that as our central task'[5]), the desire soon hit against the rigidity of the institutional design of the power-sharing settlement and a legacy of mistrust by Unionism towards republicans. When the last twenty years of republican policies and activities are examined, the party appears to have become increasingly embedded in the institutions in Northern Ireland rather than consigning them to the status of a temporary step on the inevitable road to a united Ireland. What is more, although the violent conflict between republicans and sections of the unionist community has ended, in many respects this has been replaced with a symbolic and cultural conflict. Thus the idea of gaining unionist consent for a united Ireland does not look to be forthcoming any time soon.

The main tactic adopted by republicans to pursue a united Ireland has been to engage in persuading unionists of the merits of secession from the UK. The hope is that through working together in the Assembly, Unionist politicians and the wider unionist community would come to see that republicans posed no threat to the unionist identity and that there was nothing to fear from republican aspirations for a united Ireland. Alex Maskey, Jim Gibney and Tom Hartley were tasked with reaching out to unionism and Sinn Féin even established a Uniting Ireland department in 2002 (originally called an All-Ireland department) to facilitate this. As part of these efforts, prominent republicans have repeatedly attempted to reach out to unionism. Caoimhghín Ó Caoláin, in a speech at Bodenstown in 2001, announced that republicans:

> recognise that many in the unionist community have deep fears and suspicions of republicans. We acknowledge that great hurt has been inflicted on them during the conflict, just as great hurt has been inflicted on the nationalist community. But it is in our mutual interest to build on the achievements of the peace process, achievements which we share and in which we can take pride, and to work together for reconciliation and progress on this island.[6]

Adams was even more assertive in his attempts to persuade Unionists to consider a united Ireland. He attempted to shake Unionists out of their attachment to Britain (almost akin to Marxist efforts to lift the working-class's false consciousness, which should have provided Adams with a historical clue as to how successful his efforts would be) and to convince unionism its position would improve in a united Ireland. He declared that:

> Under the Union, unionists make up fewer than 2 per cent of the Kingdom. They would constitute 20 per cent of the new Republic. They would be citizens, not mere subjects. They would have rights, not concessions. They would belong. They would be welcome. We have to persuade them of that ... Our responsibility is to ensure that unionists are comfortable and secure in a new Ireland. It is their Ireland too. So it must be a shared Ireland, an integrated Ireland, an Ireland in which unionists have equal ownership.[7]

Once unionism was reassured and productive relationships were achieved, the plan was to use the new institutions to build a transitional dynamic to a united Ireland and to advance the case by promoting the rationality of Irish unification. The primary institutional route to achieving this was to be the NSMC, a body which entails ministers from both parts of Ireland meeting to pursue shared policy interests in designated areas.[8] The republican aspiration was that:

> The All-Ireland Ministerial Council will plot a course to harmonise and strengthen the political, economic, cultural and social relationships among all sections of our people. Taken together, we can see that these institutions provide a dynamic that will transform Ireland and its people, and provide a meaningful process of national reconciliation.[9]

Upon the first meeting of the NSMC in Armagh in December 1999, a joint statement by McGuinness and Bairbre de Brún, asserted that it:

> truly marks the beginning of a new political reality on the island of Ireland. Republicans are now part of a new political administration, with elected representatives from throughout the island of Ireland. The importance of thinking, planning and acting on an all-Ireland basis cannot be overestimated.[10]

Yet given the decided lack of tangible progress in this transitional plan, over the years Sinn Féin evolved from relying exclusively on a transitional dynamic inevitably evolving as a by-product of the very existence of the NSMC and adopted more proactive measures. This entailed trying to make a case for the economic merits of unification and focused on trying to persuade politicians in the Republic of Ireland to engage in a coordinated pursuit of reunification.[11] Conor Murphy, former IRA member and both an MP and Member of the Legislative Assembly at the time, set out how republicans saw the role of the Irish government.

> The Irish government needs to assert the rights of nationalists, just as the British government asserts the rights of unionists. Earlier this year Sinn Féin launched a campaign calling for the publication of a Green Paper on Irish unity by the Irish Government. This call was made not only because the primary objective of Sinn Féin is Irish unity but because Fianna Fáil, Fine Gael, the Labour Party and the SDLP all say they are in favour of it. If that is the case then surely the logical next step is for all of us to sit down and set out a strategy to bring this about.[12]

Gerry Kelly echoed these sentiments, questioning whether 'the Irish government [is] up for this? Let's test that. The Irish government has after all a constitutional imperative to work for a united Ireland.'[13]

Sinn Féin lobbied the Irish government to undertake concrete steps to advance this, including allowing Northern Irish MPs voting rights in the Dáil, extending the voting franchise for the Irish president to include residents in Northern Ireland, formulating an all-Ireland charter of fundamental rights, and the establishment of a North-South Inter-Parliamentary Association.[14] Yet the reality was that pursuing reunification made little headway with the parties in the Republic and none have been forthcoming in joining with Sinn Féin to call for reunification.[15] Sinn Féin's response to this lack of appetite was to call for building the party's support in the Republic and increasing their vote share so that they can gain power and use this to force the issue onto the agenda. However, again this is somewhat naïve given that Sinn Féin's electoral appeal in the Republic has been more about its socialist and protest policies rather than its fervent nationalism.[16]

Perhaps the ultimate evidence of the repeated failure of the republican strategy to advance its aspiration comes from how it has come to rely on external events and exogenous shocks as an opportunistic route to reunification. Following the fallout of the 2007 economic crisis in the Republic of Ireland, a Citizens' Convention was established in 2012 to discuss possible reforms to Irish political institutions. The Convention extended invitations to Northern Irish parties (albeit no Unionist parties attended). Sinn Féin saw this as an opportunity to eliminate the 'partitionist 1937 constitution' and to create a more all-Ireland constitution – efforts which largely came to nought. The ninetieth anniversary of the first 1919 Dáil and the centenary anniversary of the 1916 Easter Rising were also deployed as events which might add impetus to calls for a united Ireland. Following the Scottish independence referendum in 2014, Martin McGuinness called for a border poll in Northern Ireland, stating that the campaign in Scotland 'showed that it is possible to discuss important constitutional issues in a spirit of respect for all sides. I believe we could do that without opening divisions which would be detrimental to the institutions.'[17]

In fact, by the 2010s republican strategies to achieve a united Ireland had almost entered the world of farce when they started a campaign called 'Irish Unity – Let the People Decide'. As part of the campaign republicans held fairs, events and family days in various border towns, which culminated in a referendum amongst those who attended the event (unsurprisingly attendees were of a decidedly republican persuasion). The results of these 'referendums' were then reported with earnest in *An Phoblacht*, such as 92 per cent in favour of a united Ireland in Crossmaglen, and over 90 per cent support in Strabane and Lifford![18]

Sinn Féin's most recent tactic for advancing a united Ireland is to take advantage of the exogenous shock of Brexit and the opportunities this possibly opens up for the party. Given that a majority of Northern Irish voters voted to remain in the EU (56 per cent) and that the DUP was the only major party to support Brexit, Sinn Féin subsequently called for a border poll to let voters decide if they would rather be part of a united Ireland within the EU or part of the UK outside the EU. The uncertainty of the future relationship

SINN FÉIN AND THE IRA

between Ireland and the UK, combined with the possibility of re-establishing a hard-border of customs controls and checks between Britain and its European frontier in Ireland, engendered cross-community disgruntlement with decisions being made in Westminster. According to Declan Kearney, Sinn Féin's National Chairperson,

> English votes have overturned the democratic will of Northern Ireland. This was a cross-community vote in favour of remaining in the EU. English voters are dragging Northern Ireland out of the EU. The British government has forfeited any mandate to represent the economic or political interest of people in Northern Ireland.[19]

Similar sentiments and language was used by McGuinness in an effort to intensify Sinn Féin's all-Ireland strategy. McGuinness argued that:

> the case for a border poll is strengthened by the outcome of this vote and by the fact that the overwhelming majority of people in the North voted to remain . . . Given that we have seen in the course of this exercise the people of the North vote to the percentage of 56% to remain in the European Union that is the next logical step and I do think that the case for [a united Ireland] has been strengthened.[20]

What is perhaps most remarkable and a significant indicator of how far Sinn Féin has moved away from its revolutionary roots while still retaining its nationalist cause, is the degree to which this strategy paralleled that used by the Scottish Nationalist Party (SNP). The SNP, as a constitutional nationalist party committed to working through the existing system, also took advantage of the fact that a majority in Scotland voted to remain in the EU, demanding a referendum on leaving the Union. The success of this strategy for the SNP was clear with the Scottish Parliament voting in favour of holding another referendum, despite holding a 'once in a lifetime' referendum three years earlier that rejected the option of secession.[21] This highlights the possibilities for Sinn Féin in terms of exploiting this tactic and, as such, the potential for an exogenous shock to advance a united Ireland cannot be dismissed. Nonetheless, Sinn Féin's rapid pouncing on this opportunity also highlights its lack of traction in achieving reunification through existing institutional channels.

So when examining the overall picture of Sinn Féin's plan to use the institutions to transition to a united Ireland, little progress has been made. Instead Sinn Féin became more embedded within the power-sharing institutions, rather than remaining aloof and using them instrumentally to transition to its desired constitutional outcome. Proof of this is in the way the party became institutionalised. The party's annual income in Northern Ireland rose from £520,740 in 2002 to a high of £1,289,335 in 2010, and it stood at £1,162,851 in 2015.[22] The number of full-time staff employed directly by the party rose from ten in 2007 to eighteen by 2015, while Sinn Féin parliamentarians went from employing an additional fifty-four members of staff to seventy-two.[23] Of course, increased wealth and personnel could well have been deployed on increased activity to pursue a united Ireland, but one indicator that this was not the case is the amount of revenue dedicated to the Uniting Ireland department. Upon its establishment in 2007 (as the All-Ireland department) this had an annual expenditure of £3,206, which rose to a high of £16,276 in 2013 before falling markedly to £6,065 in 2015. Instead, the biggest areas of expenditure were on wages, administration and organisational development.

Explaining the failure of the republican campaign for a united Ireland to date is not a difficult task. It derives in part from the institutional checks within the Belfast Agreement which inhibit major policy change without the consent of multiple veto players, notably Unionists, the Secretary of State for Northern Ireland and the general population. Institutions, although not inherently sticky, are hard to change. This is especially the case when institutional incumbents can control the timing of any reform agenda and resist pressures for change by delaying action.[24] The provision for a border poll in the Belfast Agreement states that one would be held only when the Secretary of State for Northern Ireland believes that 'a majority of those voting would express a wish that Northern Ireland should cease to be part of the United Kingdom and form part of a united Ireland'.[25] In other words, unionist public opinion retains a veto over the timing of the poll. Even with the most likely external event to trigger a border poll, the EU referendum result, both Theresa Villiers and James Brokenshire declared that this did not indicate majority support to leave the UK and that no border poll would be forthcoming.[26]

Indeed, public opinion on the possibility of a united Ireland has never had majority support following the signing of the Belfast Agreement. Although populations in both the Republic of Ireland (66 per cent in favour, 14 per cent against) and Great Britain (41 per cent in favour, 26 per cent against) are generally favourably disposed towards a united Ireland,[27] the population of Northern Ireland is much more hostile to the idea. Across the population as a whole, support for reunification has never risen above 30 per cent, and since 2010 it has actually fallen to 17 per cent. Meanwhile support for remaining part of the UK has consistently remained over 50 per cent, especially if this is based on devolved rule rather than direct rule. When these attitudes are disaggregated by religion, the picture is even starker. Unsurprisingly, Protestants are strongly opposed to reunification with never more than 5 per cent supporting the idea and overwhelming numbers preferring to remain part of the UK. More surprisingly, Catholics are evenly split between wanting reunification and wanting to remain part of the UK with devolved government. In other words, Protestants are much more adamantly against a united Ireland than Catholics are in favour of a united Ireland or against remaining under British sovereignty (see Figures 7.1 and 7.2).

Another reason for the failure of republicanism to advance a united Ireland

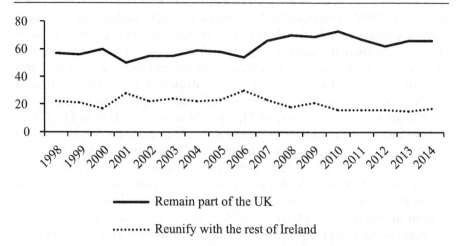

Figure 7.1 Percentage support towards different options for the future of Northern Ireland, 1998–2015

Source: Northern Ireland Life and Times Survey <http://ark.ac.uk/nilt/>. The options available to respondents changed in 2007 from 'remain part of the UK' to 'remain part of the UK with direct rule' or 'remain part of the UK with devolution'. These have been aggregated here to allow comparison over time. The survey was not administered in 2011 and so this is an imputed value as the mid-point between 2010 and 2012.

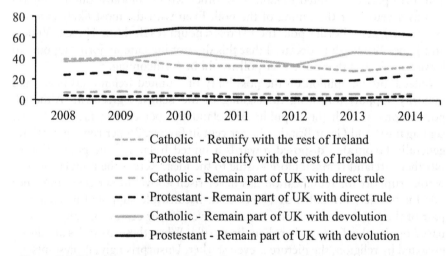

Figure 7.2 Percentage support of Catholics (in grey) and Protestants (in black) for different options for the future of Northern Ireland, 2008–2014

Source: Northern Ireland Life and Times Survey <http://ark.ac.uk/nilt/>. The survey was not administered in 2011 and so this is an imputed value as the mid-point between 2010 and 2012.

has been that republicans actually saw an increase in tension with Unionist politicians in recent years and therefore it seems naïve to think that their strategy of persuasion could be successful. A cultural conflict emerged between republicans and their Unionist counterparts and this has remained stubbornly in place, even after major breakthroughs like the St Andrews Agreement of 2006 and the Hillsborough Agreement of 2010. This can be seen in debates over when, if ever, should the Union Jack flag be flown from public buildings; what rules should govern partisan parades that celebrate nationalist or unionist history but which are often seen by the other community as attempts to assert control over a particular territory; and how should Northern Ireland deal with the legacy of its violent past.

Instances of tension between the two communities post-Belfast Agreement have manifested at the local level, with notable examples including: violent stand-offs between 1995 to 2000 over whether unionists should be allowed to march down the predominantly nationalist part of the Garvaghy Road; rioting within working-class unionism over the removal of the Union Jack from Belfast City Hall in 2013; and the failure of Sinn Féin and the DUP to agree over how to deal with the legacy of the past in 2013/2014 which almost led to a collapse in the Assembly. The ability for cultural clashes to emerge over relatively innocuous proposals is remarkable. One such example was the proposal by the Alliance Party in 2000 that St Patrick's Day should become a public holiday in Northern Ireland, a policy that aimed to unite communities given that everyone likes a day off work! However, republicans complained that the Assembly's proposal contained the phrase 'calls on Her Majesty's Government' and sought permission from Britain for recognition of an Irish holiday. Ulster Unionists amended the proposal to list it as an official flag day, so that the Union Jack would be flown from all public buildings every St Patrick's Day. Meanwhile, Ian Paisley of the DUP, declared that he would recognise St Patrick's Day only because St Patrick was actually British and had been 'hijacked by Fenians' who had distorted his legacy.

It is a little puzzling why more than twenty years after the Belfast Agreement was accepted by all parties (except the DUP), and following a decade of stable power sharing (which included the DUP in a leading role), cultural and symbolic issues became so destabilising and intractable. This is not to suggest that these are unimportant but rather given that the parties had already accepted extensive constraints on their behaviour and learnt to pursue and sell difficult compromises with former adversaries, why was compromise on these symbolic issue so difficult to find? In part this is down to the nature of the power-sharing institutions, which create an incentive for the electorate to reward parties that are seen as offering the greatest protection of their interests against possible encroachment from the opposing community, provided they endorse exclusively peaceful politics that does not damage the prosperity of Northern Ireland.[28] While there were big incentives to end violence, participate exclusively within politics and endorse power sharing, such incentives do not hold for moderating identity stances. Once Sinn Féin gave up violence, their radical history became somewhat of an electoral asset and allowed them to be seen as the best placed party to protect nationalist interests, eclipsing the SDLP. Similarly, the DUP utilised its traditional rejectionist policy stance to overtake the UUP. Being tough on identity and cultural politics allows both parties to play to their core supporters without being seen to reject the new institutions entirely.

In addition, tension between the two communities rose due to the perception within unionism that the peace process has cost them more and benefitted them less, whereas nationalists are more likely to view it as having benefitted both communities equally.[29] This is hardly surprising given that the restructuring of Northern Ireland essentially entailed a redistribution of power away from Unionist dominance towards more equal participation and opportunity. But it is against a backdrop of the perception that there have already been enough sacrifices to Irish nationalists, and republicans in particular, that Unionist leaders are reluctant to compromise further on symbolic issues relating to their identity and tradition. Unionists compromised on those issues that were necessary to extract a ceasefire from the IRA and persuade Sinn Féin to the consent principle for a united Ireland. However, compromising on flags, parades and the investigation of historical violence seem less necessary now than these other sacrifices were in 1998 and 2007. Additionally, the ability for Unionist leaders to make any compromises on symbolic issues is hampered by ongoing electoral competition between the DUP and UUP, which are both vying to be seen as the strongest voice for unionism in Northern Ireland.

Attempts to resolve such conflict have made some progress, but have done little to reconcile the two communities in the way that Sinn Féin needs if its plan for unity through consent is to be successful. Policy initiatives such as 'A Shared Future' (2005), the Stormont House Agreement (2014), and 'A Fresh Start' (2015) have helped to reduce any ongoing paramilitary activity and stabilised the Assembly following various economic crises and cultural conflicts, but in reality they have done little to deal with the source of the problems. There still remains ongoing and fundamental disagreement over the legacy of the past, combined with incentives for political leaders to exploit these cultural differences. In fact, it has been argued that the very nature of the settlement and the nature of institutions established by the British and Irish governments, inherently laid the foundation for such crises to occur.[30] The Assembly itself tends to focus more on day-to-day business and divisions between the political groupings are fairly well entrenched and often manifest in various policy splits.[31]

Reynolds has argued that power-sharing systems are usually transitional in nature and lead to new political systems in the longer term as a state reincorporates all groups into the political system.[32] Often this has been about transitioning to a system of rule that favours those groups who have historically been outside the reins of power, such as black communities in South Africa and Zimbabwe. Yet the Northern Irish case may well challenge the dominant thinking that power-sharing systems lead in this direction. To the extent that Northern Ireland is changing from consociationalism to a different system of government, it seems more likely to shift to a model with an official opposition and government rather than shifting towards reincorporation into an all-Ireland form of government. Such a model was already being considered under the inbuilt provisions of reviewing the functioning of the Belfast Agreement and it has become more embedded as an option with the decision of the UUP and the SDLP to sit in opposition rather than take up their ministerial seats following the 2016 Assembly election.[33]

Sinn Féin's response to its inability to advance the goal of a united Ireland in the way that it hoped is to call for republicans to change their expectations on a united Ireland. Instead the party is now looking for alternative ways to court Unionism. What is interesting to note is that the inability to bring a united Ireland closer does not appear to have hampered the level of republican moderation. It would be overly harsh to say that the aspiration for a united Ireland has been reduced to the level of rhetoric, but it does appear that the party is struggling to fulfil its vision in the way that it intended. Although clearly the possibility of pursuing its goals through the new institutions was necessary in order for the movement to moderate, the inability to actually realise those goals (in the medium term, at any rate) has not led to backsliding on their moderation or led to particularly disgruntled supporters. Sinn Féin's vote share has continued to rise since the Belfast Agreement, only dropping slightly in Northern Ireland in 2015 and 2016 but rising in the Republic of Ireland. This has certainly helped to insulate the leadership somewhat from internal criticisms over the failings of its united Ireland strategy. In other words, for moderation through inclusion to occur, the *possibility* of achieving its goal through the political system was necessary, but actually *realising* this goal was not necessary.

Lessons for Elsewhere

Previously, studies of Northern Ireland often failed to locate themselves within a wider comparative context, either in terms of drawing on comparative lessons to better illuminate Northern Ireland or in terms of teasing out the lessons of Northern Ireland for comparative theory.[34] Yet with the peace process there has been a boom in attempts to export its lessons to other contexts with political leaders, officials and academics all looking to apply lessons to other instances of conflict. For example, Sinn Féin officials have advised FARC, ETA and the PKK on ending their conflicts.[35] Many British and Irish officials have advised other governments on negotiating an end to conflict.[36] There is now an important body of literature that looks to place Northern Ireland within a comparative context and draw out generalisable lessons.[37] Therefore, it would be academically naïve and negligent not to place the moderation of Sinn Féin and the IRA in its comparative context and look to see what lessons it holds for elsewhere, albeit while remembering that context is important in any complete understanding of the outcomes that occurred.[38]

The transformation of Irish republicanism has crucial lessons as a 'least likely' case in that this transformation was highly unlikely to occur but the theory of moderation through institutional inclusion holds anyway.[39] In the 1970s, the radicalism of Irish republicanism seemed so deeply embedded as to be intractable. The British government believed republicanism was too radical and committed to revolutionary goals to engage in meaningful negotiations. Indeed many in the republican leadership were deeply militarist and would only accept complete British withdrawal and reunification, and this had to be secured by the IRA not Sinn Féin. In spite of these preconditions, the theory that inclusion within a strong framework of liberal democratic institutions extracts moderation held in this unlikely case. Therefore, moderation through inclusion is a valuable pathway for the transformation of violent separatists and it is worth turning our attention to examine what this indicates for wider debates.

The first major lesson is that it is not necessary for a radical separatist group to give up its goals or values in order to become moderate actors. This is important because common to any radical group that undergoes a moderate transformation is a deep suspicion from its critics about whether the transformation is genuine or not. Declaring a ceasefire or agreeing to participate in elections is often not adequate proof of moderation for critics. The fear is that radical groups will merely use elections instrumentally to undo democracy and that moderation is primarily a strategic guise to win popular support for an unchanged radical programme. The case of the Islamic Salvation Front in Algeria is living proof of the justification for such anxieties. Therefore groups are expected to condemn their past behaviour, give up goals that challenge the state's authority and espouse a fundamental change in values before any transformation is accepted as credible.

Such a view is often seen from governments when contemplating whether to negotiate with radical separatists. Governments and politicians often refuse to negotiate unless separatist groups give up trying to secede or cease denying the existing state's right to rule over a territory. For example, when José María Aznar was prime minister of Spain he initially refused to negotiate with ETA and Herri Batasuna in the late 1990s, even though conditions for a ceasefire looked promising, because Basque radicals refused to compromise on core demands around self-determination and because of their attachment to a rigid form of ethnic nationalism.[40] In 2000, after the PKK declared an unsteady ceasefire and changed its strategy from seeking independence to seeking autonomy within Turkey, the Turkish government refused to negotiate due to ongoing Kurdish attachments to a distinct identity and the possibility that this would lead to a return to separatist demands over time.[41] After Hamas won the 2006 Palestinian legislative elections, Israel refused to recognise the result because Hamas continued to reject the right of Israel to exist.[42]

Yet the case of Irish republicanism shows that insisting on value change as part of separatist moderation is unnecessary and actually may even be harmful to the possibility of negotiating peace. Many separatist groups, even those engaged in violence, espouse a commitment to democracy. Given there is nothing inherently anti-democratic in making an alternative claim to sovereignty, such groups do not need to change their values as they are already compatible with the principles of political pluralism. Instead, behavioural change to give up the use of violence and other revolutionary tactics is sufficient. In other words, moderation has two dimensions: a 'strategic behaviour' dimension and a 'values and goals' dimension. In order to become a moderate group, radical separatists do not necessarily have to change their values and goals but only their strategic behaviour provided they already have a commitment to democracy.

This draws attention to the next crucial lesson from the pathway to moderation outlined here, which is that moderation occurs when internal demands for moderation by a separatist group are met with the supply of a principled avenue to moderation by the state.[43] Through increased institutional inclusion a dynamic developed within republicanism that led to internal reappraisals in a moderate direction. Yet to realise this dynamic in full it was necessary that the British government (and the Irish government in coordination with Britain) supplied a space into which republicans could move to pursue their goals with low political risk. In other words, demand needed to meet supply in order for moderation to occur. This has important implications for debates around how democratic states should respond to anti-system and separatist threats.

State responses to violent ethno-national challenges vary in their degree of tolerance and, in reality, it is difficult to find the conditions elsewhere that enabled such a tolerant response from Britain towards Irish republicanism. Pedazhur classifies how democracies respond to anti-system threats and categorises state responses as either 'militant democracies', 'defending democracies' or 'immunised democracies'.[44] Militant democracies tend to respond to threats militarily and with political suppression, while immunised democracies tend to engage more in promoting education, civil society and other political measures to counter the threat. Defending democracies lie in-between these extremes. Others have made similar distinctions in the degree of militancy or tolerance in democratic state responses.[45]

Britain's highly tolerant and immunised response to the threat from Irish republicanism was crucial to its moderation, but the conditions that allowed such a response are hard to find elsewhere. Britain's long history of robust democratic institutions and its tolerance for the pursuit of secession were made possible because of the relative political distance of Westminster from the outcomes in Northern Ireland. In addition, Britain's political culture is one which accepted the idea of self-determination for former British colonies by the middle of the twentieth century. In contrast, states with weaker democratic institutions and with the most profound challenges to their political authority tend to adopt the most militant responses, which in turn further entrenches the conflict. Turkey's response to Kurdish nationalism and Israel's response to Palestinian demands for a separate state are typical here. In both these instances, levels of political tolerance for the goal of separatism are minimal. Some limited cultural recognition may be given, such as language rights for Kurds or Arabs, but generally speaking the idea of accepting any policy that challenges the borders of the unitary state is unthinkable. To use Lustick's language, the state and political elites are not willing to cross the hegemonic threshold embedded in policy that would contemplate a contraction of Turkey's or Israel's borders and, therefore, tolerance for the separatist goals is unthinkable.[46]

Without tolerance there is no political space for the rebel group to move into, and it becomes entrenched in its militancy, which reinforces the state's response. The range of options open to the state in all these cases is hampered and tolerance is not politically viable. For example, southeast Turkey is an electoral battleground for the ruling Justice and Development Party (AKP) and so it is reluctant to allow a powerful Kurdish political movement to emerge. In addition, the political culture of Turkey which is in part founded on the principle of overarching Turkish identity and territorial integrity, restricts the possibility of contemplating self-determination for minorities. The strategic security concerns of Israel restrict its willingness to consider a two-state solution to any meaningful degree, much as India's security concerns ensure it will only give limited decentralisation to Kashmir but consider little else. The wealth of the Basque region and the potential for setting a precedent for other regions in Spain ensure that the government is only willing to decentralise power, but not allow secession. No such factors restricted the range of options open to the British state. Indeed Canada, another Westminster model of democracy, may be the only recent case of allowing the possibility of secession through consent to occur with the referendum on independence for Québec in 1995.

This is not to say that it is entirely the state's responsibility to set out a tolerant policy framework in all cases. There may be little actual indication that a separatist group is willing to consider alternative routes to violence. For example, the PKK has squandered real opportunities for negotiation and preferred to pursue militarism in order to shore up its own power.[47] ETA sustained its armed campaign longer than any other separatist group in Europe and this, combined with swings in Spanish policy in terms of tolerance and suppression according to which government was in power, ensured that demand and supply for moderation never met. Attempts at negotiations with the FARC in Colombia during the late 1990s ran aground amid militant threats over their demands, combined with the FARC having too many vested interests in maintaining the conflict to make negotiations a success. But setting aside the nature of the separatist group, failing to respond in a tolerant fashion to the political values of the radical groups shuts down the possibility of the negotiated pathway to moderation outlined here.

Therefore, a further important lesson from the Northern Irish case is the need to separate the political and military dimensions of the separatist threat. There are often substantial differences between state responses to terrorism and state responses to political threats,[48] and this was certainly the case in the way in which Britain responded strongly to the IRA but tolerantly to Sinn Féin. Söderberg Kovacs states that the transformation of Irish republicanism cannot be included in debates about rebel-to-party transformations because Sinn Féin was always a political party and it was the IRA that stopped fighting, but this misses the point.[49] Not only was there extensive cross- and dual membership between the two groups, but it was the very fact that these two strands could be separated that enabled the dynamic of moderation through inclusion to occur. Tolerance of Sinn Féin could sit alongside tough anti-terrorist legislation, thus squeezing the IRA while simultaneously bringing Sinn Féin into ever closer and deeper engagement with the moderating power of an established framework of liberal democratic institutions. In contrast, a case like Turkey fails to distinguish between Kurdish political parties and the PKK, treating both as a fundamental threat to the founding principle of the territorial integrity of the state. Yet failing to make this distinction shuts off an avenue to moderation, something which is often overlooked.

The other important aspect where the case of Irish republicanism can inform wider debates is in the consolidation of rebel-to-politician transformations. An important aspect of these debates has been around how to make such transformations 'stick' and how to prevent backsliding into violence.[50] It would be a mistake to look at Irish republicanism and assume that once the Belfast Agreement was signed the party smoothly and inevitably stayed on the moderate path. Clearly, there were points where officials and the public feared violence would resume and splits within the IRA show that some republicans wanted to return to violence as well.[51] Yet in spite of the fragility of the process at times and the prolonged nature of the implementation phase of the peace agreement, moderation did stick and this gives the case of Irish republicanism privileged insights into how such a process was possible.

The sequencing of moderation was significant for republicanism. It is worth noting that accepting participation and agreeing to work through existing institutions occurred before giving up violence. This in itself is not surprising and is also seen elsewhere, such as how dealing with weapons was one of the final aspects of the rebel-to-politician transformation of the FMLN in El Salvador too.[52] Attempts to force rebel groups to give up arms completely prior to negotiations can seem misguided from this perspective and may jeopardise possible breakthroughs. Republicans viewed such demands as tantamount to surrendering as well as fearing that this would remove their leverage prior to any negotiations occurring. As such, demilitarisation and removing paths back to violence permanently are more likely to be successful when undertaken as part of the negotiation process rather than demanded as a precondition to negotiations.

Yet the real reason for the binding nature of republican moderation is the institutional framework that was in place which enabled the conversion of republicans from spoilers to stakeholders. Sustained institutional contact did not just extract moderation in the first instance, but it also locked republicans into the moderate path by lowering the risks for their ongoing participation. As such, this adds further evidence to the importance of power-sharing institutional designs in helping to commit rebels to moderate paths.[53] The main reason why republicans ultimately never backed away from the new institutions, even though they undoubtedly came close at times, was that their interests were now served by making these institutions a success. If republicans wished to advance a united Ireland or if they wished to rise to a position of political influence, it was necessary to strengthen and work through the new institutional framework. It is precisely this inability to align a spoiler's interests behind a peace deal that leads to failure to secure moderation.[54]

A recurring theme throughout the interviews for this book was the surprising, unexpected and dramatic nature of the transformation that republicanism underwent – from IRA bombers and political pariahs to forming one half of the 'Chuckle brothers' and working sincerely and productively for its constituents in both parts of Ireland. Yet the drama of this transformation should not blind us from explaining it, and a close scrutiny highlights the importance of inclusion within a strong framework of liberal democratic institutions as central to moderation. Although a slow and gradual process, it was one that was powerful. Indeed the biggest threat from Irish republicanism today is more likely to come from an excoriating speech about austerity than any violent confrontation with opposing groups. This is not to say that Northern Ireland has put all its Troubles behind it, but certainly the emergence and sustenance of Irish republicans as moderate actors has gone a long way to doing so.

NOTES

1. The obvious examples here are Powell's, *Great Hatred, Little Room*, Mansergh's 'The Background to the Irish Peace Process', and repeated speeches and public statements by Martin McGuinness, including 'The Future of the Union'. This view is also standard in journalistic understandings of the end of the conflict, such as Taylor's *Provos*, and many academic understandings, such as Schulze, 'The Northern Ireland Political Process'.
2. This is the thrust of Powell's 'bicycle' theory of negotiations that momentum and forward drive leads to success, as outlined in *Great Hatred, Little Room* and further elaborated in *Talking to Terrorists*. The choreography of negotiations as central to the success of the peace process is also a major theme of Dixon, *Northern Ireland*.
3. Schwedler, *Faith in Moderation*; Wickham, 'The Path to Moderation'; Tezcür, *The Paradox of Moderation*.
4. Of course, nor is there any reason to dismiss this interpretation entirely either. However, the bigger point is that it is close to impossible to know with certainty the 'true' motivations of senior republicans. Therefore, it is preferable to explore and interrogate their stated motivations.
5. Caoimhghín Ó Caoláin quoted in *AP*, 22 January 2009, p. 17.
6. Caoimhghín Ó Caoláin, Speech at Bodenstown, June 2001.
7. Gerry Adams quoted in *AP*, 22 January 2009, pp. 9–11.

8. In some areas policies were agreed together but implemented separately (agriculture, education, environment, health, tourism and transport), while in other areas policies are implemented on an all-Ireland basis (waterways, food safety, common EU programmes, Irish language, trade development between the North and South, and much to the laughter of many Unionists due to highlighting how marginal the policies were, lighthouses).

9. *AP,* 25 November 1999, p. 3.

10. 'First Meeting of the All Ireland Ministerial Council', Sinn Féin Press Release, 13 December 1999 <http://www.sinnfein.org/releases/pr121399.html>.

11. See, for example, the recurring theme in many speeches given at the Sinn Féin conference on Irish unity in July 2011 that partition created an inefficient duplication of services which hindered economic growth. Reported in *AP,* July 2011.

12. Murphy, Speech at Bodenstown, June 2005.

13. Kelly, Speech at Bodenstown, June 2006.

14. Sinn Féin, *A Republic for All* <http://www.sinnfein.ie/a-republic-for-all-policy>.

15. Enda Kenny, Taoiseach and leader of Fine Gael, called for a border poll for the first time following Britain's referendum decision to leave the EU but quickly clarified that he meant this should be strived for in the medium term, not immediately. 'Kenny says Border poll should be considered in Brexit talks', *Irish Times,* 18 July 2016.

16. See, for example, Marsh and Cunningham, 'A Positive Choice, or Anyone but Fianna Fáil?'.

17. 'Scottish referendum: Sinn Féin's Martin McGuinness calls for Northern Ireland border poll following Scotland result', *Belfast Telegraph,* 19 September 2014.

18. For example, see *AP* in February and March 2013.

19. 'Sinn Féin to "intensify" demand for united Ireland vote following Brexit', *Irish Times,* 24 June 2016.

20. 'Brexit results: Sinn Féin's Martin McGuinness calls for border poll on united Ireland', *Independent,* 24 June 2016 <http://www.independent.co.uk/news/uk/politics/brexit-northern-ireland-eu-referendum-result-latest-live-border-poll-united-martin-mcguinness-a7099276.html>.

21. Nicola Sturgeon, the SNP leader, later reluctantly rolled back on holding a second independence referendum following the poor showing of the SNP in the 2017 general election, when they lost twenty-one seats to the resurgent Conservative and Labour parties in Scotland. Many within the SNP and outside the party interpreted this decline as stemming from voter fatigue with the SNP's desire to hold another independence referendum, despite a seeming overall majority wanting to remain within the Union. This is perhaps another lesson for Sinn Féin to take on board from the recent Scottish experience. Nonetheless, this does not change the bigger point that nationalist parties will often seek to exploit contingent political developments to further their secessionist agenda.

22. Sinn Féin, *Six County Report & Financial Statements.* Various years available at Electoral Commission, UK <http://www.electoralcommission.org.uk/find-information-by-subject/political-parties-campaigning-and-donations/political-parties-annual-accounts>.

23. Ibid.

24. Capoccia, 'When do Institutions "Bite"? Historical Institutionalism and the Politics of Institutional change'.

25. *Belfast Agreement,* 1998, schedule 1, paragraph 2.

26. 'Theresa Villiers rules out Sinn Féin border poll call', *BBC News,* 24 June 2016 <www.bbc.co.uk/news/uk-northern-ireland-366221201>; 'Adams Still Hopeful of Border Poll', *The Newsletter,* 18 July 2016. Brokenshire's rejection of holding a poll came in spite of the leaders of both Fine Gael and Fianna Fáil in the Republic

of Ireland declaring support for the possibility over the coming years following Britain's exit from the EU.

27. RTE/BBC, *Northern Ireland Cross Border Survey*, 2–16 October 2015 <http://downloads.bbc.co.uk/tv/nolanshow/RTE_BBC_NI_Cross_Border_Survey.pdf>; *Guardian*/ICM, *Attitudes in Britain on the Future of Northern Ireland*, 17–19 August 2001.

28. Mitchell et al., 'Extremist Outbidding in Ethnic Party Systems is Not Inevitable'.

29. See the Northern Ireland Life and Times Survey, 'Has the Good Friday Agreement benefited unionists or nationalists more? (GOODFRI), 1998–2005 <http://www.ark.ac.uk/nilt/results/polatt.html#gfa>.

30. Todd, 'Contested Constitutionalism?'.

31. Interview with Sean Farren; interview with Alex Attwood.

32. Reynolds, 'A Constitutional Pied Piper'.

33. See the role and outputs of the Assembly and Executive Review Committee, for examples of this <http://www.niassembly.gov.uk/assembly-business/committees/assembly-and-executive-review/>.

34. McGarry and O'Leary, *Explaining Northern Ireland*.

35. *AP*, 20 October 2015; 'Sinn Féin "heavily involved" in push for ETA ceasefire, says Gerry Adams', *The Guardian*, 6 September 2010; 'Irish republicans to hold peace summit with Kurdish and Basque separatists', *The Guardian*, 10 February 2011.

36. The most obvious example here is Jonathan Powell who, after Blair left office, went on to form a consultancy company Inter Mediate that focuses on aiding peace processes, but many other officials have also used their expertise to advise other contexts too.

37. Tonge, *Comparative Peace Processes*; Bew et al., *Talking to Terrorists*; McEvoy, *Power-Sharing Executives*, are just three of the best recent such works but there are also many others.

38. On the importance of context when generalising the Northern Irish case, see O'Kane, 'Learning from Northern Ireland?'.

39. On least likely cases and their uses, see Gerring, 'Is There a (Viable) Crucial-Case Method?', p. 232.

40. Whitfield, *Endgame for ETA*, pp. 81–85.

41. Unal, 'Strategist or Pragmatist'.

42. 'Hamas Sweep to Palestinian Elections, Complicating Peace Efforts in Mideast', *Washington Post*, 27 January 2006.

43. Whiting, 'Moderation without Change'.

44. Pedazhur, *The Israeli Response to Jewish Extremism and Violence*.

45. Rummens and Abts, 'Defending Democracy'.

46. Lustick, *Unsettled States, Disputed Lands*.

47. Tezcür, 'When Democratization Radicalizes'.

48. Müller, 'Militant Democracy'.

49. Söderberg Kovacs, 'Rebel-to-Party Transformations in Civil War Peace Processes'.

50. Deonandan et al., *From Revolutionary Movements to Political Parties*.

51. Interview with Jonathan Phillips; ICM survey for the *Sunday Mirror* in July 1999 found that 42 per cent of respondents feared a return to violence.

52. Wood, *Forging Democracy from Below*.

53. See also Walter, *Committing to Peace* and Hoddie and Hartzell, *Strengthening Peace in Post-Civil War States*.

54. Steadman et al., *Ending Civil Wars*.

BIBLIOGRAPHY

LIST OF INTERVIEWEES

Alex Attwood
Ken Bloomfield
Robin Butler
Matt Carthy
John Chilcot
Bernard Donoughue
Mark Durkan
Sean Farren
William Fitall
David Goodall
Peter Hain

Douglas Hurd
Bill Jeffrey
Tom King
Eamonn McKee
Tom McNally
Martin Mansergh
Danny Morrison
Jonathan Phillips
Joe Pilling
Jim Prior
Quentin Thomas

ARCHIVES

Dáil Éireann Debates
Hansard Record
Linen Hall Library Northern Ireland Political Collection
The National Archives, UK (NA)
National Archives of Ireland (NAI)
Public Record Office of Northern Ireland (PRONI)
WikiLeaks US Cables

SINN FÉIN DOCUMENTS

Éire Nua. The Social and Economic Programme of Sinn Féin (1971).
Peace with Justice: Proposals for Peace in a New Federal Ireland (1974).
A Scenario for Peace (1987).
The Sinn Féin/SDLP Talks: January–September, 1988 (1988).

Freedom (1991).
Setting the Record Straight (1994).
Towards a Lasting Peace in Ireland (1994).
Submission to the Mitchell Commission (1996).
Policing in Transition: A Legacy of Repression, an Opportunity for Justice (1996).
A Police Service for a New Future. Submission to the Commission on Policing (1998).
A Republic for All (2015).
In addition, manifestos, constitutions and financial accounts across the life of the party were consulted.

IRA DOCUMENTS

Provisional IRA, *Freedom Struggle* (Dublin: Provisional IRA, 1973).

NEWSPAPERS AND MAGAZINES

An Phoblacht (AP)
Belfast Telegraph
Evening Press
The Guardian
Hibernia

The Independent
Irish Independent
The Irish Times
News Letter
Republican News (RN)

REFERENCES

Acemoglu, D. and J. A. Robinson, *The Economic Origins of Dictatorship and Democracy* (Cambridge: Cambridge University Press, 2005).
Adams, G., *Hope and History. Making Peace in Ireland* (Kerry: Brandon Publishers, 2003).
Adams, G., *The Politics of Irish Freedom* (Kerry: Brandon Publishers, 1986).
Alexander, G., 'Institutions, Path Dependence and Democratic Consolidation', *Journal of Theoretical Politics*, 13(3) 2001, pp. 249–270.
Alexander, G., *The Sources of Democratic Consolidation* (Ithaca: Cornell University Press, 2002).
Alonso, R., *The IRA and Armed Struggle* (London: Routledge, 2007).
Arthur, P., *Special Relationships. Britain, Ireland and the Northern Ireland Problem* (Belfast: The Blackstaff Press, 2000).
Aughey, A., 'The Art and Effect of Political Lying', *Irish Political Studies*, 17(2) 2002, pp. 1–16.
Aughey, A., *The Politics of Northern Ireland. Beyond the Belfast Agreement* (London: Routledge, 2005).
Aughey, A. and C. Gormley-Heenan, 'The Anglo-Irish Agreement: 25 Years On', *The Political Quarterly*, 82(3) 2011, pp. 389–397.

Augusteijn, J., 'Motivation: Why did they Fight for Ireland? The Motivation of Volunteers in the Revolution', in J. Augusteijn (ed.), *The Irish Revolution 1913–1923* (Basingstoke: Palgrave, 2002), pp. 103–120.

Barry, R., *2016 Assembly Election: Transferred Votes. Northern Ireland Assembly Research and Information Service Briefing Note*, 37/16 (Belfast, 2016). Available at: <http://www.niassembly.gov.uk/globalassets/docu ments/raise/publications/2016-2021/2016/general/3716.pdf> (last accessed 22 September 2016).

Barry, R., *2017 Assembly Election. Transferred Votes. Northern Ireland Assembly Research and Information Service Briefing Note*, 23/17 (Belfast, 2017). Available at: <http://www.niassembly.gov.uk/globalassets/docu ments/raise/publications/2017-2022/2017/general/2317.pdf>.

Bean, K., *The New Politics of Sinn Féin* (Liverpool: Liverpool University Press, 2007).

Bean, K. and M. Hayes, 'Sinn Féin and the New Republicanism in Ireland: Electoral Progress, Political Stasis, and Ideological Failure', *Radical History Review*, 104 2009, pp. 126–142.

Beresford, D., *Ten Men Dead. The Story of the 1981 Irish Hunger Strike* (London: Grafton, 1987).

Bermeo, N., 'Myths of Moderation: Confrontation and Conflict during Democratic Transitions', *Comparative Politics*, 29(3) 1997, pp. 305–322.

Berti, B., *Armed Political Organizations. From Conflict to Integration* (Baltimore: Johns Hopkins University Press, 2013).

Bew, P., M. Frampton and I. Gurruchaga, *Talking to Terrorists: Making Peace in Northern Ireland and the Basque Country* (London: Hurst and Co., 2009).

Bogdanor, V., *Devolution in the United Kingdom* (Oxford: Oxford University Press, 2001).

Bourke, R., *Peace in Ireland. The War of Ideas* (London: Random House, 2003).

Bourke, R., 'The Politicization of the IRA', *Times Literary Supplement*, 5 March 2008.

Bowyer Bell, J., 'Societal Patterns and Lessons. The Irish Case', in R. Higham (ed.), *Civil Wars in the Twentieth Century* (Lexington: University of Kentucky Press, 1972), pp. 217–226.

Brancati, D., 'Decentralization: Fuelling the Fire or Dampening the Flames of Ethnic Conflict and Secessionism', *International Organization*, 60(3) 2006, pp. 651–685.

Breen. R., 'Class Inequality and Social Mobility in Northern Ireland, 1973 to 1996', *American Sociological Review*, 65(3) 2000, pp. 392–406.

Breen, R., 'Why is Support for Extreme Parties Underestimated by Surveys? A Latent Case Analysis', *British Journal of Political Science*, 30(2) 2000, pp. 375–382.

Brown, K. and C. Hauswedell, *Burying the Hatchet. The Decommissioning of*

Paramilitary Arms in Northern Ireland (Bonn: Bonn International Centre for Conversion, 2008).

Capoccia, G., 'Anti-System Parties. A Conceptual Reassessment', *Journal of Theoretical Politics*, 14(1) 2002, pp. 9–35.

Capoccia, G., *Defending Democracy. Reactions to Extremism in Interwar Europe* (Baltimore: Johns Hopkins University Press, 2010).

Capoccia, G., 'When Do Institutions "Bite"? Historical Institutionalism and the Politics of Institutional Change', *Comparative Political Studies*, 49(8) 2016, pp. 1095–1127.

Clancy, M. A. C., *Peace Without Consensus. Power Sharing Politics in Northern Ireland* (Surrey: Ashgate, 2010).

Clifford, B., *Northern Ireland: What is it? Or Professor Mansergh Changes his Mind* (Belfast: Belfast Magazine, 2011).

Coakley, J., 'National Identity in Northern Ireland: Stability or Change?', *Nations and Nationalism*, 13(4) 2007, pp. 573–597.

Cochrane, F., 'Irish-America, the End of the IRA's Armed Struggle and the Utility of "Soft Power"', *Journal of Peace Research*, 44(2) 2007, pp. 215–231.

Committee of Inquiry into Police Interrogation Procedures in Northern Ireland, *Report of the Committee of Inquiry into Police Interrogation Procedures in Northern Ireland* (London: HMSO, 1979).

Compton, P. A., *The Contemporary Population of Northern Ireland and Population Related Issues* (Belfast: Queens University, 1981).

Cox, M., 'Bringing in the "International": The IRA Ceasefire and the End of the Cold War', *International Affairs*, 73(4) 1997, pp. 671–693.

Cunningham, K. G., 'Divide and Conquer or Divide and Concede: How Do States Respond to Internally Divided Separatists?', *American Political Science Review*, 105(2) 2011, pp. 275–297.

Deonandan, K., D. Close and G. Prevost (eds), *From Revolutionary Movements to Political Parties: Cases from Latin America and Africa* (New York: Palgrave Macmillan, 2007).

Di Palma, G., *To Craft Democracies: An Essay on Democratic Transitions* (Berkeley: University of California Press, 1990).

Diehl, P. F. (ed.), *A Road Map to War: Territorial Dimensions of International Conflict* (Nashville: Vanderbilt University Press, 1999).

Dixon, P., 'British Policy Towards Northern Ireland 1969–2000: Continuity, Tactical Adjustment and Consistent "Inconsistencies"', *British Journal of Politics and International Relations*, 3(3) 2001, pp. 340–368.

Dixon, P., *Northern Ireland. The Politics of War and Peace* 2nd edn (Basingstoke: Palgrave Macmillan, 2008).

Downs, G. and S. J. Steadman, 'Evaluation Issues in Peace Implementation', in S. J. Steadman, D. Rothchild and E. M. Cousens (eds), *Ending Civil Wars. The Implementation of Peace Agreements* (Boulder: Lynne Rienner Publishers, 2002), pp. 43–69.

Dumbrell, J., 'The New American Connection: President George W. Bush and Northern Ireland', in M. Cox, A. Guelke and F. Stephen (eds), *A Farewell to Arms? Beyond the Good Friday Agreement* 2nd edn (Manchester: Manchester University Press, 2006), pp. 357–366.

Dumbrell, J., 'The United States and the Northern Irish Conflict 1969–94: From Indifference to Intervention', *Irish Studies in International Affairs*, 6 1995, pp. 107–125.

Dunleavy, P., *Democracy, Bureaucracy and Public Choice. Economic Explanations in Political Science* (London: Harvester, 1991).

Dunphy, R., *The Making of Fianna Fáil Power in Ireland, 1923–1948* (Oxford: Oxford University Press, 1995).

English, R., *Armed Struggle: The History of the IRA* (London: Pan, 2004).

English, R., *Radicals and the Republic. Socialist Republicanism in the Irish Free State 1925–1937* (Oxford: Clarendon Press, 1994).

Erk, J. and L. Anderson, 'The Paradox of Federalism: Does Self-Rule Accommodate or Exacerbate Ethnic Divisions?', *Regional and Federal Studies*, 19(2) 2009, pp. 191–202.

Evans, G. and B. O'Leary, 'Northern Irish Voters and the British-Irish Agreement: Foundations of a Stable Consociational Settlement', *The Political Quarterly*, 71(1) 2000, pp. 78–101.

Evans, J. and J. Tonge, 'From Abstentionism to Enthusiasm: Sinn Féin, Nationalist Electors and Support for Devolved Power-Sharing in Northern Ireland', *Irish Political Studies*, 28(1) 2013, pp. 39–57.

Ezrow, L., C. De Vries, M. Steenbergen and E. Edwards, 'Mean Voter Representation and Partisan Constituency Representation: Do Parties Respond to the Mean Voter Position or to their Supporters?', *Party Politics*, 17(3), pp. 275–301.

Fahey, T., B. C. Hayes and R. Sinnott, *Conflict and Consensus. A Study of Values and Attitudes in the Republic of Ireland and Northern Ireland* (Leiden: Brill, 2006).

Fair Employment Commission for Northern Ireland, *Profile of the Monitored Workforce* (Belfast: Fair Employment Commission for Northern Ireland, 1990–1998).

Farrell, M., *Northern Ireland. The Orange State* 2nd edn (London: Pluto Press, 1990).

Farren, S., *The SDLP: The Struggle for Agreement in Northern Ireland, 1970–2000* (Dublin: Four Courts Press, 2010).

Farren, S. and D. Haughey, *John Hume. Irish Peace Maker* (Dublin: Four Courts Press, 2015).

FitzGerald, G., *All in a Life* (Dublin: Gill and Macmillan, 1991).

Frampton, M., *The Legion of the Rearguard. Dissident Irish Republicanism* (Dublin: Irish Academic Press, 2010).

Freeden, M., *Ideologies and Political Theory. A Conceptual Approach* (Oxford: Clarendon, 1996).

Freeden, M., 'Is Nationalism a Distinct Ideology?', *Political Studies*, 46(4) 1998, pp. 748–765.

Gallagher, M., 'The Pact General Election of 1922', *Irish Historical Studies*, 22(84) 1979, pp. 404–421.

Garry, J., 'Consociation and its Critics. Evidence from the Historic Northern Ireland Assembly Election 2007', *Electoral Studies*, 28(3) 2009, pp. 458–466.

Garvin, T., *1922: The Birth of Irish Democracy* (New York: St. Martin's Press, 1996).

Gerring, J., 'Is There a (Viable) Crucial-Case Method?', *Comparative Political Studies*, 40(3) 2007, pp. 231–253.

Gormley-Heenan, C., *Political Leadership and the Northern Ireland Peace Process* (Basingstoke: Palgrave Macmillan, 2007).

Guelke, A., 'The United States, Irish Americans and the Northern Ireland Peace Process', *International Affairs*, 72(3) 1996, pp. 521–536.

Hart, P., *The IRA at War, 1916–1923* (Oxford: Oxford University Press, 2003).

Hartzell, C. A. and M. Hoddie, *Crafting Peace. Power Sharing Institutions and the Negotiated Settlement of Civil Wars* (University Park: Pennsylvania State University Press, 2007).

Hartzell, C. A., M. Hoddie and D. Rothchild, 'Stabilizing the Peace After Civil War: An Investigation of Some Key Variables', *International Organization*, 55(1) 2001, pp. 183–208.

Hayes, B. C. and I. McAllister, 'Sowing Dragon's Teeth: Public Support for Political Violence and Paramilitarism in Northern Ireland', *Political Studies*, 49(5) 2001, pp. 901–922.

Hayes, B. C. and R. Sinnott, *Conflict and Consensus. A Study of Values and Attitudes in the Republic of Ireland and Northern Ireland* (Leiden: Brill, 2006).

Higley, J. and M. Burton, *Elite Foundations of Liberal Democracy* (Lanham: Rowman & Littlefield Publishers, 2006).

Hoddie, M. and C. A. Hartzell (eds), *Strengthening Peace in Post-Civil War States. Transforming Spoilers into Stakeholders* (Chicago: University of Chicago Press, 2010).

Huntington, S. P., *The Third Wave. Democratization in the Late Twentieth Century* (Norman: University of Oklahoma Press, 1991).

Independent Commission on Policing for Northern Ireland, *A New Beginning: Policing in Northern Ireland. The Report of the Independent Commission on Policing for Northern Ireland* (Belfast: Independent Commission on Policing for Northern Ireland, September 1999).

Kalyvas, S. N., *The Rise of Christian Democracy in Europe* (Ithaca: Cornell University Press, 1996).

Kerr, M., *The Destructors. The Story of Northern Ireland's Lost Peace Process* (Dublin: Irish Academic Press, 2011).

Kerr, M., *Imposing Power-Sharing. Conflict and Coexistence in Northern Ireland and Lebanon* (Dublin: Irish Academic Press, 2005).

Kissane, B., 'Defending Democracy? The Legislative Response to Political Extremism in the Irish Free State, 1922–39', *Irish Historical Studies*, 34(134) 2004, pp. 156–174.

Kissane, B., 'Electing Not to Fight: Elections as a Mechanism of Deradicalisation after the Irish Civil War 1922–1938', *International Journal of Conflict and Violence*, 6(1) 2012, pp. 41–54.

Kissane, B., *Explaining Irish Democracy* (Dublin: University College Dublin Press, 2002).

Kissane, B., *New Beginnings. Constitutionalism and Democracy in Modern Ireland* (Dublin: University College Dublin Press, 2011).

Kissane, B., *The Politics of the Irish Civil War* (Oxford: Oxford University Press, 2005).

Kitschelt, H., *The Transformation of European Social Democracy* (Cambridge: Cambridge University Press, 1994).

Knox, C., 'Emergence of Power Sharing in Northern Ireland: Lessons from Local Government', *Journal of Conflict Studies*, 16(1) 1996, pp. 7–29.

Labour Force Survey, *Religion Report* (Belfast: Statistics and Social Division, Policy Planning Unit, 1990–1998).

Laffan, M., *The Partition of Ireland, 1911–1925* (Dundalk: Dundalgan Press, 1983).

Laffan, M., *The Resurrection of Ireland. The Sinn Féin Party 1916–1923* (Cambridge: Cambridge University Press, 1999).

Levitsky, S. and L. Way, 'International Linkage and Democratization', *Journal of Democracy*, 16(3) 2005, pp. 20–34.

Levitsky, S. and L. Way, 'Linkage versus Leverage. Rethinking the International Dimensions of Regime Change', *Comparative Political Studies*, 38(4) 2006, pp. 379–400.

Linz, J. and A. Stepan, *The Problems of Democratic Transition and Consolidation: Southern Europe, South-America and Post-Communist Europe* (Baltimore: Johns Hopkins University Press, 1996).

Lustick, I., *Unsettled States, Disputed Lands: Britain and Ireland, France and Algeria, Israel and the West Bank-Gaza* (Ithaca: Cornell University Press, 1993).

Lynch, T. J., *Turf War. The Clinton Administration and the Northern Ireland* (Hampshire: Ashgate, 2004).

Lynn, B., 'Tactic or Principle? The Evolution of Republican Thinking on Abstentionism in Ireland, 1970–1998', *Irish Political Studies*, 17(2) 2002, pp. 74–94.

McAllister, I., 'The Armalite and Ballot Box. Sinn Féin's Electoral Strategy in Northern Ireland', *Electoral Studies*, 23 2004, pp. 123–142.

McEvoy, J., *Power-Sharing Executives: Governing in Bosnia, Macedonia, and Northern Ireland. Nationalist and Ethnic Conflict in the 21st Century* (Philadelphia: University of Pennsylvania Press, 2014).

McGarry, F., *The Rising. Ireland: Easter 1916* (Oxford: Oxford University Press, 2010).

McGarry, J. and B. O'Leary, 'Consociation and its Critics: Northern Ireland after the Belfast Agreement', in S. Choudhry (ed.), *Constitutional Design for Divided Societies: Integration or Accommodation* (Oxford: Oxford University Press, 2008), pp. 369–408.

McGarry, J. and B. O'Leary, *Explaining Northern Ireland: Broken Images* (Oxford: Oxford University Press, 1994).

McGarry, J. and B. O'Leary, *Policing Northern Ireland. Proposals for a New Star* (Belfast: The Blackstaff Press, 1999).

MacGinty, R., 'American Influences on the Northern Irish Peace Process', *Journal of Conflict Studies*, 71(2) 1997, pp. 31–50.

McGrattan, C., 'Dublin, the SDLP, and the Sunningdale Agreement. Maximialist Nationalism and Path Dependency', *Contemporary British History*, 23(1) 2009, pp. 61–78.

McGrattan, C., 'Modern Irish Nationalism: Ideology, Policymaking and Path-Dependent Change', in A. Guelke (ed.), *The Challenges of Ethno-Nationalism. Case Studies in Identity Politics* (Basingstoke: Palgrave Macmillan, 2010), pp. 177–190.

McGrattan, C., *Northern Ireland. 1968–2008. The Politics of Entrenchment* (Basingstoke: Palgrave, 2010).

McGuinness, M., 'The Future of the Union: Northern Ireland', *London School of Economics and Political Science Public Lecture*, 30 April 2012.

McIntyre, A., 'Modern Irish Republicanism: The Product of British State Strategies', *Irish Political Studies* 10(1) 1995, pp. 97–121.

McKearney, T., *The Provisional IRA. From Insurrection to Parliament* (London: Pluto, 2011).

Mainwaring, S., 'Transitions to Democracy and Democratic Consolidation: Theoretical and Comparative Issues', in S. Mainwaring, G. O'Donnell and J. Samuel Valenzuela (eds), *Issues in Democratic Consolidation: The New South American Democracies in Comparative Perspective* (Notre Dame: Notre Dame University Press, 1992), pp. 294–341.

Mair, P., *The Break-Up of the United Kingdom. The Irish Experience of Regime Change* (Glasgow: Centre for the Study of Public Policy, 1978).

Major, J., *Interview on Sunday 10 February 1991*. Available at <http://www.johnmajor.co.uk/page2041.html>.

Mansergh, M., 'The Background to the Irish Peace Process', in M. Cox, A. Guelke and F. Stephen (eds), *A Farewell to Arms? Beyond the Good Friday Agreement* 2nd edn (Manchester: Manchester University Press, 2000), pp. 24–40.

Marsh, M. and K. Cunningham, 'A Positive Choice, or Anyone but Fianna

Fáil?', in M. Gallagher and M. Marsh (eds), *How Ireland Voted 2011* (Basingstoke: Palgrave, 2011), pp. 172–204.

Mattest, M. and B. Savun, 'Fostering Peace after Civil War: Commitment Problems and Agreement Design', *International Studies Quarterly*, 53(3) 2009, pp. 737–759.

Mitchell, G. J., *Making Peace* (New York: Alfred A. Knopf, 1999).

Mitchell, P., G. Evans and B. O'Leary, 'Extremist Outbidding in Ethnic Party Systems is Not Inevitable: Tribune Parties in Northern Ireland', *Political Studies*, 57(2) 2009, pp. 397–421.

Moloney, E., 'The IRA', *Magill*, September 1980.

Moloney, E., *A Secret History of the IRA* (London: Allen Lane, 2002).

Moloney, E., *Voices from the Grave. Two Men's War in Ireland* (London: Faber and Faber, 2010).

Müller, J. W., 'Militant Democracy', in M. Rosenfeld and A. Sajó (eds), *Oxford Handbook of Comparative Constitutional Law* (Oxford: Oxford University Press, 2012), pp. 1253–1269.

Müller, W. C. and K. Strøm, 'Political Parties and Hard Choices', in W. C. Müller and K. Strøm (eds), *Policy, Office or Votes? How Political Parties in Western Europe Make Hard Decisions* (Cambridge: Cambridge University Press, 1999), pp. 1–35.

Murray, G. and J. Tonge, *Sinn Féin and the SDLP. From Alienation to Participation* (London: C. Hurst, 2005).

Muttarak, R., H. Hamill, A. Heath and C. McCrudden, 'Does Affirmative Action Work? Evidence from the Operation of Fair Employment Legislation in Northern Ireland', *Sociology*, 47(3) 2012, pp. 560–579.

Northern Ireland Office, *The Future of Northern Ireland. A Paper for Discussion* (London: Stationery Office, 1972).

O'Boyle, G., 'Bombings to Ballots: The Evolution of the Irish Republican Movement's Conceptualisation of Democracy', *Irish Political Studies*, 26(4) 2011, pp. 593–606.

O'Clery, C., *The Greening of the White House* (Dublin: Gill and Macmillan, 1997).

Ó Dochartaigh, N., *From Civil Rights to Armalites. Derry and the Birth of the Irish Troubles* (Cork: Cork University Press, 1997).

Ó Dochartaigh, N., 'The Longest Negotiation: British Policy, IRA Strategy and the Making of the Northern Ireland Peace Settlement', *Political Studies*, 63(1) 2013, pp. 202–220.

O'Donnell, G., P. Schmitter and L. Whitehead, *Transitions from Authoritarian Rule. Comparative Perspectives* (Baltimore: Johns Hopkins University Press, 1986).

O'Duffy, B., 'British and Irish Conflict Regulation from Sunningdale to Belfast. Part I: Tracing the Status of Contesting Sovereigns', *Nations and Nationalism*, 5(4) 1999, pp. 523–542.

O'Duffy, B., 'British and Irish Conflict Regulation from Sunningdale to Belfast.

Part II: Playing for a draw 1985–1999', *Nations and Nationalism*, 6(3) 2000, pp. 399–435.

O'Huiginn, S., 'Peace Comes Dropping Slow', in S. Farren and D. Haughey (eds), *John Hume. Irish Peacemaker* (Dublin: Four Courts Press, 2015), pp. 143–154.

O'Kane, E., 'Learning from Northern Ireland? The Uses and Abuses of the Irish "Model"', *British Journal of Politics and International Relations*, 12(2) 2010, pp. 239–256.

O'Leary, B., 'The Labour Government and Northern Ireland, 1974–9', in J. McGarry and B. O'Leary, *The Northern Ireland Conflict. Consociational Engagements* (Oxford: Oxford University Press, 2004), pp. 194–216.

O'Leary, B., 'Mission Accomplished? Looking Back at the IRA', *Field Day Review*, 1 2005, pp. 217–246.

O'Leary, B., 'The Nature of the Agreement', *Fordham International Law Review*, 22(4) 1998, pp. 1628–1667.

Osborne, R. D., 'Progressing the Equality Agenda in Northern Ireland', *Journal of Social Policy*, 32(3) 2003, pp. 339–360.

Pedazhur, A., *The Israeli Response to Jewish Extremism and Violence: Defending Democracy* (Manchester: Manchester University Press, 2002).

Pierson, P., 'Increasing Returns, Path Dependency, and the Study of Politics', *American Political Science Review*, 94(2) 2000, pp. 251–267.

Powell, J., *Great Hatred, Little Room. Making Peace in Northern Ireland* (London: Bodley Head, 2008).

Powell, J., *Talking to Terrorists. How to End Armed Conflicts* (London: Bodley Head, 2014).

Pridham, G., 'The International Context of Democratic Consolidation: Southern Europe in Comparative Perspective', in R. Gunther, P. N. Diamandouros and H.-J. Puhle (eds), *The Politics of Democratic Consolidation – Southern Europe in Comparative Perspective* (Baltimore: Johns Hopkins University Press, 1995), pp. 166–203.

Przeworski, A., 'Some Problems in the Study of the Transition to Democracy', in G. O'Donnell, P. Schmitter and L. Whitehead (eds), *Transitions from Authoritarian Rule* (Baltimore: Johns Hopkins University Press, 1986).

Przeworki, A. and J. Sprague, *Paper Stones. A History of Electoral Socialism* (Chicago: Chicago University Press, 1986).

Pyne, P., 'The Third Sinn Féin Party 1923–1926: I. Narrative Account', *The Economic and Social Review*, 1(1) 1969, pp. 29–50.

Rees, M., *Northern Ireland: A Personal Perspective* (London: Methuen, 1985).

Regan, J., *The Irish Counter Revolution, 1921–1936* (Dublin: Gill and Macmillan, 1999).

Reiss, M., *Negotiating with Evil. When to Talk with Terrorists* (New York: Open Road Integrated Media, 2010).

Reynolds, A., 'A Constitutional Pied Piper: The Northern Irish Good Friday Agreement', *Political Science Quarterly*, 114(4) 1999–2000, pp. 613–637.

Rhodeen, P., *Peacerunner. The True Story of How an Ex-Congressman Helped End the Centuries of War in Ireland* (Dallas: BenBella Books, 2016).

Roberts, H., 'Sound Stupidity: The British Party System and the Northern Ireland Question', *Government and Opposition*, 22(4) 1986, pp. 315–335.

Ruane, J. and J. Todd, *After the Good Friday Agreement. Analysing Political Change in Northern Ireland* (Dublin: University College Dublin Press, 1999).

Ruane, J. and J. Todd, 'Path Dependence in Settlement Processes: Explaining Settlement in Northern Ireland', *Political Studies*, 55(2) 2007, pp. 442–458.

Rummens, S. and K. Abts, 'Defending Democracy: The Concentric Containment of Political Extremism', *Political Studies*, 58(4) 2010, pp. 649–665.

Sanders, A., *Inside the IRA. Dissident Republicans and the War for Legitimacy* (Edinburgh: Edinburgh University Press, 2011).

Schedler, A., 'What is Democratic Consolidation?', *Journal of Democracy*, 9(2) 1998, pp. 91–107.

Schmitt, D. E., 'The US War on Terrorism and its Impact on the Politics of Accommodation in Northern Ireland', in C. Farrington (ed.), *Global Change, Civil Society and the Northern Ireland Peace Process* (Basingstoke: Palgrave Macmillan, 2008), pp. 54–72.

Schulze, K. E. 'The Northern Ireland Political Process: A Viable Approach to Peace Building?', *Irish Political Studies*, 12(1) 1997, pp. 92–110.

Schwedler, J., 'Can Islamists Become Moderates? Rethinking the Inclusion-Moderation Hypothesis', *World Politics*, 63(2) 2011, pp. 347–376.

Schwedler, J., *Faith in Moderation: Islamist Parties in Jordan and Yemen* (Cambridge: Cambridge University Press, 2006).

Smith, D. J. and G. Chambers, *Inequality in Northern Ireland* (Oxford: Clarendon, 1991).

Smith, M. L. R., *Fighting for Ireland? The Military Strategy of the Irish Republican Movement* (London: Routledge, 1995).

Söderberg Kovacs, M. and S. Hatz, 'Rebel-to-Party Transformations in Civil War Peace Processes 1975–2011', *Democratization*, 23(6) 2016, pp. 990–1008.

Spencer, G., *From Armed Struggle to Political Struggle. Republican Tradition and Transformation in Northern Ireland* (London: Bloomsbury, 2015).

Spencer, G., 'Negotiations and Positions: An Interview with Sir John Chilcot', in G. Spencer (ed.), *The British and Peace in Northern Ireland* (Cambridge: Cambridge University Press, 2015).

Steadman, S. J., 'Spoiler Problems in Peace Processes', *International Security*, 2(2) 1997, pp. 5–53.

Steadman, S. J., D. Rothchild and F. M. Cousens (eds), *Ending Civil Wars. The Implementation of Peace Agreements* (Boulder: Lynne Rienner Publishers, 2002).

Sutton, M., *Bear in Mind these Dead . . . An Index of Deaths from the Conflict in Ireland*. Available at <http://cain.ulst.ac.uk/sutton/book/index.html>.

Taylor, P., *Provos: The IRA and Sinn Féin* (London: Bloomsbury, 1997).

Tezcür, G. M., *The Paradox of Moderation: Muslim Reformers in Iran and Turkey* (Austin: University of Texas Press, 2010).

Tezcür, G. M., 'When Democratization Radicalizes: The Kurdish Nationalist Movement in Turkey', *Journal of Peace Research*, 47(6) 2010, pp. 775–789.

Thatcher, M., 'Speech to Conservative Party Conference', 12 October 1984.

Thatcher, M., 'Speech to Finchley Conservatives. 25 Years as MP', 20 October 1984.

Thompson, J. E., *American Policy and Northern Ireland. A Saga of Peacebuilding* (Westport: Praeger, 2001).

Todd, J., 'Contested Constitutionalism? Northern Ireland the British-Irish Relationship Since 2010', *Parliamentary Affairs*, forthcoming. DOI: 10.1093/pa/gsw019.

Todd, J., 'Institutional Change and Conflict Regulation: The Anglo-Irish Agreement (1985) and the Mechanisms of Change in Northern Ireland', *West European Politics*, 34(4) 2011, pp. 838–858.

Todd, J. and J. Ruane, 'Beyond Inequality? Assessing the Impact of Fair Employment, Affirmative Action and Equality Measures on Conflict in Northern Ireland', in G. K. Brown, A. Langer and F. Stewart (eds), *Affirmative Action in Plural Societies. International Experiences* (Basingstoke: Palgrave Macmillan, 2012).

Toft, M. D., *The Geography of Ethnic Conflict: Identity, Interests and the Indivisibility of Territory* (Princeton: Princeton University Press, 2003).

Tonge, J., *Comparative Peace Processes* (Polity: Cambridge, 2014).

Tonge, J., 'Sinn Féin and the 'New Republicanism' in Belfast', *Space and Polity*, 10(2) 2006, pp. 135–147.

Tonge, J., P. Shirlow and J. McAuley, 'So Why Did the Guns Fall Silent? How Interplay, not Stalemate, Explains the Northern Ireland Peace Process', *Irish Political Studies*, 26(1) 2011, pp. 1–18.

Trumbore, P., 'Electoral Politics as Domestic Ratification in International Negotiations: Insights from the Anglo-Irish Peace Process', *Irish Studies in International Affairs*, 12 2001, pp. 113–131.

Unal, M., 'Strategist or Pragmatist: A Challenging Look at Ocalan's Retrospective Classification and Definition of PKK's Strategic Periods Between 1973 and 2012', *Terrorism and Political Violence*, 26(3) 2013, pp. 419–448.

Van Engeland, A. and R. M. Rudolph (eds), *From Terrorism to Politics* (Hampshire: Ashgate, 2008).

Walter, B., 'Building Reputation: Why Governments Fight Some Separatists but not Others', *American Journal of Political Science*, 50(2) 2006, pp. 313–330.

Walter, B. F., *Committing to Peace. The Successful Settlement of Civil Wars* (New Jersey: Princeton University Press, 2002).

Waterman, H., 'Political Order and the "Settlement" of Civil Wars', in

R. Licklider (ed.), *Stopping the Killing: How Civil Wars End* (New York: New York University Press, 1993).

White, R. W., *Ruairí Ó Brádaigh. The Life and Politics of an Irish Revolutionary* (Bloomington: Indiana University Press, 2006).

Whitfield, T., *Endgame for ETA. Elusive Peace in the Basque Country* (London: Hurst, 2013).

Whiting, M., 'Moderation without Change. The Strategic Transformation of Sinn Féin and the IRA in Northern Ireland', *Government and Opposition*, forthcoming. DOI: http://dx.doi.org/10.1017/gov.2016.19.

Whyte, J., 'How Much Discrimination was there Under the Unionist Regime, 1921–68?', in T. Gallagher and J. O'Connell (eds), *Contemporary Irish Studies* (Manchester: Manchester University Press, 1983).

Whyte, J., *Interpreting Northern Ireland* (Oxford: Clarendon, 1990).

Wickham, C. R., 'The Path to Moderation: Strategy and Learning in the Formation of Egypt's Wasat Party', *Comparative Politics*, 36(2) 2004, pp. 205–228.

Wilson, A. J., *Irish America and the Ulster Conflict, 1968–1995* (Belfast: The Blackstaff Press, 1995).

Wood, E. J., *Forging Democracy from Below: Insurgent Transitions in South Africa and El Salvador* (Cambridge: Cambridge University Press, 2000).

Zartman, W., 'The Timing of Peace Initiatives: Hurting Stalemates and Ripe Moments', in J. Darby and R. McGinty (eds), *Contemporary Peacemaking: Conflict, Violence and Peace Processes* (Basingstoke: Palgrave Macmillan, 2003), pp. 19–29.

INDEX